THE REPRODUCTIVE BARGAIN

Studies in Critical Social Sciences Book Series

Haymarket Books is proud to be working with Brill Academic Publishers (www.brill.nl) to republish the *Studies in Critical Social Sciences* book series in paperback editions. This peer-reviewed book series offers insights into our current reality by exploring the content and consequences of power relationships under capitalism, and by considering the spaces of opposition and resistance to these changes that have been defining our new age. Our full catalog of *SCSS* volumes can be viewed at www.haymarketbooks.org/category/scss-series.

THE REPRODUCTIVE BARGAIN

Deciphering the Enigma of Japanese Capitalism

HEIDI GOTTFRIED

Haymarket
Books
Chicago, IL

First published in 2015 by Brill Academic Publishers, The Netherlands.
© 2015 Koninklijke Brill NV, Leiden, The Netherlands

Published in paperback in 2016 by
Haymarket Books
P.O. Box 180165
Chicago, IL 60618
773-583-7884
www.haymarketbooks.org

ISBN: 978-1-60846-644-3

Distributed to the trade in the US through Consortium Book Sales and
Distribution (www.cbsd.com) and internationally through Ingram Publisher
Services International (www.ingramcontent.com).

This book was published with the generous support of Lannan Foundation and
Wallace Action Fund.

Special discounts are available for bulk purchases by organizations and
institutions. Please call 773-583-7884 or email info@haymarketbooks.org for more
information.

Cover design by Jamie Kerry of Belle Étoile Studios and Ragina Johnson.

Printed in the United States.

Entered into digital printing July 2021.

Library of Congress Cataloging-in-Publication Data is available.

Contents

Preface

Wither Japanese Capitalism: Closely Watched Trains

> The station, a vast organism, which houses the big trains, the urban trains, the subway, a department store, and whole underground commerce – the station gives the district this landmark which, according to certain urbanists, permits the city to signify, to be read. The Japanese station is crossed by a thousand functional trajectories, from the journey, to the purchase, from the garment to food: a train can open onto a shoe stall.
> BARTHES 1982, 38

Like most visitors to Japan, my trip begins at the nexus of air and rail in the Narita International Airport. The railroad and the airport are symbolic hubs emblematic of Japan's modernity; both represent sites of private and state interventions building the new nation-state and sites of post-war contentious politics over the economic fate of the nation. Railroads are remnants of the prewar military complex, the infrastructure for industrial modernization, thrusting Empire into their territories, and epitomizing the iconic Japanese corporate networks (*kiretsu*) that own rail-lines to combine transportation with urban commerce in department stores at the terminus. From the earliest rail-line of the Edo period linking Yokohama and the new capital in Tokyo, to the nationalization of many rail-lines in 1906, the construction of railroads and later airports parallel stages of capitalist development. At the turn of the 20th Century, Japan built an extensive railway system throughout the colonies, consolidating the physical empire and supporting the circulation and transmission of art, material culture, and cross-border exchanges (Kleeman 2014, 7, 18). Japan's postwar model crystallizes in the twin development of rail and air transport. To ensure reliable transportation in their effort to rebuild capitalist productive capacity in 1949, the US General HQ issued a directive to reorganize much of the rail system by forming the Japanese National Railways (JNR), a state-owned public corporation. The Liberal Democratic Party (LDP) realized its postwar economic agenda, introducing and expanding high-speed rail including the line to Narita airport, with little input from unions and despite strike activity throughout the 1960s. Following a neo-liberal playbook, JNR was dismantled and privatized in 1987.

This book follows the arc of my own intellectual journey in search of an explanation for the rise and decline of secure employment in an increasingly precarious Japan. In the spring of 1998, I board the Shinkansen, aka bullet train; it speeds along past barely noticeable vegetable farms and rice paddies, and slows down as dusk covers the Tokyo cityscape before stopping at "a vast organism" known as Tokyo Station. Amidst the blur of jetlag I merge with the swarm of thrumming people on the move in all directions despite the late hour. We join hundreds of thousands of passengers boarding trains daily. Overwhelmed, I try to find my way in this enclosed city within the city. On this first, and then on subsequent trips, Tokyo Station never loses its velocity and vitality, its dizzying array of offerings, its allure. From this location, I would embark on follow up research visits to the temporary-help agency Manpower's offices at the heart of the financial district in Tokyo, then to their new head-quarters in Yokohama, still in close proximity to workers and clients linked by frequent trains leaving Tokyo Station. On the same track, the new Manpower offices herald the global processes of work (dis)placement and dislocation – now enclosed in a shopping mall.[1] But I always return to the main train stations in Tokyo metropolitan area.

At multiple train hubs around Tokyo, it is possible to "read," as Roland Barthes' postmodern travelogue invites the reader to do, an "empire of signs" of the setting sun. Whether standing on the platform or walking in and around the station, I apply my ethnographic imagination to discern from the chaos the "functional trajectories" behind the endless chain of exchange: people on their way to work traversing the vast warren of underground passageways; an almost invisible encampment of blue plastic tarps nestled between trees shielding casual labor and the unemployed in bucolic Ueno Park; a tent village rising up in Hibiya Park where more than 500 temp workers protest their precarious existence made worse after the collapse of Lehman brothers;[2] and a depart-ment store, seamlessly located inside the station, that mirrors and sells the material objects and desires of global capitalism. The Japanese train station is a landmark for the circulation of networks, where private and public lines/ lives intersect, and where the everyday comes into contact with the complexity of labor and commerce; it is emblematic of the rapid, accelerated pace of the state-led modernization project that built these nodes at the center of this now declining empire.

---

1 David Fasenfest cheekily called the emergence of mall complexes, the mauling of Japanese cityscapes.

2 In the months preceding the event through March 2009, 300,000 non-regular workers lost their job. The tent village garnered public support and attention. There were 1500 volunteers who came to the aid of the protesters, and who raised 23 million yen ($210,000) in donations, over a five-day period (Malinas 2014).

Parallel to my first scholarly foray deconstructing Japan's economic miracle, the airport, upon closer inspection, reveals a turbulent history of the post-war settlement in the shadows of its imperial entanglements. At the onset of my journey, I land at Narita Airport, a paragon of efficiency, fairly easy to navigate from arrival to departure. In the expanse between the airport and Tokyo lies a forgotten history, also a part of the revved up engine that propelled Japan's muscular economy to its global zenith. Using the powers of eminent domain, the state expropriated farmers' land in the mid-1960s, and then privatized the airport authority in the early years of the new millennium. Only from an historical perspective can we view the specter of capitalism among the phantom warriors; helmeted Left-wing students joining local farmers in their fight against the police for control of the land surrounding the airport (Nathalie-Kyoko Stucky 2013). As the violence escalated farmers took a stand on, and literally in, their land by constructing large fortresses and burrowing themselves underground.

Japanese documentary filmmaker, Shinsuke Ogawa, who formed the film collective Ogawa Productions (Ogawa Pro),[3] was committed to a "cinema of protest." The collective created a pastiche film-making style consisting of historical re-enactments, Japanese-inspired ghost stories, abstract images of plant-life, scenes of landscapes changing with the seasons, and scientific narration, all in the service of documenting the everyday world of the farmer. The films were calls to action as well as documents of a time, place, and a people's fading way of life. An ethnographic spirit infused the filmmaking process and the collective viewing of farmers' swirling demonstrations on the "battle front" in Sanrizuka, cultivating the culture and history of rice production in *Magino Village – A Tale/The Sundial Carved with a Thousand Years of Notches*. These Japanese films were central to the resistance among farmers and left-wing students fighting against the Japanese authorities' expropriation of land to build the Narita International Airport in the mid-1960s. Though the films did not stop the government, they did radicalize and change the lives of student protesters and farmers who continued to seek redress regarding the constitutionality of the government's use of eminent domain to seize the land. Even after the spectacle of demonstrations and armed struggles disappeared, the farmers and their advocates continued their campaign to reclaim the fertile land until 2003, when Japan's Supreme Court, deferentially ruled on the constitutionality of the state's action. That same year, the government passed a law

---

3   Ogawa Pro's filmmaking style belongs to an experimental tradition in which art expresses utopian possibilities; an avant-garde sensibility aimed at finding a new visual language for the production and reception of this art form and new way of life.

that enabled the privatization of the airport.[4] By 2007, dwindling numbers of farmers, only nine percent of the working population, attested to the rapid economic transformation already underway. Through such traces we can see how Narita signifies a history of state-led development in the first instance, and the impact of neo-liberal state retreat on the lives and livelihoods, in the last. An analysis of sedimented histories informs the rise and decline of this economic juggernaut.

The book's timing coincides with the return of Shinzo Abe to the office of Prime Minister. I was on sabbatical at Ochanomizu University when I watched, as if in slow motion, Abe's fall from grace. The unfolding of events parallels another episode from Japan's early post-war history: in 1960, then Prime Minister Kishi Nobusuke, Abe's grandfather, was forced to resign after the massive assembly of snake-dancing demonstrators protested the passage of the controversial security treaty with the US (Haberman 1987). It brings to mind *The Eighteenth Brumaire of Louis Bonaparte*'s opening passage: "Hegel remarks somewhere that all great, world-historical facts and personages occur, as it were, twice. He has forgotten to add: the first time as tragedy, the second as farce" (Marx 1852). The disgraced Abe's short tenure of only one-year, characterized by ministerial gaffes, especially the widely reported statement by the health minister referring to women as "birth-giving machines," seemed to doom his political fate at the start of the 2007 New Year.

The anxiety fueling pro-natalist political rhetoric of the ruling Liberal Democratic Party made visible contradictions buried beneath the smooth surface glossed by the narrative of economic success. Abe's decisive electoral victory at the polls in 2012 bears witness to a country reeling from the many years of economic malaise, compounded by the triple disasters of 3/11. The political promise of the Democratic Party of Japan (DPJ), following on the heels of the global financial meltdown in 2009, was never realized in the few years of their administration. Their lack of governing experience in the face of entrenched institutional interests and weak civil society organizations left a political vacuum filled by the return of Prime Minister Abe. In office one-year, Abe's rhetoric echoed the militarism of his grandfather, a chief architect of empire building in the 1930s (Fackler and Sang-Hun 2013, A6); and his economic policy, Abe-nomics, abandoned social commitments of the old employment model in favor of a neo-liberal political agenda. Speaking at Davos in 2014, Prime Minister Abe acknowledged that women's economic role was underutilized, and pledged that women should compose 30 percent of senior

---

4 http://en.wikipedia.org/wiki/Narita_International_Airport (downloaded October 7, 2013).

posts by 2020, but provided no specific details (such as childcare and parental leave) on how to achieve these goals.[5] Several months later, a cabinet shakeup brought five women into the cabinet, a symbolic gesture from Abe, looking to shore up his steep decline in favorability ratings. The politics and rhetoric were aimed at jumpstarting the lackluster economy without putting into place a set of social policies.

The reversal of political and economic fortunes is an occasion for my reflection on this empire of the setting sun. Current literature on imperial formations has tracked the genealogies of empire, both its historical antecedents and its contemporary imperial forms (Steinmetz 2013; Stoler 2013; Hardt and Negri 2001). Empire marks both the symbolic and historic role of Japan's military and economic domination in the region. What's left behind has escaped notice in much analysis of Japan's present crisis. Stoler's (2013) elegiac rumination on imperial ruin and ruination evokes the ghostly, brutal, and violent residues of colonial rule. She reminds us that imperial power resides in often overlooked and seemingly imperceptible residues. Her rubric of "imperial formations" shifts the point of emphasis from a fixed form of sovereignty to an "ongoing quality of processes of decimation, displacement, and reclamation" (Stoler 2013, 8). Similarly, Japan's vestiges of colonialism cast a long shadow on the scarred lives and landscapes within and across countries in East Asia (Chae 2013). Through the lens of imperial formations, it becomes possible to see how Japan established its economic hegemony and then lost its way in the twilight of the 20th century.

Japan's imperial project both emulated and rejected Western models of empire: on the one hand, Japan's political elite commandeered the idea of gunboat diplomacy from the West (Chae 2013, 402) in order to accomplish the annexation of its first colony in Taiwan (1895), followed by Sakhalin and Kurile Islands and Manchuria (1905), Korea (1910), and swaths of China and the Pacific Islands (1919) at the turn of the 20th Century (Kleeman 2014, 1–2); and on the other hand, the state articulated both an ethno-historical discourse that emphasized a common Asiatic cultural and racial identity and a colonial narrative in which Japan claimed control over ancient Korea to justify its colonial rule (Chae 2013, 404–5). Though the territorial expansion was more limited in scale and scope than either British or French Empires, the close geographic proximity fostered more frequent flows and exchanges of people, ideas, and

---

5 "Abe Says Women are Key to Japan's Future, Bloomberg Businessweek, Jan. 23, 2014 http://www.businessweek.com/videos/2014-01-22/abe-says-women-are-key-to-japans-future#r=lr-sr (accessed on January 23, 2014).

material culture with the East Asian region (Kleeman 2014, 2).[6] More specifically, these dual aspects of Japanese expansion entailed what Kleeman (2014, 4) calls "colonial disregard," to describe "the process of erasure" whereby the Meiji administrative powers concealed internal colonization of peoples from Hokkaido to Okinawa; and "colonial regard," to describe the "mimcry of Western superpowers." The legacy of imperialism resonates in contemporary nation-building. Empire is inscribed in the rise and decline of Japan's economic policies and employment system.

The train station was my point of departure for reflecting on the enigma of Japanese capitalism. Parallel to my own intellectual foray, the narrative of the book begins in the late 1990s, when the weakness of the Japanese model became more apparent in the midst of lingering economic malaise. The Tokyo Station and its locale are emblematic of the unraveling of the old bargain. Like the Narita Airport, private enterprises, in partnership with local authorities, are restructuring space in the area surrounding Tokyo Station in the central business district of Marunouchi, which accommodates 230,000 workers toiling away in high-rise office buildings mostly owned by Mitsubishi, one of the biggest corporate conglomerates currently controlling nearly 40 percent of the land (Languillon-Aussel 2014); their holdings date to the Meiji Restoration and Taisho periods "when pre-existing daimyo (aristocratic estates) adjacent to the Imperial Palace were decommissioned and sold off" (Rowe 2011, 1280). After the asset price bubble collapsed, private developers actively reshaped and redefined public spaces (Languillon-Aussel 2014). During the past two decades, Japanese capitalism has morphed into a new dreamscape for private interests.

---

6   The borders of Japanese empire extended beyond the confines of East Asia. Japan projected Empire in a southern expansion as far away as the Brazilian interior. Immigration served the purposes of imperial power. The Japanese state encouraged rural laborers to emigrate, thereby dispersing surplus labor from the countryside and defusing possible social unrest among workers faced with dispossession (Jacobowitz 2014).

Acknowledgements

Much like the figure of Beatrice, I met many who guided me along the way on my intellectual journey in Japan. My initial foray grew out of the research activities of graduates students at Purdue University. Working with Nagisa Kato Hayashi pushed me to apply for the SSRC Abe Fellowship. I am grateful to Nagisa who kept the initial project on track as we tried to navigate sign-less streets during our joint enthographic outings. Nagisa not only served as a guide through the dizzying social, political and physical geography of that nation's capital, but also served as an interlocutor who helped me analyze the sometimes opaque Japanese economic system. Both Hiroko Hirakawa and Laurie Graham pointed me in new directions and toward new insights engendered by conversations about their dissertations. Purdue was a kind of purgatorio – shorn of its religious imagery; here Robert Perrucci took on the role of Virgil whose foresight and support enabled me to embark on the next stage of this long-term project.

With generous funding from the SSRC Abe Fellowship and with the generosity of Karen Shire, and her colleagues (particularly Kazuko Tanaka and William Steele) at the International Christian University (ICU), I enjoyed a bucolic setting at the northern reaches of sprawling Tokyo. ICU gave me the time and the space to immerse myself in Japanese studies. Karen Shire was more than a host. Karen, Peter and Freddy opened their home to me on several occasions, and kept me from losing my bearings on the city streets and in the transportation networks. Catching a glimpse of Peter on the crowded platform of Shinjuku Station, allowed the three weary travelers to disembark from the Narita Express and to continue on the next two legs of what became a routine transit nexus. The Mitaka Station was the first, and then the last place, literal bookends, where I conducted research for this manuscript. Finally, Karen introduced me to her colleague, Kazuko Tanaka, who's political and personal commitments have inspired generations of students in addition to influencing feminist scholars and activists.

Kazuko was an important collaborator on the next stage of the project, funded by the Center for Global Partnership of The Japan Foundation. In conjunction with Anne Zacharias-Walsh, we developed a two-year project on working women's organizations. Our partnership spanned the personal and the political. Over the duration of that project and subsequently, I came in contact with numerous labor and feminist activists. I apologize in advance for my inability to recall the names of all of the dedicated activists who contributed to this book. There are many deserving of mention, including: Hirohiko Takasu, Seichii Yamasaki, Jo Nakajima, Matt Noyes and Emiko Aono, Midori Ito, Makiko Matsumoto, Kazuko Tanaka, Naoko Takayama, Daiki Hiramori, Chie Matsumoto, Akai Jinbu, Natori Manabu, Makoto Kawazoe, Kiyoko Ban, and Noriko Nakatani. Special thanks are due to Chie Matsumoto and Seichii Yamasaki, translators extraordinaire.

Much is owed to my friends and my colleagues in the GLOW network. The ideas for this book were nurtured in my relationships with GLOW members. GLOW has been an intellectual home; whether sharing dinner at a long table illuminated by the flickering light of dusk in Provence or debating core concepts in-between home-cooked meals and soaking in the *onsen* at Mari's lovely house. I can never repay my intellectual debt to GLOW, especially Joan Acker, Karin Gottschall, Ilse Lenz, Mari Osawa, Karen Shire, and Sylvia Walby. Other GLOW members extended our network further: Keiko Aiba, Sawako Shirahase, Yuko Ogasawara, Diane Perrons, Monika Goldmann, Ann Witz, and Ursula Mueller.

The latter stage of the book is based on research conducted when I was on sabbatical at the Institute for Gender Studies (IGS), Ochanomizu University. I have fond memories of my daily visits, greeted by the guards at the gate, and welcomed by the helpful staff. I learned a lot from interacting with the students and from the discussions with Ruri Ito, Mariko Adachi, Nobuko Nagase, and Kaoru Tachi. In one reconnaissance of the district, I discovered a fateful sandwich sign advertising Mahlzeit Bakery – a curiosity, a German-style bakery tucked away in Tokyo. Visiting the bakery and the bakers became an almost daily ritual – in fact, the baker asked how my family enjoyed the bread, assuming that my daily rations could feed a family.

Several people have deepened my knowledge of Japanese society, labor politics, and precarious employment. Their work goes further than a mere bibliographical citation: David Slater, John Campbell, Andrew Gordon, Leah Vosko, Sarah Swider, Kimoto Kimiko, Anne Allison, Kevin Hewison, Arne Kalleberg, Dennis Arnold, and Joe Bongiovi.

The final chapters of this book were written after my return from a research visit made possible by a grant from The Douglas A. Fraser Center, Wayne State University, and with support from Marick Masters, Director of Labor@Wayne.

Denis Wall deserves a special thank you for his thorough copy-editing and sociological imagination. His thoughtful queries forced me to rethink ideas already published. I incorporated many of his suggestions, though I take full responsibility for the final text.

Of course it is customary to end with salutary remarks about one's family. I have profited immensely from conversations with Penelope Ciancanelli, who despite her Italian surname, is part of our adopted family. Penny's comments are so woven into the fabric of the argument; it is hard to draw a line between her ideas and my own. Her encouragement at a critical stage kept me from abandoning the book. Molto bene, Penny.

What to say about my partner and my son. I want to thank Bernhard for indulging my interest in Japanese culture, particularly the enchantments of Studio Ghibli. Our visit to the Museum, a short taxi ride from Mitaka Station, revealed the workings of imagination. Totoro will forever stand as a sentry guarding those precious memories of that visit, and a reminder of the delights experienced in our joint viewing of each Miyazaki animation. It was on this trip, during a three-month hiatus, that Bernhard's early film-work had a meaningful impact on me and my work. The short films that he narrated while I was away in Japan, reminded me of home.

The book is dedicated to my partner of many years – the actual number remains in dispute. David Fasenfest accompanied me on my first trip to Japan, and returned home with Bernhard while I stayed behind to conduct my research. He supported me in many other ways too numerous to identify and even to remember. The 2014 trip to Naoshima was the prelude to the last stage of my research in Japan. Nothing could prepare us for Tadao Ando's underground museum, Chichu, illuminated by natural light, the island's natural beauty interspersed with monumental sculptures, the Hiroshi Sugimoto photographs hanging on the walls of the floor below our hotel room, and the sparkling sake and other local delicacies.

To them, and to my friends and colleagues, I say: Domo arigato.

List of Tables

The Enigma of Japanese Capitalism: An Historical Introduction

On 3/11, a catastrophic series of events sent tremors across the Japanese nation. It took the devastating aftermath to expose the hidden fault-lines embedded in Japan's once vaunted postwar economic system. Three weeks into the crisis, "Braving Heat and Radiation for Temp Job" (Tabuchi April 9, 2011), reported on day laborers and migrants risking their lives for a job cleaning irradiated water leaking from the Fukushima Dai-ichi nuclear power plant. In the months following the disaster, the intense media scrutiny focusing attention on the cleanup efforts made day laborers' precarious employment more transparent, and thus, newsworthy. Though the media's glare has faded, periodic updates reveal the deplorable working conditions at the plant. The tsunami and nuclear disaster at the Fukushima plant shook up society, revealing the vulnerabilities that lay dormant in society. Three years after the disaster, a front-page article in *The New York Times* headlined a story about a labor intermediary company advertising jobs specifically aimed at destitute, unskilled workers (Tabuchi March 19, 2014). Homeless and unemployed men, society's cast-offs, were hired as temp workers to clean-up the dangerous irradiated site. The presence of these informalized workers during the recovery puts in stark relief a chronic problem of precarious work, challenging the dominant image of Japan represented symbolically by the middle-class salaryman.

Three "lost" decades have taken their toll, leaving nothing untouched in their wake. When the tsunami washed away whole villages, Japan's social structure already resembled the US in terms of its income inequality (GINI Index of 0.329 for Japan vs. 0.378 for the US), its overall poverty rate (15.7 percent vs. 17.3 percent), the poverty rates for children (14.2 percent vs. 21.6 percent) and for seniors (21.7 percent vs. 22.2 percent) (Blow 2011). In another sign of the changing times, youth's inability to gain a foothold in the labor market became evident as unemployment reached 10.4 percent of men and 8.0 percent of women and nonstandard employment hovered at one-quarter of men's and more than one-third of women's total employment (JSJ 2014, 49).[1] It is now well documented that young men and women no

---

1   While the nomenclature of standard/nonstandard employment has applicability to Japan, its general usage is problematic for several reasons: labor standards vary even among workers

longer can expect to find a permanent job right out of school. Brinton (2011) chronicles the uncertain fate of the current generation of young non-elite men "Lost in Transition." Changing economic circumstances undermine social and cultural conditions felt acutely by young men who are being denied the normal entry into the labor market. Despite these trends over the past three decades (Ishida and Slater 2010), theories characterizing Japan's variety of capitalism have underestimated the depth and even the extent of old fissures and the possibilities of new class and gender fault-lines in society.

The story of Japanese capitalism, held up as a model for economic prosperity and growth, underplayed nonstandard employment and women's unpaid reproductive labor in the narrative of success. Once celebrated as a high trust system generating a high economic performance, Japan seemed to lose its way so spectacularly in what some have called the "Lost Decade" of the 1990s. Japan's accelerated growth stalled on the shoals of the Lost Decade, never to fully recover from its economic tailspin. Such a precipitous decline, punctuated by the extensive spread of precarious employment, is hard to square with the former narrative of economic success. The economic success story masked inherent contradictions only coming to light during the prolonged recession. The forms taken by the decades-long crises and the current efforts at resolution must be understood in terms of the specific features of this variety of coordinated capitalism which has dictated events.

This juxtaposition of rapid economic success against subsequent failure has eluded theorists' attempts to explain the enigma of Japanese capitalism. Some economists treat Japan as such an exceptional case that no general economic theory is applicable (for a critique see Boyer 1998, 156). Others attribute superior economic performance to distinctive features of Japan's culture or political system. Challenging these conventional neo-classical economic accounts, William Tabb (1995) anatomizes Japan's postwar system built on historically-specific institutional features: including, its developmentalist state implementing a broad industrial policy; its trade unions embedded in corporate structures; and its electoral politics dominated by the Liberal Democratic Party (LDP). Institutional complementarities in this coordinated variety of capitalism formed "a unique social structure of accumulation, or system of regulation, or

---

in the same categories and across countries; the standard employment relationship has been limited to a small number of workers, primarily men in the unionized manufacturing sector, and differs in countries with strong labor regulation and unions; the standard employment relationship never existed in the global South nor among women, but rather was a function of a particular class and gender bargain in the west after WWII; and not all nonstandard work is precarious (Bernhardt 2014).

societal reproduction that set it apart from other nations and in important respects from Japan's own past and its future" (Tabb 1995, 6). By the early 1990s, the asset bubble had burst unwinding conditions that had supported the system's coherence and rendering unviable previous accommodations that heretofore were propitious for the political economy. Tensions between state and economy produced dysfunctions, as an increasingly globalist orientation of Japan's industrial titans began to conflict with nationally-bound state bureaucracies that had guided capital allocation (Tabb 1995, 6–7).

Yet, conventional accounts have misdiagnosed the crisis because they failed to integrate gender in their analysis of class-based institutions coordinating economic governance. The institutional architecture distinguishing varieties of capitalism and social structures of accumulation missed a central feature of the postwar economy, namely its embedded reproductive bargain. This reproductive bargain had sustained and made possible the economic miracle. Consistent with Tabb (1995, 7–8), those very characteristics of a social structure of accumulation that had stabilized (regulated) the system and that had supported societal reproduction over time came to be fetters on adjustments when confronted with new conditions. My perspective focuses on the dramatic increase of nonstandard employment, which I argue is rooted in the design of the institutional architecture supporting pillars of the Japanese employment system, the reproductive bargain, and its mode of regulation. The concept of reproductive bargain simultaneously delimits the structures of social relationships linking production and social reproduction in the context of institutional arrangements between family/household, the state and the economy, with a dynamic understanding of agents and agency of individuals and groups (re)negotiating these relationships.

A reproductive bargain composes an historical ensemble of institutions, ideologies, and identities around social provisioning and care for human beings. My usage of ensemble echoes Lefebvre's reading of Marx, referring to the totality of spheres of labor activity existing in dynamic relationship to each other. The interrelations between spheres are historically contingent and open, "even as they are inextricably interwoven with each other" (cited in Harvey 2011, 128). The variability of gender relations is based on historical bargains, likely to vary both across time and place. That is, strategies and choices around market and domestic options are shaped within a set of concrete constraints (Kandiyoti 1988, 285). In Japan, the institutional buttresses of the reproductive bargain that had stabilized and enabled economic success during the expansionary 1960s became fetters on societal reproduction manifest in declining fertility, labor shortages, and restrictions on immigration during the recessionary 1990s, and thereafter. By identifying the institutional logic of a corporate-centered male-breadwinner reproductive bargain, this book offers a framework to explain escalating precarious work (as effect) in the Japanese labor market, and social precarity (as affect) in society more generally.

This introduction lays out the argument in four main sections. The first section identifies the specific historical conditions at the heart of Japan's postwar capitalist development. It was the particular national and international circumstances faced by Japan during the period after the Second World War through the 1950s that set the stage for the consolidation of political power of the LDP and the "domestication of labor," putting an end to this turbulent era, that forged the negotiated reproductive bargain. An examination of the historical settlement allows for an analysis of the establishment of company citizenship privileging the male breadwinner in calculations for welfare benefits in exchange for men working long hours in relatively secure jobs at core industrial firms. In contrast the bargain relies on women's unpaid reproductive labor in the family and increasingly on women's waged work in nonstandard jobs.

Over the next three sections, the introduction documents the trajectories of Japanese capitalism. In the second section, using the concept of reproductive bargain, the analysis makes explicit the usually implicit agreement over the organization of tangible benefits and responsibilities provided by the state for families and for citizens (Pearson 1997), in order to reveal the connections between "the public and the private, the individual and the social, market work and family work" (Cobble 2007, 102). Looking more in-depth at state and society relations, the formation of Japanese capitalism was founded on institutions of hegemonic rule, most notably through the ideology of the salaryman coupled with the enforcement of nationalist policies. Then turning to the employment system, the third section shows how the regulatory system solidified the male-breadwinner model of Japan's corporate-centered welfare system. The slowing of economic growth and intensified global competition put pressure on the former class and gender compromise holding up the old bargain. As a result, precarious employment already a feature of the postwar system became a more visible trend. Finally, the fourth section reveals signs of the reproductive bargain unraveling manifested in the processes of widespread labor precaritization. Precarity is defined both as effect and as affect, in order to distinguish between employment forms and social forces, respectively.

The book uncovers vulnerabilities already built into the economic model now becoming more acute. Rather than merely a residual dimension of Japanese employment practices and structures, the perspective outlined here indicates that nonstandard employment represents a key component of work transformation and underscores the salience of class, gender, sexuality and nationality in the process of Japan's on-going restructuring. By deciphering the terms of this reproductive bargain the book seeks to solve the enigma of Japanese capitalism.

Forging a Reproductive Bargain in Postwar Japan

Japan's current economic crisis is linked to the state's nation-building project consolidating capitalism over the past half century. Though Japan's imperial ambitions were extinguished in the ashes of defeat, the Japanese state embarked on an ambitious modernization project in an effort to rebuild the war-torn nation and to ensure an adequate supply of labor channeled into burgeoning industrial sectors. The state's rebuilding of economic infrastructure and pro-ductive capacity, decimated during the Second World War, occurred in the context of the country's imperial entanglements and complex histories, both within the region and vis-à-vis the United States.

At the war's end, America played a pivotal role in the establishment of the Japanese employment and political systems and in laying the groundwork for Japan's accelerated economic growth. In this view, Japan's economic miracle was neither an inevitable outcome of a collectivist ethos derived from Confucianism nor of hierarchical relations inherited from feudalism (West 2003, 3). Instead, Yusaku Horiuchi (2013) attributes Japan's spectacular postwar growth to a structural break in 1958. Internationally, the Cold War climate motivated the US to pursue several foreign policy goals vis-à-vis Japan: the US saw Japan as a strategic partner in Asia, as a key geo-political location for sta-tioning American troops, and as an ideological bulwark against communism looming in China and the Soviet Union. A treaty signed in 1951 gave the US the right to establish military bases in Japan and to call on Japan for aid in case war broke out in the region (Global Nonviolent Action Database) – the renewal of the treaty, referred to by its acronym ANPO, has been a source of contestation provoking waves of protest from the outset to the present time.

Domestically, political alliances brought together conservative politicians and business interests, expressed in the newly founded Liberal Democratic Party (LDP) formed by the merger of two competing conservative parties in 1955 (Tsukamoto 2012, 401). Soon after, the LDP had secured more than 60 percent of the seats in the 1958 election of the Lower House, and dominated electoral politics for the next fifty years (Samuels 1981). However, Horiuchi (2013) expresses skepticism that the LDP's victory alone was the decisive factor explaining double-digit growth on the eve of the next decade. Rather, Horiuchi persuasively argues that the new security relationship forged with the US fundamentally altered Japan's economic prospects. An adjunct to the security alliance was an economic pact in which the US absorbed a large share of Japan's exports, facilitated bank loans, and provided subsidies, relieving the Japanese state of considerable outlays for defense spending. The ruling LDP then directed "savings" toward domestic economic purposes to shore up political patronage, solidifying their hold on government power. Overall, the economic miracle was rooted in "good" institutions and favorable policies, but also enjoyed exceptional international circumstances providing the conditions for sustained growth (Horiuchi 2013).

America's role also shaped the institutional development and trajectory of "coordinated capitalism" (Yomamura and Streeck) and the corporate-centered welfare system in Japan. From his headquarters "in the fortress-like Dai-ichi Insurance Building," the Supreme Commander for the Allied Powers, General Douglas MacArthur, "exercised tsar-like power over the entire country" (Literature, Science and the Arts 2013, 55; also see Dower 2000), from the end of the war until 1952 (Tsukamoto 2012, fn. 6, 416). Under his authority, a new constitution was written and labor laws, modeled on the US National Labor Relations Act, were passed (Gould 1984). During the Occupation, the Japanese working hours regime was substantially revised by the 1947 Labor Standards Act, which imposed a six-day, 48-hour work week, and provided for six days of statutory vacation for workers employed at least one-year (West 2003, 6). These labor laws alone did not create the conditions for the subsequent economic boom and the consensus bargain.

Labor volatility and insecurity dominated early postwar reconstruction. Harsh working conditions led restive workers to mount strikes throughout this period, and union membership peaked at around 45 percent. Militant class conflict might have changed the course of history if the Occupation forces had not prohibited a general strike, canceled by the organizers in February 1947, and if the US military presence had not posed as a potent deterrent. At midnight on January 30, 1947, an estimated 2,400,000 workers were poised for a general strike. These transportation, utilities and postal service workers demanded the tripling of wage increases and the resignation of Yoshida Shigeru's conservative government. A work stoppage of this magnitude could have brought down the government. Acting to preserve the status quo and to keep a lid on worker's mobilization, General MacArthur banned the strike: he is quoted as saying that "he could not permit 'so deadly a social weapon' as a general strike in the present impoverished and emaciated condition of Japan" (The Sydney Morning Herald 1947). The volatile politics of the era was apparent in the splintering and reconsolidation of political parties; the Socialist

Party of Japan (SPJ) even spent ten-months leading a coalition government from April 1947 to February 1948.[2] Then the SPJ's influenced waned in the midst of red purges during the era. The suppression/repression of domestic communist parties, left-leaning unionists and students was a part of the domestic "security" alliance.

By the end of the decade a massive protest against the security treaty threatened the fragile alliance between Japan and the US (Horiuchi 2013). Prime Minister Kishi Nobusuke, one of the architects of LDP's conservative industrial and foreign policy (Samuels 1981), had made strengthening and ratifying the security treaty with the US foremost among his top priorities. In one of the largest protests of the era, a coalition led by Sohyo, the Socialist Party, and Zengakuren, the national student association, brought together organized labor, leftist groups, and more broad-based civil society organizations, including the Federation of Japanese Women's Organizations, the Association of Japanese Literary Persons, the YMCA, cultural groups, and many academics. Staging rallies, car parades, and limited strikes across cities in Japan, the main actions occurred in front of the Diet in Tokyo. On November 27, 1959 the coalition amassed thousands of protestors with the intention of presenting petitions against the treaty. Spontaneously, protestors burst into the Diet, spending the rest of the day singing, dancing, and occupying the building (Global Nonviolent Action Database 2014). Despite further mass mobilizations, the Diet passed the treaty in short order after Nobusuke authorized the police to extricate Socialist Party MPs from the parliament on May 19, 1960. Protests continued and intensified, leading to general strikes and culminating in a rally of more than 120,000 people at the symbolic center of the government. In the face of mounting pressure, Nobusuke resigned, defusing this politically volatile situation. By 1960, the LDP was ensconced in office, propped up by US economic aid.

This brief political history marked two major turning points that put Japan on its economic path.[3] At critical junctures, the employment model could have turned out differently. The US Occupation forces along with US

---

2   For an excellent blow-by-blow account of the political machinations of the period, see Samuels (1981).

3   The statist project has a long history, dating back to the Meiji period. After toppling the nearly 260-year old Shogunate dynasty, the leaders of that "revolution" began fashioning a modern nation-state in 1868. To consolidate control, the capital was moved from Kyoto to Tokyo, and the modern prefectures replaced the former feudal fiefdoms. By the end of the 1890s, Japan had consolidated the central government, allowing the state to pursue its twin agendas of militarization and industrialization in the inter-war period (Tsukamoto 2012, 400).

economic aid buttressed the establishment of the LDP's stronghold on the levers of government. Once the LDP had solidified power, the state dictated rapid modernization aimed at building physical infrastructure for the reconstruction of the economy, and fostered an ensemble of institutions, ideologies and identities, promoting a social bargain that structured women's and men's inclusion in, and exclusion from, public arenas of work and politics. Japan's state-led modernization was a cultural as well as an economic and political project.

State and Society: The Formation of Japanese Capitalism

Japanese capitalism "operated through a broad configuration of disciplinary institutions, hegemonic rule through creation of social consensus and normativity, and forcing of individual and collective identities in complex relation to one another" (Yoda 2006, 35). Hegemonic rule in modern Japan involved the policing of bodies and boundaries through the enforcement of a strict border regime around the notion of Japaneseness, and through the heteronormativity of the salaryman and professional housewife, which provided the material basis of and cultural conditions for hegemonic masculinity of the corporate-centered male-breadwinner model.

The ideology of the salaryman was at the center of this model of capitalism and the male-breadwinner reproductive bargain. While the term salaryman dates back to the Taisho period (1912–26), the expression of masculinity signified by this construct gained currency in circulation during the 1960s (Roberson and Suzuki 2003, 7). By one estimate, salarymen accounted for less than 10 percent of the employed workforce in the pre-war period, increasing to around 50 percent of household heads by 1955 and 75 percent in 1970. Though this estimate exaggerates the "real" number of salarymen by including all full-time male employees receiving a monthly salary in the category, it underscores the ideological centrality of the middle-class, heterosexual citizen worker in Japanese culture and politics (Dasgupta 2003; 2013). The image of salaryman, or male breadwinner, both allowed and compelled men to devote long hours as workers in capitalist corporations and fulfill roles as taxpayers (Roberson and Suzuki 2003), whereas women were expected to occupy positions out of the labor force as "good wives and wise mothers" on behalf of the nation (Uno 1993). Many of the same themes embodied in the image of masculinity also constituted the core composition of adulthood; that is, taking responsibility toward society, family and work organization (Cook 2013, 33). The Japanese welfare system based entitlements on this male-breadwinner model whereby women typically derived rights and benefits as wives and mothers rather than principally as workers (Gottfried 2009).[4] This configuration of class, gender, sexuality and nationality informed the inscription of the ideal family and worker, which participated in the structuring of hierarchies and exclusions (Bergeron and Puri 2012, 497).

A national(ist) narrative filtered modern subjects through the binary of Japanese/non-Japanese based on the exclusion of (colonial) "Others." To sustain this juxtaposition, the modern state reinvented a tradition of an authentic monolithic culture. Glenda Roberts summarizes the new research on "the formation of modern Japanese identity" in the following way: "The meaning of 'Japaneseness' was created from the new nation-state, linking nation, family, and the Japanese way of life. The next step, linking blood and culture, was made explicit in 1940 by Kada Tetsuji, who argued for a biological or genetic basis for the 'distinctiveness and superiority of the Japanese people'" (1999, 399).[5] In particular, the construction of Japaneseness erased the recognition of other subject positions and fostered a kind of historical amnesia for forgetting Japan's colonial past. "In the process Japan turn[ed] increasingly inwards as it [grew] to seek its national identity by distancing itself from the other that is the West, while the rest of Asia is silenced" (Endo 2006, 1).

The Immigration and Control Law and strict enforcement created a border regime, regulating the mode of entry, the movement of bodies within and across nations, and restricted the terms and conditions of living and working in Japan, that undergirded this inward turn. Even the revised Immigration and Control Law of 1990 accorded a special status to those with Japanese heritage, *Nikkeijin*, consisting principally of Latin Americans, mostly from Brazil and Peru (Roberts 1999, 399). As overseas descendants of Japanese, *Nikkeijin* were allowed to stay in Japan as "spouses or children of Japanese nationals or as 'long-term residents' without limitations on work" (Ito 2005, 56). The subsequent lifting of restrictions gave workers with specific skill sets temporary visas, ensuring their return after a brief training/work stint. The border regime managed populations by regulating whom and under what conditions people could be incorporated into the "body politic" (Mahler and Pessar 2006, 40).

---

4   The male-breadwinner model privileges married women with children over single mothers in the distribution of welfare benefits. Unable to rely on a safety net and unable to access favorable tax deductions, single mothers must work to secure the livelihood of their family. Due to the gender wage gap, single mothers are the category of women with the highest rates of full-time employment, and the highest rates of poverty.

5   Based on a review of Michael Weiner's introductory chapter from *Japan's Minorities: The Illusion of Homogeneity*.

Restrictions on immigration circumscribed the supply of labor available for low-wage reproductive labor. Through exclusion and selective inclusions, the Japanese state enforced the boundaries and terrain on which social consensus and class and gender compromises were negotiated.

The Japanese Employment System: Regulating Labor, Labor Regulations

The corporate-centered welfare form of capitalism was forged against the backdrop of postwar reconstruction in Japan. By the end of the 1950s, and solidified on the eve of the new decade, the ensemble of institutions composing the Japanese variety of capitalism had taken root. The state paved the way for the establishment of institutions supporting consensus bargaining that tied workers' livelihoods to corporate-centered welfare capitalism. Consensus bargaining in Japan and in Germany had roots in the particular security alliance with, and economic aid from, the US. Both countries faced a similar set of circumstances favoring economic growth: export-manufacturing sectors built on male industrial citizenship and a reproductive bargain centered on the ideological construction of the "professional housewife."

In Japan this corporate-centered reproductive bargain established a strong form of company citizenship coordinating worker's interest with the economic prosperity of their particular firms. Weak labor organization at the national level, and high fusion of labor representation with employers at the enterprise level deprived labor of a strong political lever for realizing a social bargain. Unions settled for strong internal labor markets that ensured job security and an age-graded system of rewards for their members in large industrial companies. This bargain between labor and capital extended rights and real benefits for company citizens at the enterprise, effectively abolishing traditional boundaries between white and blue-collar workers – the latter had been "paid on a daily basis and had limited access to corporate welfare and limited prospects for promotion" (Imai 2014, 3). The male-breadwinner reproductive bargain channeled benefits to company citizens who enjoyed the three treasures of lifetime employment, age-graded wage increases, and generous bonuses and allowances.

As one of the central pillars of the Japanese employment model, the courts substantively supported the norm of lifetime employment as far back as the 1950s. Later, Japan's courts applied a strict legal standard, "an abuse of rights" approach, to determine whether an employer had just cause for dismissing a worker (West 2003, 10). There is strong historical evidence suggesting that the courts' actions "were not enforcing longstanding pre-existing norms, as lifetime employment was simply not present in prewar Japan" (West 2003, 13). West, among other legal scholars (Foote 1996; Kagan 2000), find that the courts uniformly enforced the no-dismissal rule in the general case, while permitting dismissal in cases in which workers attempted to renege on the labor-management bargain (2003, fn. 42, 15). Statutory protections against unfair dismissal apply under limited circumstances. The Labor Standard's Act (LSA) (art. 19) prohibits dismissal in the case of workers recuperating from work-related injuries and women workers on maternity leave – a provision that equated pregnancy with disability. West argues that it was not principally the LSA, but rather it was the judiciary that established limits on dismissal, grounded in the guaranteed right to work in article 27 of the Constitution (West. 2003, 9). Japanese judges have restricted employer's right to dismiss workers without strong justification (Koshiro 2000), in effect upholding the practice of lifetime employment relationships. In 2003, many of these common law principles were codified. The revised Labor Standard's Act stipulated that dismissal had to be based on "reasonable grounds" and to be acceptable "in light of social norms" (West 2003, 11). This doctrine was applied broadly. It extended to fixed-term contract employees, as courts have long held that the renewal of fixed-term contracts on a regular basis may create a "regular employment" relation (West 2003, 12). For the most part, nonstandard employment was not covered by these legal norms, though the courts went as far as providing legal protection for workers on fixed term contracts in limited cases shown to be of a regular employment arrangement. In this way, the courts upheld the corporate-centered welfare system by bolstering job security for those workers in standard employment.

More generally, Japan's regulatory regime has relied on informal "administrative guidance" (Kagan 2000 228), minimizing the role played by the judicial and legal system in "making" law. Regulated enterprises and their industry associations are involved in formulating regulation. According to Kagan (2000, 228), "Ramseyer (119) suggests an additional reason: in Japan's parliamentary political structure, dominated by the national bureaucracy and an almost continuously powerful Liberal Democratic Party (LDP), regulatory bureaucrats have faced strong incentives not to deviate from policies favored by the LDP, and judges have faced strong incentives to defer to those bureaucratic decisions." The court's posture toward labor law has been less deferential vis-à-vis the state and employers. Yet refusal to work overtime or to transfer, a notable aspect of the employment bargain, represented justified grounds for dismissal of workers, according to court legal interpretations.

Under the umbrella of weak national labor regulation, the employment system supported job security for a core workforce and minimal social protections for other workers. Job security of regular employees working in large Japanese companies was underwritten by the less visible inferior working conditions further down the job hierarchy and the production chain throughout the postwar period. Economic expansion that followed during the 1960s stabilized employment relationships for many men who moved into more secure industrial employment in unionized enterprises, while these same enterprises and their subcontractors employed men in nonstandard employment as a flexible labor force (Slater 2009).

Alongside burgeoning industrial giants in auto and electronic, agriculture and textiles saw their fortunes decline throughout the 1960s and 1970s. State industrial planning accelerated the transformation of agriculture. A glance at the employment structure over a twenty-year span 1950–1970, confirms the major upheaval; a shift from nearly half (48.3) in agriculture to only 13.4 percent. Likewise, industrial production employed only 22.6 percent of the working population in 1950, and grew to 37.2 percent by 1973 (see Table 1.1).[6] In some regions of the country, farming no longer could support a family's livelihood. As a result, both the husband and the wife combined part-time farming and factory work generating income for family sustenance.[7] Japan's economy is notable for the relatively large share of women working full-time at jobs in the manufacturing sector, particularly in the textile industry. Historically, the textile industry was a key sector propelling the economic miracle until its decline in the face of global competition and from the move of Japanese companies to reap low-wage labor in other parts of Asia. Until the 1970s, textile workers enjoyed relatively stable employment and good benefits, though these never reached the generous levels found in auto, steel, and other major manufacturing sectors. An empirical and qualitative study of textile workers' everyday lives and livelihoods suggests that the dual-earner female career model co-existed with the ideology of the male breadwinner.

---

6 Japan's employment structure contrasts with two other economic powerhouses, the US and Germany. Already by 1950s, the US was a postindustrial economy, with more than half of employment in services, only 13.0 percent in agriculture, and 33.3 percent in industry. By 1973, services accounted for nearly two-thirds of total employment, and industrial employment fell less than one-percent. Germany began the 1950s with a large share of employment in industry (43.0 percent), adding a few percentage points twenty years later. Interestingly, Japan's service sector exceeded the industrial sector by 1973; whereas Germany's employment structure was evenly divided around 46 percent in each.

7 A personal conversation, on July 31, 2014, with Professor Kimiko Kimoto of Hitotsubashi University, reminded me of gaps in the narrative of the Japanese economic miracle. Too often, automobile and steel dominate accounts characterizing the employment system in Japan.

Women entered their husband's three-generation family homes and, with their added income, contributed to sustaining the compound family form. In these working class communities, few women were full-time housewives. Since the 1980s and 1990s, the downsizing of the textile industry has left many women out of work and underemployed. By the 2000's with minimal prospects for stable employment and the downsizing of factories, women shifted their employment from manufacturing to low-wage, insecure employment in retail and care. Even prior to global relocation of textile plants, mechanization transformed the labor process and led to the replacement of workers by machines.

More generally, since the mid-1970s, when shocks from the global energy crisis sent tremors throughout this oil-dependent nation, the increased rate in nonstandard employment and the absolute number employed in nonstandard work became a more noticeable feature of staffing strategy. Japan's flexible mass production model further incorporated nonstandard employment, chiefly among women, as a cheap labor buffer to manage high personnel costs associated with the lifetime employment system and with the embedded male breadwinner reproductive bargain. The economic downturn during the 1990s fueled even further the erosion of standard in favor of nonstandard

TABLE 1.1   *Employment structure, 1950–1973*

		US	Germany	Japan
Agriculture				
	1950	13.0	22.2	48.3
	1960	8.2	13.8	30.2
	1973	4.1	7.2	13.4
Industry				
	1950	33.3	43.0	22.6
	1960	34.3	48.2	28.5
	1973	32.5	46.6	37.2
Services				
	1950	53.7	34.8	29.1
	1960	57.5	38.0	41.3
	1973	63.4	46.2	49.4

SOURCE: MADDISON (1987) CITED IN VIDAL, FORTHCOMING.
Notes: Percentage of total employment.

employment (see Appendix Tables 1.1 through 1.5). More insecure work replaced secure employment as represented by the salaryman previously at the center of the Japanese model.

To fully understand precarity after the initial Lost Decade, this section looked back at the historical foundation of Japanese capitalism. In brief, Japan's celebrated economic miracle had supported company citizenship for a core male workforce in large enterprises, and had depended on less secure and less visible precarious employment among workers outside these firms. While the promise of lifetime employment has not disappeared as either a practice or an expectation, it has become an unstable pillar of the Japanese employment system as more regular jobs are converted into nonstandard positions and as new jobs increasingly are created as nonstandard work arrangements, thereby undermining the former reproductive bargain. Though the ideology of the LTE continues to underpin Japanese corporate culture and expressions of hegemonic masculinity (Dasgupta 2013, 4), the terms of the bargain no longer apply in light of the growing numbers of workers whose working lives have become much more precarious and are made more visible in the wake of the devastating tsunami that hit Japan on 3/11.

Unraveling Bargains: The Crisis of Reproduction

After the tsunami swept away entire towns and destroyed former resident's livelihoods, another face of precarious work appeared when temporary workers risked their lives for a job cleaning irradiated water. In the wake of the disaster unleashed by the tsunami, a clearer picture of the underlying faultlines of inequality emerged against the background of old fissures.[8] The tsunami cleared the way for seeing social ruptures and economic dislocations that were already part of the great transformation in progress.

A similar epochal change on the eve of the last century inspired Marx and Engels' (1848) prescient observation: "Constant revolutionizing of production, uninterrupted disturbance of all social conditions, everlasting uncertainty and agitation distinguish the bourgeois epoch from all earlier ones. All fixed, fast-frozen relations, with their train of ancient and venerable prejudices and opinions, are swept away, all new-formed ones become antiquated before they can

---

8   Jennifer Robertson (2012) questions the use of "post" as a prefix in reference to the 3/11 disaster, and instead advocates for the use of "inter-disaster" to suggest continuity of the postwar government's "incapacity" to acknowledge its war-time atrocities and its current inability to adequately address the social consequences of inequality in the aftermath of the tsunami.

ossify. All that is solid melts into air, all that is holy is profaned, and man is at last compelled to face with sober senses his real conditions of life, and his relations with his kind." This description evoked the damage and ruination of sociality in the churning that occurs as a result of the "constant revolutionizing" of the forces and relations of capitalist production. "All that is solid melts into air," as reinterpreted by Marshall Berman (1988), characterizes the self-destructive nature of modernization and post-modernization, as capitalism further dissolves everything with which it comes into contact and tethers all social relations to its calculable logic. Such a picture emerges in Anne Allison's post-disaster elegy in her recent book *Precarious Japan*:

> the sea of mud that pummeled what had been solid on the coastline signaled something else: a liquidization in socio-economic relations that started in the mid-1990s (but actually before) with the turn to flexible employment and its transformation of work and the workplace (2013, 7).

What Marx and Engels did not, and could not, foresee is the crisis of reproduction and the renegotiation of an historical reproductive bargain occurring as the conditions of uncertainty and precariousness seep into all areas of work and life.

The case of Japan opens a window from which to observe inherent crisis tendencies and increasing risks associated with neo-liberal global capitalism. The more recent developments in Japan foreshadow risks posed by an old social contract designed around a set of employment relations and economic conditions no longer applicable for a growing number of workers worldwide. Nonstandard precarious work, hidden in the representation of the economic miracle, now reshapes employment relations and social reproduction in fundamental ways. The changing nature of work may herald the formation of a new precariat class, based both on the loss of long-term employment commitments at the root of organizational career-paths, and on the disconnection from old forms of social protection and sociality (Standing 2011).

Precaritization is a feature of contemporary capitalism. Precarity registers not only in the churning of workers into and out of the labor market, but also is linked to the ways we work (Hewison and Kalleberg 2008) and inhabits our senses (Allison 2013). As a widespread "social form" (Chang 2011), precarity reflects increasingly market-mediated conditions of uncertainty and insecurity, materially and existentially (Arnold and Bongiovi 2013), both as affect and as effect. But precarity (as affect) needs to be distinguished from precarious work (as effect); they map different dimensions of social, cultural, and economic phenomena.

According to Grossberg, affect "describes complex articulations among imagination, bodies, and expressions" (Grossberg 2013, 461). As "embodied affect," Allison describes how precarity "registers on the senses in the first place – as a sense of being out of place, out of sorts, disconnected." In this latter sense, precarity is a disposition of self vis-à-vis society, following Butler, who reserves precarity for identifying that "class" relegated to the margins by the state (as cited in Allison 2014, 64–65). Overall, precarity as affect consists of two different but interdependent meanings: an objective empirical condition and a subjective response. The objective condition is the acute sense of loss; loss not only of stable employment, but also loss of social moorings for grounding identities.[9] Precarity also is expressed through a range of subjective and corporeal responses, including despair and paralysis and/or hope and renewed energy for reimagining one's place in the social order. These two instantiations of precarity as affect shape the structure of feelings and actions (Chun 2014).

As effect, precarious work refers to an employment relationship, typically lacking both implicit (derived from past practices) and explicit (arising out of contractual rights) guarantees for long-term employment (Kalleberg 2011). Most fully, Vosko (2010, 2) defines precarious work as insecure, unstable and uncertain, and further considers the "social processes that go into daily and intergenerational maintenance of the working population" (Vosko 2006, 17). In other words, precarious work is associated with few or minimal benefits (health care, education, housing allowances). Whether working in the shadows or in the formal economy, precarious work has the effect of diminishing worker's ability to establish a workplace presence and identity, to organize collectively at a single workplace, and to secure both their own livelihood and that of their families. In this latter sense, precarious work represents an employment status, often delimited through the absence of social protections and of legally established rights, increasing risks and responsibilities borne by workers and their families with regard to social reproduction.

The process of precaritization spreads conditions of insecurity, acutely experienced and embodied by nonstandard workers who must improvise a sense of belonging in the midst of institutional uncertainty, and who must navigate the social, cultural and cognitive uncertainties of being socially excluded and disconnected from a fixed place of work and work group. The spread of precarity and the growth of precarious work are both a symptom and symptomatic of shifting risks from state and economy to individuals and families. Fewer workers have access to social protections tied to occupational and employment status that was the basis of securing consensus at the center of

---

9   Denis Wall pointed out this important distinction to me.

the old reproductive bargain. Social precarity deprives people of establishing a long-term career, a vocation, and a livelihood; it is a corrosive condition eroding the foundations for sustaining an identity.

Precarity as affect has a potentially empowering effect, as nonstandard workers challenge the way we work and live in a capitalist society. Nonstandard work, much like informal caring labor, represents both "a locus of exploitation and a site from which resistant subjects and alternative visions might emerge" (Weeks 2007, 234). The affective dimension of precarity operates "as a potential source of alternative epistemologies and ontologies" (Weeks 2011, 236–237). Impelling workers' organizing activity are both the objective conditions of nonstandard precarious employment and the subjective influence of precarity on one's structure of feelings. The structure of feeling can motivate positive action when workers have a sense of hope and when they recognize that their own situation is not of their own making, but rather is rooted in economic structures and political decisions.

Positive forces for change are emerging from civil society. Shaken by nationalist rhetoric and by announcements to restart nuclear power plants, waves of citizens' movement address the fragile ecosystem by routinely occupying public spaces in cities throughout Japan. In addition to the citizens' movements, new community unions coalesce in diverse places, spaces and at different scales, each operating alongside traditional unions and locating in the spaces between work and civil society. These new unions, representing unemployed and nonstandard workers, organize around precarious employment status and precarity in everyday life (e.g., uncertainties are related to livelihood insecurity of households, to the loss of social moorings, and to the lack of social benefits, and the resultant deleterious effects on health and well-being). It is this precarious existence that can enable workers to take action and that prompts them to re-imagine organizational strategies and forms.

Conclusion: Precarity in Japan

Japan's current economic misfortunes cannot be understood in isolation from the historical residues of the country's imperial entanglements and international engagements. Residues of empire continue to be lodged in insular policies toward immigration, in restrictive pathways to citizenship, and in exclusion of "foreign others" from a sense of social belonging. During the latter half of the 20th century the nation-building exercise promoted class and racial homogeneity coalescing around Japaneseness that marked who could belong to the bounded community or the nation. It is in this historical context that

I interpret more recent employment trends, and situate Japan's industrial model in "domestic" politics and international relations.

In this chapter, and in the remainder of the book, a gendered institutional analysis of Japanese capitalism offers a lens to explain patterns of inequalities. By introducing the concept of reproductive bargain, the book seeks to denaturalize and make visible the hidden abode of reproduction. The concept of reproductive bargain highlights the emergence of social settlements established in different national contexts over the past half century. Each reproductive bargain scaffolds a set of organizing principles and governing codes regulating the distribution of responsibilities, rights and relations between women and men within and between spheres of production and social reproduction, with implications for gender, ethnicized groups, and class relations. The specific configuration of class, gender, sexuality and nationality inscribe an ideal, heteronormative family form and male citizen-worker, contributing to structures of hierarchy and patterns of exclusion.

Behind the enigma of Japanese capitalism is a set of institutions seemingly corresponding to modernity. An examination of the times, from the end of the war to the late 1950s, in this chapter highlighted the development of coordinated capitalism. More specifically, the chapter identified the historical factors and actors driving rapid economic growth just a decade since the devastation wrought by the Second World War. The role of the LDP, supported by US foreign aid and favorable trade policies, gave the party the necessary leverage to take hold of political power, which lasted for 50 years. Since the mid-1950s, the LDP survived in office by coordinating business and farm interests and patronage enabled by and fuelling economic expansion. US Occupation forces, in its military capacity policing and curtailing labor militancy and in its administrative imposition writing labor laws, laid the groundwork for Japan's employment relations system. These critical turning points set the conditions for negotiation of the reproductive bargain. Class and gender intersect and interact in different ways depending on the terms of the reproductive bargain. The current unraveling of the reproductive bargain and widespread precarity in Japanese society are rooted in the tensions between production and social reproduction.

The Enduring Enigma of Japanese Capitalism

The book consists of six chapters presenting historical, ethnographic and statistical data on the institutional features of Japanese capitalism, which contributed first to the economic miracle and then to the subsequent decline.

Each chapter unfolds in an historical chronology marking critical turning points when political choices, once locked in an institutional logic then moving path-dependently thereafter. The analysis concentrates on the decades before and after the bubble burst in the 1990s. Yet, I approach "the decade [of the 1990s] in relations to broader historical trends of globalization and postmodernization that followed completion of Japan's postwar high-speed economic growth" (Yoda and Harootunian 2006, 6–7). The introductory chapter traveled back to early postwar Japan in search of the origins of Japanese capitalism. The institutions associated with the Japanese model came into existence at the end of WWII in the midst of reconstruction. Contrary to the picture of consensus bargaining, political tumult at the time threatened the social order. The volatile era ended in the late 1950s, with the development of new political-economic institutions. This first chapter followed the historical forces at play leading to the onset of the Japanese economic miracle.

Chapter 2 deconstructs the former narrative of the Japanese economic miracle to shed light on this almost invisible pillar of the employment system by tracing the historical development of nonstandard employment. "Gendering Work: Deconstructing the Economic Miracle" first appeared at a critical conjuncture in the late 1990s. One could not know at the time that signs of precarity would, in fact, become an enduring feature of Japanese capitalism. Now in retrospect, the economic miracle seems more like a chimera. Versions of the Japanese employment model heretofore had not provided an adequate explanation of the depth and even the extent of old social fissures in society. Analysis in this chapter focuses on employment trends spanning the forty-year period from 1960 to the mid-1990s, when the reproductive bargain took root. By deconstructing the economic miracle, Chapter 2 traces the emergence of dualization of the labor market. It finds that nonstandard work represented a larger and faster growing share of total employment, with women accounting for most of the change, especially before the bubble economy burst. Less visible, but no less important, nonstandard employment flourished unprotected yet not unregulated.

Into the second decade after the recession began, I applied the concept of reproductive bargain to identify the roots of precarious employment in this variety of coordinated capitalism. Chapter 3 reflects back on the historical construction of the reproductive bargain as part of Japanese capitalism during the 1950s to help explain why a country once celebrated as an economic miracle lost its way. The slowing of economic growth along with intensified global competition put pressure on the former class and gender compromise that was holding up the old bargain. As a result, part-time employment, already a feature of the postwar system, became a more visible trend even before the recession of the 1990s began. Reproductive bargains reflect the terms of compromise made about the gender division of labor, at work, and by implication, at home. Making explicit the usually implicit reproductive bargain reveals hidden dependencies and helps to account for women's relative position in paid employment and unpaid caring work. Institutionalized employment relations systems produce and are built on different bargains over the distribution of and the responsibility for the costs of reproduction. Identifying the terms of the reproductive bargain illuminates the less visible factors and forces influencing patterns of precarious work and life.

Chapter 4 moves the analysis to the organizational level, presenting an in-depth case study of agency temporary employment. It tracks the transformation of the temporary-help industry and the socio-demographics of this one-type of precarious employment. Though the extent of agency temporary work declined as a consequence of the world financial crisis, the age and gender composition of the labor force shifted as a result of the changing reproductive bargain making different groups of workers available for precarious work. Agency temporary firms do not simply respond to larger economic, political, and social forces, but also actively pursue a business model recreating the boundaries of employment relationships for different cohorts of male and female workers. The erosion of the male breadwinner model contributed to the new socio-demographics of agency temporary employment.

Comparative institutional analysis is a method for disentangling how gender matters in determining similarities and differences between coordinated and deregulated varieties of capitalism. A comparison between Japan, Germany and Sweden, in Chapter 5, broadens the conceptual template for understanding trajectories of capitalist development. The extent of the accumulated disadvantages, and patterns of precarious work, depends on employment protection and caring support that developed as part of the reproductive bargain. The male-breadwinner reproductive bargain compromised women's positions and standardized employment contracts around the needs, interests and authority of industrial male citizens. A focus on compromises and bargains makes visible the differentiated gender and class effects of work transformation in each country. The comparison puts in sharp relief those features "unique" to the Japanese employment system, and those institutional governance principles similar across the three countries.

Returning to contemporary Japan, Chapter 6 finds the "lost generation" of youth in today's labor market. It asks the question whether youth constitute a new precariat class in the making. Current statistical data from the first two decades of the new millennium indicate that the promise of lifetime employment is just that, an unfulfilled promise, and becoming less of a reality for young men. Relatively high rates of unemployment and the persistence of nonstandard employment in work biographies, signal the enduring crisis in Japanese capitalism. Evident are both tragic responses as some individuals turn inward, and hopeful signs as some unemployed youth organize against precarious conditions. In particular, the growing number of young men in precarious work challenges the dominant image of Japan represented symbolically by the heteronormative, middle-class, citizen worker in Japanese culture and politics.

The final chapter discusses politics and policies in light of the "Lost Decade" and its aftermath. Kingston (2004) asks 'what was lost in the Lost Decade?' The answer lies in the publics' skepticism about formal institutions solving problems and addressing growing social inequality. An inept government fueled ordinary citizens' demands for a more democratic society. Through Japan's "quiet transformation," civil society organizations sowed the seeds for new politics in response to the current crisis. Under the specter of ruin following the triple disasters, workers and their communities have coalesced around a new form of politics to address current and future risks. Precarious work and precarity present new prospects for and hurdles in front of labor movements. This last chapter identifies available policy tools and assesses whether old alliances and bureaucratic stasis will continue to limit state-based policy innovation. The extent to which civil society organizations can reshape the political landscape are then also examined.

The book reprises articles published over the past 16 years, coinciding with the temporal unfolding of the Japanese economic crisis. Research visits in 2007 and again in 2014, primarily to revisit temporary help agencies and new reform movements, allowed me to update the research and to reflect on my initial findings. The final chapter returns to Japan for a prospective view of new risks associated with precarious work in light of the current labor movement. Taken together, the analysis allows for an assessment of the consolidation and the decline of Japanese capitalism.

APPENDIX TABLE 1.1   *Regular and non-regular employees 2011* (10,000)*

	Employees excluding executives	Regular	Non-regular	Part-time/ temporary	Others
Total	4918	3185 (64.8)	1733 (35.2)	1181	552
Male	2745	2200 (80.1)	545 (19.9)	260	279
Female	2173	985 (45.3)	1188 (54.7)	916	273

SOURCE: THE JAPAN INSTITUTE FOR LABOUR POLICY AND TRAINING, JAPANESE WORKING LIFE PROFILE 2012/2013. TOKYO, JILPT, 2013, P. 33.
* Does not include data from Iwate, Miyagi, and Fukushima Prefectures affected by Tsunami.

APPENDIX TABLE 1.2   *Share of short-time (> 35 hr/wk) employees (non-agriculture) (10,000)*

	1980	1990	2000	2010	2011*
Total	390	722	1053	1415	1384
Male	134	221	298	449	432
Female	256	501	754	968	954
Share %					
Total	10.0	15.2	20.0	26.6	27.1
Male	5.2	7.5	9.4	14.6	14.7
Female	19.3	27.9	36.1	43.0	44.1

SOURCE: THE JAPAN INSTITUTE FOR LABOUR POLICY AND TRAINING, JAPANESE WORKING LIFE PROFILE 2012/2013. TOKYO, JILPT, 2013, P. 34.
* Does not include data from Iwate, Miyagi, and Fukushima Prefectures affected by Tsunami.
Share short-time = # of short-time/#total employees (excludes temporary disabilities) × 100

APPENDIX TABLE 1.3   *Female part-time and ratio to total number of female workers (10,000)*

	1987	1990	2000	2010	2011*
Total female	1507	1695	2014	2233	2148
Part-time female	469	584	846	923	906
Ratio	31.1	34.5	42.0	41.3	42.2

SOURCE: THE JAPAN INSTITUTE FOR LABOUR POLICY AND TRAINING, JAPANESE WORKING LIFE PROFILE 2012/2013. TOKYO, JILPT, 2013, P.35.
* Does not include data from Iwate, Miyagi, and Fukushima Prefectures affected by Tsunami.

APPENDIX TABLE 1.4   *Ratio of part-time workers (>30 hr/wk), by gender and country*

	Year	Japan	US	UK	Germany	France
Male	2000	7.4	7.7	8.6	4.8	5.5
Male	2011	10.3	8.4	11.7	8.5	5.9
Female	2000	29.1	18.0	40.8	33.9	24.9
Female	2010	34.8	17.1	39.3	38.0	22.6
Ratio of women among PT	2000	73.1	68.1	79.4	84.5	78.8
Ratio of women among PT	2011	71.0	65.6	74.7	79.2	77.2

SOURCE: THE JAPAN INSTITUTE FOR LABOUR POLICY AND TRAINING, JAPANESE WORKING LIFE PROFILE 2012/2013. TOKYO, JILPT, 2013, P. 36.

APPENDIX TABLE 1.5   *Labor force status 1965–2010 (10,000)*

	1965	1970	1980	1990	2000	2010
Male						
Total employed	2852	3091	3394	3713	3817	3615
Self-employed	666	692	658	607	527	433
Family worker	223	186	112	93	63	34
Employee	1963	2210	2617	3001	3216	3133
Unemployed	32	38	71	77	196	207
Labor force participation (%)	81.7	81.8	79.8	77.2	76.4	71.6
Unemployed (%)	1.1	1.2	2.0	2.0	4.9	5.4
Female						
Total employed	1878	2003	2142	2536	2629	2642
Self-employed	273	285	293	271	204	146
Family worker	692	619	491	424	278	155
Employee	913	1096	1354	1834	2140	2329
Unemployed	25	21	43	47	123	127
Labor force participation (%)	50.6	49.9	47.6	50.1	49.3	48.5
Unemployed (%)	1.3	1.0	2.0	2.2	4.5	4.6

SOURCE: THE JAPAN INSTITUTE FOR LABOUR POLICY AND TRAINING, JAPANESE WORKING LIFE PROFILE 2012/2013. TOKYO, JILPT, 2013, MALE WORKERS P. 20, FEMALE WORKERS P. 21.

Gendering Work: Deconstructing the Narrative of the Japanese Economic Miracle[1]

> It was there that the sleight-of-hand lawyers proved that the demands lacked all validity for the simple reason that the... company did not have, never had had, and never would have any workers in its service because they were all hired on a temporary and occasional basis... and by a decision of the court it was established and set down in solemn decrees that the workers did not exist.
>
> GARCIA-MARQUEZ 1970, 307

New staffing arrangements and production systems arose in response to problems brought on by global economic pressures. In search of solutions, many turned their gaze eastward to the apparent Japanese economic success story. Japan was the paradigmatic reference, implicitly or explicitly, for much of the comparative research on economic restructuring in the 1980s. A kind of "Orientalism" marked the treatment by scholars, governmental leaders, and executives who cast Japanese management methods as the path to economic recovery. The narrative of the Japanese miracle, however, masked the existence of a gendered work regime and a male-breadwinner reproductive bargain. By examining nonstandard employment among women we deconstruct this narrative.

Analysis in this chapter focuses on employment trends beginning in 1960 to the mid-1990s. Nonstandard work constituted a large and rapidly growing share of total employment, and women accounted for most of the change, especially before the bubble economy burst. Three primary institutional domains are discussed in order to help explain this gendered pattern of labor market experiences in Japan: the labor market, the family, and the state. Institutional legacies set conditions for the development of Japanese capitalism and the male breadwinner reproductive bargain, which favored men as full-time wage earners and women as part-time wage workers and full-time caregivers. This chapter highlights a work phenomenon that presaged more fundamental problems now apparent in the economy.

---

1   Research in this chapter is derived from early work appearing in Gottfried and Hayashi, 1998.

Nonstandard employment had been a key but understudied feature of the Japanese employment system. A voluminous literature seeking to understand or export lessons from Japan's economic success story characterized employment experiences of core full-time workers in the largest firms, and associated rapid economic growth of the 1960s and early 1970s with this primary labor market segment staffed by male employees (Gordon 1985; for a comprehensive summary see Lie 1996). An analysis of so-called "traditional" Japanese employment practices, including the lifetime/permanent employment system (LTES) and the seniority-based promotion and wage system (*Nenko-joretsu*), had diverted attention away from nonstandard employment, a relatively neglected pillar of the Japanese employment system. By almost exclusively focusing on traditional employment practices the gendered subtext of the economic miracle had been obscured.

Reading for this subtext sheds light on the less visible parts of the economic miracle. Chalmers, in one of the few studies of nonstandard employment at the time, documented what we now know as the skewed and limited picture that emerged from analysis of select labor market segments. Examining industrial relations in this relatively unknown portion of Japan's private sector workforce, she found that the *nenko* system, quality circles and concepts of welfare corporatism are "irrelevant in the peripheral context" (1989, 247). Evidence that the peripheral workforce is becoming a permanent part of the employment system confirms her prescient predictions. Although Chalmers' study filled in a missing piece of the narrative, it left unexplored the gendered work regime and reproductive bargain. Gender entered into her analysis as a demographic characteristic rather than as an explanatory factor behind the economic miracle; that is, she did not examine why women made up the majority of the nonstandard labor force.

An exemplary account by Mary Brinton (1993) probed the economic miracle narrative to reveal how family relations, educational structures and work organization together constituted a human capital system that disadvantaged women and advantaged some men in the paid labor force. However, Brinton's focus on human capital development paid insufficient attention to the broader social forces that gave rise to women's participation in nonstandard employment. A promising approach by Rosenfeld and Birkelund (1995, 130) examined the relationship between the state and part-time work, arguing that "where the organizational power of labor is strong and recent political history is dominated by leftist political regimes (such as the Scandinavian countries), a large public service sector has emerged, which together with the family policy of these countries seems to favor part-time work among women." They too found high levels of female part-time employment, but concluded that Japan did not conform to their general model. The authors unfortunately failed to further explore the reasons behind this apparent anomaly.

This chapter deconstructs the narrative of success, indicating that nonstandard employment represented a key component of the Japanese employment system from the outset.[2] Institutional legacies have set conditions for the development of the Japanese employment system which favored men as full-time wage earners and women as part-time wageworkers and full-time, unpaid caregivers. First, lifetime employment promised job security to a segment of male workers in exchange for high productivity and long hours in sunrise industries. In order to maintain lifetime employment among a small core of male workers, employers hired women workers and some men in nonstandard employment. The weakness of labor in general and enterprise bargaining in particular sustained the dual labor market structure. Second, the negotiation of employment contracts assumed and contributed to the development of a reproductive bargain between a male breadwinner expected to devote extensive time to the firm and a "professional housewife" expected to dedicate herself to the management of household affairs. Finally, (pro)active state policies have underwritten and supported traditional employment practices and household arrangements. The Japanese economic miracle is best understood as a gendered work regime and reproductive bargain arising out of the relationships between capital, labor and the state.

The Japanese Employment System and the Hidden Bargain

The myth of the LTES had obscured the facts about the Japanese employment system. While the 1990s recession required scholars to reassess their understanding of the Japanese model, there was already some recognition of the limits of the employment system prior to this economic downturn. For example, it had already been noted that the system covered only a minority of workers at about one-third of the total workforce, that "lifetime" ended around age 55, that many benefits accrued only after a minimum service of about 10 years, and that Japanese firms had always used peripheral workers as a numerically

---

2   This article draws on three main sources of data: (i) interviews conducted with government officials, temporary placement employees, and company managers of Manpower Inc. to document changes in industrial relations; (ii) government documents including legislative records, and government white papers from the Ministry of Labor (1974, 1988, 1990, 1994, 1996) to track changes in labor law; and (iii) published statistics to chart nonstandard employment.

flexible buffer (Chalmers 1989; Kato and Steven 1995, 75–76). Still, analyses of Japanese employment practices, for the most part, have left hidden the reproductive bargain underpinning the system. We maintain that the inclusion of women in less secure employment arrangements contributed to making the Japanese miracle possible.

The current employment situation dates back to the early-1970s when oil shocks reverberated throughout the oil-dependent nation (Dore 1986, 14–15; Wood 1989). In the aftermath of the initial 1973–75 oil shocks, Japanese firms introduced two main types of flexibility: lean management (*genryo keiei*) and internal flexibility (handling reductions in labor demand). Lean management and just-in-time production enabled private enterprises to make adjustments to market and technological change "more quickly, smoothly and cheaply" (Wood 1989, 2). Numerical flexibility grew in importance between 1970–75 when short-time employment rose by 3.2 percent overall and 5.2 percent among women, who lost ground as regular employees.

The recession that followed in 1993–1995 burst the expansionary real estate bubble, undermining the material basis and shaking the foundations of the LTES. Private enterprises, with the aid of the interventionist state,[3] pursued economic restructuring by intensifying gender differentiation of job assignments, which reinforced already segmented labor markets. On the one hand, large firms attempted to preserve the LTES for their core workforce, who, although smaller in number, continued to enjoy lifetime employment. On the other hand, the burden of the LTES increased the appeal of nonstandard employment leading to reforms of the lifetime employment system in general, and driving firms to accelerate their use of nonstandard employees. The increase of nonstandard employment for both men (17.1 percent) and women (21.8 percent) between 1982–1992 confirms the latter trend; the sharpest rise of short-time employment occurred during the early 1990s at a rate surpassed only during the period immediately following the oil crisis.

Men in large firms have experienced organizational restructuring in the form of departmental consolidation, the shift to a more ability-based wage/ promotion system such as Honda's introduction of an ability-based system on an experimental basis, shorter work hours, and generous severance packages for workers of all ages (Beck and Beck 1994). Large firms increasingly shed core workers through a number of existing mechanisms: for example, older employees have been dispatched to smaller subcontracting companies in the Keiretsu

---

3 A government White Paper issued by the Ministry of Labor in 1995 formally acknowledged the economic burden of the LTES, exhorting employers to save on pensions, insurance and wages by relaxing the job security system.

orbit; the retirement age has been lowered; and white collar workers have been reassigned to production work (also see Berggren 1995). According to one worker we interviewed, assembly workers at the largest Japanese electronic auto-parts company had been redeployed as gardeners in slack periods. It was the increased use of nonstandard employees, which represented a modification that sought to preserve the famed business practice of the LTES for core male workers.

Beyond the core, workers who fell outside the protective shield of the LTES experienced less job security and more economic uncertainty. In particular, small firms expected male employees to work long hours for lower wages and with either minimal or no bonuses.[4] Industrial relations was less formal and institutionalized and more coercive due to the absence or weakness of labor organization (Chalmers 1989, 238–240). Women were more likely to work in small firms (37.0 percent) or in family enterprises (19.3 percent) and/or as nonstandard workers, places and statuses which do not accord lifetime employment. Those women who found employment in large firms most typically worked as Office Ladies (OLS), a position without a formal port of entry into internal labor markets (Lo 1990). Instead, employers viewed OLS as "temporary" positions to be filled by young women prior to marriage or childbirth. The small size of the Japanese welfare state has worked against employment opportunities for women. Japanese women with college degrees have found jobs in the state sector, but not in the numbers of their counterparts in many European countries. The government accounted for only 6.0 of the female share of the labor force in Japan.

Japanese women's inability to secure employment in large firms restricted their access to "long and broad "internal labor markets. Initial job placement determines to a large extent an individual's economic future, as underscored by a senior Manpower executive:

> The society in Japan is such that women are still expected to marry and to not work after they married, to raise a family. If you finish your schooling, technical or university, and you accept a job. You are given a couple of years to corral a husband. If you don't succeed at that you lose face. And you lose the job. You are given a second chance in a second company somewhere somebody will hire who has been through a couple of years of that. The second chance you get, you get another couple of years. If you

---

4   The lack of bonuses depressed the overall pay packet for workers in small enterprises along
    the supply chain, since: "Twice-yearly bonuses have typically constituted about 25 percent of
    the total yearly cash payments made to [core] workers since the 1960s" (Brinton 1993, 133).

haven't made it by that time, you lose that job and there is no third chance. And so there exists in Japan a reasonably large group of women with four years of administrative experience, mature in their outlook and in their lifestyle, committed to their profession, because this isn't so important any more. And their skills are outstanding. They are professional people. And we can just go out and scoop those people up as temporary workers and they're terrific workers.... A company can't have then on their payroll for social reasons but can bring them in as temporary workers.[5]

In addition, Japanese workers who exit from the labor market "prematurely" suffered harsh penalties in terms of future advancement. Women, more than men, were disadvantaged by such practices. For example, women reentering the labor market after a leave of absence due to marriage or to birth of a child find that few firms hire employees at the mid-level of the organizational hierarchy. Whether or not women willingly "choose" temporary work, a Manpower executive acknowledged the societal constraints on women's participation in primary labor markets:

> More of them than we in the West would expect are willing to continue in temporary work. There is a substantial number that still want to reconnect with a long-term career development possibility. It's hard to do that. The average length of service in Manpower Japan is much longer than it is in the United States.

Not only were women less likely to find jobs with firm-specific internal labor markets, but they also saw their promotional prospects limited by cultural expectations. Organizational culture compelled workers to put in long hours at work (longer than the average for many other industrialized countries) and to remain for several hours after work to socialize with workmates; only those unencumbered by family responsibilities could satisfy these norms/requirements. It constrained women in more subtle ways as well. Others have written about how masculine corporate culture from the board room to the factory floor (Roberts 1994; Kondo 1990; Saso 1990; Gupta 2013) doomed women to jobs at the lower end of occupational hierarchies. Institutionalized labor market practices and organizational culture rewarded full-time male workers, and served as inflexible barriers for advancement among women who did not fit the standard employment model in Japan.

---

5   All quotations are based on interviews conducted by the authors in Milwaukee, London, Stockholm, Frankfurt and Tokyo.

Likewise, potentially positive neo-Fordist arrangements, such as team work, job rotation, and functional flexibility were available to workers in a subset of occupations and in a subset of industries only. Though flexible and team-oriented work was fairly extensive in Japan, these practices were concentrated in a few industries such as automobile, steel and electronics (Locke et al. 1995, 148). Similarly, large firms were more likely than small ones to organize work around teams and to rotate jobs (Locke et al. 1995, 149): the majority of Japanese firms (98 percent) with over 1,000 employees did so while just over half of medium size firms and few small size firms offered job rotation. In addition, a select group of industries (for example, finance, insurance and utilities) rotated jobs among employees (Brinton 1993, 127). The distribution of these arrangements was skewed toward men in core industries (Jenson 1989; Smith and Gottfried 1998).

Labor market institutions and organizational culture created full-time employment for core male workers and part-time employment for female workers. The weakness of organized labor was partially responsible for labor market dualism. Like other countries where organized labor had been relatively weak (e.g., the US), there was no statutory principle of equal treatment between full-time and part-time jobs in Japan. This meant that many part-time workers failed to qualify for benefits, often earned low wages, and were excluded from standardized work rules and legally sanctioned labor protections. Moreover, the fragmentation of labor representation through enterprise-bargaining and the difficulties of organizing small firms deprived workers of an effective negotiating mechanism, preempted the diffusion of unionization to non-regular workers (Chalmers 1989, 242, 249), and diminished labors' ability to stem the tide of casualization.

Mapping Nonstandard Employment

This section documents the upward trend of nonstandard employment relative to regular employment, and maps this gender-differentiated pattern from 1960 to 1994. The evidence reveals the gendered construction of such work arrangements and builds on the feminist literature on women's work in Japan (Lenz 1996; Fujimura-Fanselow and Kameda 1995; Hunter 1993; Kawashima 1987).

At the beginning of the decade of the 1990s, part-time (*paato-taimu*) employment overlapped with regular employment: nearly 12 percent of *paatos* worked weekly hours equivalent to full-time employees, another 14 percent worked just 10 percent fewer hours than full-time employees (Post-Kobayashi

1992, 37), yet the majority worked less than regular employees. The main difference between part-time and regular employees stemmed from the nature of
employment contracts and subsequent status of benefits, wages, and job security (Roberts 1994, 181). For example, Brinton (1993, 137) found that about one-
third of female part-time workers in large firms received short-term contracts
lasting two months or less. Regardless of firm size, fewer than 10 percent of
female part-time workers had secured long-term employment contracts of a
year or more in duration.

The creation of *paato* jobs allowed companies to save on wages and fringe
benefits: a *paato* earned about 70 percent of the average hourly wage of full-
time female employees who in turn earned on average about 60 percent of a
full-time male employee in 1993.[6] These numbers have not changed significantly, as will be discussed in the next chapter. Wage increases based on length
of service grew more slowly for *paatos*: 106.2 yen after five years as compared to
133.4 yen for regular female employees. The wage gap increased over the life
span between men and women, rising 11 percentage points from 1976–1987 in
the service sector (Post-Kobayashi 1992, 38). But this wage differential underestimated the earnings gap because it excluded both fringe benefits and social
wages negotiated at the enterprise-level.

Short-time *paato* jobs constituted a significant and growing share of wom-
en's paid labor. Though short-time employment only became overwhelmingly
female-dominated at the end of the 1960s, the share of short-time relative to
total employment grew more for female employees than their male counterparts throughout the period beginning in the late-1950s (see Table 2.1). The
percentage of short-time female employment increased fourfold from 8.9 percent in 1960 to 32.5 percent in 1994 (column 4, Table 2.1), while it only doubled
from 5.2 percent to 10.5 percent for men over the same period (column 5,
Table 2.1). The distribution of short-time employment by age also differed by
gender: for men, *paato* employment served as a temporary measure before
entry into permanent positions and at exit points from the labor market,
whereas for women *paato* employment spanned their life cycle – except for
women at the point of entry (15–24) when they experienced unusually high
rates of full-time labor force participation rates (Roberts 1994). Just over one-
fifth of Japanese women in *paato* employment occupied unskilled manufacturing jobs (Brinton 1993) and another one-third worked in wholesale, retail
and restaurant services (Kurokawa 1995, 81).

---

6 In 1988 Japan reported a large female-to-male hourly earnings ratio of 48.9 percent for
   manual manufacturing indicating high wage inequality (O'Connor 1996, 83).

TABLE 2.1 *Employment by short-time status and gender, 1960–1994*

Year	Total			Short-time employment			
	Number employed ('000)	Percent women	Percent short-time	Female short-time as a percent of all women employed	Male short-time as a percent of all men employed	Percent of all short-time employees who are women	
1960	2,106	30.3	6.3	8.9	5.2	42.9	
1965	2,713	31.4	6.2	9.6	4.6	48.8	
1970	3,222	33.1	6.7	12.2	4.0	60.2	
1975	3,556	32.0	9.9	17.4	6.4	56.1	
1980	3,886	34.0	10.0	19.3	5.2	65.6	
1981	3,951	34.4	10.0	19.6	5.0	67.3	
1982	4,012	34.5	10.4	20.5	5.0	68.3	
1983	4,119	35.2	10.5	21.1	4.8	70.7	
1984	4,181	35.5	11.1	22.1	5.0	70.7	
1985	4,231	35.8	11.1	22.0	5.1	70.7	
1986	4,296	36.1	11.7	22.7	5.5	70.0	
1987	4,346	36.4	11.6	23.1	5.1	72.1	
1988	4,454	36.7	12.0	23.6	5.2	72.4	
1989	4,592	37.3	13.1	25.2	5.9	71.8	
1990	4,748	37.8	15.2	27.9	7.5	69.4	
1991	4,906	38.2	16.3	29.3	8.3	68.6	
1992	5,018	38.5	17.3	30.7	8.9	68.2	
1993	5,099	38.5	18.2	31.8	9.8	67.1	
1994	5,135	38.7	18.8	32.5	10.5	66.9	

Arubaito jobs apply to both men and women who work nonconventional hours. The term often combines with student (*gakusei*) to indicate that young high school and college students typically fill *arubaito* jobs. Such jobs have been viewed as short-time, temporary positions for young entrants into the labor market, but they are no longer reserved for students. Over the 1970s and 1980s, men and women with college degrees who previously might have found jobs in large firms have settled for combining several *arubaito* jobs as they wait for more permanent employment.[7] *Arubaitos* were likely to receive hourly wages in excess of *paatos* but, like *paatos*, they rarely gained full membership in the company and shared much in common with current temporary workers. However, the uncertainty of *arubaito* positions has not, until recently, translated into lifelong economic disadvantages.

Temporary employment has been growing in importance, although it remains a small percentage of overall nonstandard employment. In 1995 temporary-help firms dispatched approximately 630,000 agency temporary workers throughout the Japanese economy accounting for 1.26 percent of total employment. The largest temporary-help firm, Manpower, employed over 77,000 "field staff" (*haken-shain*). The percentage of field staff registered with Manpower grew by 72 percent (40,711 to 70,120) while the percentage of clients increased by 46 percent (23,841–34,809) from 1990–94. Manpower/Japan reported that the biggest users of contract temporary employees included the "Big Ten Shoshas" (trading companies), such as Mitsui, Mitsubishi, and the Nippon Telegraph and Telephone (NTT). For example, the communications giant, NTT, employed 10,000 field staff from Manpower in 1995. Overall, women constituted the vast majority of all applicants for agency temporary jobs at 95 percent; among these 40 percent were married, and 67 percent were between 25 and 34 years old. The bulk of assignments (58 percent) lasted for less than five days (interview at Manpower).

In general, agency temporary workers were treated differently than similar workers in the same user company because wages and conditions of employment were negotiated between the individual temporary employee and the temporary service agency (Bronstein 1991; Gottfried 1992). Temporary employees received lower wages than regular employees, risked dismissal at the end of a fixed-term contract regardless of the hours worked or tenure with a company, and did not have formal access to a client firm's internal labor market. More specifically, agency temporary employment was found in a narrow range of occupations in Japan. A legal requirement – stipulated by Dispatching Labor Law of 1985 (*Rodosha Haken Jigyo Ho*) – restricted agency temporary work to

---

7   Based on interviews with women workers conducted by the authors.

16 administrative and clerical occupational titles. As the Japanese Manpower spokesperson noted, only Japan, at the time, prohibited temporary-help companies from dispatching workers to industrial areas of production. State regulation explains in part the extremely high concentration of women in agency temporary employment.

Paato-taimu and *haken* jobs have evolved from a mere tool of temporary relief from market fluctuations to a permanent part of a firm's organizational structure. The reliance on numerical forms of flexibility was evident in the changing ratio of part-timers to full-timers. Part-timers barely existed prior to the early 1960s; the first instance dates back to 1954 when a large department store in Tokyo began hiring female part-timers (Post Kobayashi 1992). Yet the numbers of short-time employees remained rather small until the mid-1970s: only 6.3 percent of workers held short time contracts in 1960. More than three decades later the percentage of short-time employees in non-agricultural industries had tripled to 18.8 percent of total employment.

Similarly, temporary employment grew steadily from 1960 to 1970, then suddenly jumping several percentage points between 1975 and 1980 (column 2, Table 2.2). The rate dropped slightly at the height of the 1990 recession, but this decline was short-lived and temporary employment remained fairly constant, until the financial crisis contagion spread in 2008. Temporary employment tended to fluctuate in accordance with the business cycle. A spokesperson for Manpower Inc. at international headquarters in America confirmed this trend for Japan as well as for other countries in which they operate. In response to a question about the growth picture at Manpower as of 1994, the spokesperson cautioned that:

> At this moment, I would say, it's a, it's exceptionally positive. However, it changes like the weather. In such a short time-period it can change drastically according to primarily economic conditions. It's a cyclical business. And although one philosophically could make a case for using temporary workers in a down economy, it doesn't work out that way very well in factories and offices. The result is that our business is not good during recession periods.

Interviews with upper-level Manpower managers in several world cities repeated this view, arguing that temporary employment was "usually an early indicator of coming out of recession."

Japanese economic restructuring was reflected in the normalization and feminization of nonstandard employment. Tables 2.1 and 2.2 provided strong evidence of the contrasting experience between men's work and women's

TABLE 2.2 *Employment status by gender, 1960 to 1994*

Year	Women			Women as percent of all temps	Men		
	Percent regularly employed	Percent temp workers	Percent daily workers		Percent regularly employed	Percent temp workers	Percent daily workers
1960	87.6	8.1	4.3	46.0	91.7	4.3	4.0
1965	86.5	9.0	4.6	55.2	93.1	3.4	3.5
1970	86.3	9.4	4.3	63.0	94.4	2.7	2.8
1975	85.6	10.0	4.4	66.7	95.0	2.4	2.6
1980	82.2	13.4	4.5	71.4	94.8	2.8	2.4
1981	82.1	13.6	4.3	72.0	94.9	2.8	2.3
1982	81.5	14.3	4.3	73.1	95.0	2.8	2.3
1983	80.7	15.1	4.3	73.5	94.8	3.0	2.2
1984	80.7	15.1	4.2	73.7	94.9	3.0	2.1
1985	80.8	15.2	4.0	73.8	94.9	3.0	2.1
1986	81.1	14.9	3.9	73.7	95.0	3.0	2.1
1987	80.7	15.6	3.7	73.1	94.8	3.3	1.9
1988	80.6	15.6	3.7	72.8	94.6	3.4	2.0
1989	80.6	15.7	3.6	73.4	94.6	3.4	2.0
1990	80.9	15.5	3.6	72.5	94.6	3.6	1.9
1991	81.5	14.9	3.6	72.1	94.6	3.6	1.8
1992	81.7	14.9	3.4	72.5	94.8	3.6	1.6
1993	81.6	15.0	3.4	71.9	94.7	3.7	1.6
1994	81.9	14.8	3.3	71.8	94.7	3.7	1.6

work, underlining the gendered pattern of nonstandard and standard employment. For example, the rate of women's regular employment ratcheted downward from 87.6 percent in 1960 to 80.7 percent in 1983. The rate seesawed before reaching 81.9 percent by 1994 (column 1, Table 2.2). Women lost ground during the period. The opposite held true for men whose regular employment either grew incrementally or remained constant and high for most of the period. Men as a group experienced consistently high rates of regular employment (column 5, Table 2.2).

The biggest change over the time period 1960–1994 and between men and women occurred in the temporary employment category; temporary employment grew for women (column 2, Table 2.2), but remained at a low level for men (column 6 Table 2.2). A slight reduction among women in 1986 probably resulted from legal restrictions on agency work; only Manpower was allowed to operate under this legislative mandate. As a result, Manpower thrived as a virtual monopoly for years. The international spokesperson for Manpower acknowledged the boon to business as well as the unforeseen consequences of their leading position when he stated that:

> And while this has some very comfortable advantages, you can also ask ATT what happens when that stops. We spent years building an organization that isn't used to competition. And so when the law changed and everyone saw this huge fat plum out there in Japan, practically everyone wanted a piece of it so the competition mushroomed instantly.

Once the ban was lifted several years later Manpower lost market share, although the number of temporary workers increased overall. The Manpower spokesperson characterized their competitors as follows:

> The... strongest competition was Japanese. There are Japanese trading companies that only serve their own subsidiaries. They will have a very substantial business... Sony, they have so many corporate bodies, and so many total employees, so if they just take their human resources department and turn it into a temporary help service or make a part of it a temporary help service and then they service just those companies as a corporate umbrella, then it's a substantial business.

Nonstandard work was steadily becoming standard fare for women. The gendered pattern of nonstandard employment can be explained by reference to the reproductive bargain.

The Reproductive Bargain

The Japanese employment system was based on a breadwinner reproductive bargain, which regulated action and identity through a socio-cultural consensus on sexual relations in the family and the integration of men and women into the labor market (Pfau-Effinger 1993). Women and men entered the labor market facing different domestic responsibilities and different employment opportunity structures. Employment opportunity structures for women were constructed in relationship to mandatory motherhood. Because of restrictive cultural values about women's familial and domestic roles, as well as ideologies about the gender-specificity of job tasks, female workers had been confined to occupational and industrial positions that were subordinate to those of male workers.

An historical overview of the emergence of the reproductive bargain and supporting gender ideology indicated that the strengthening of women's domestic position occurred at the point in which women no longer fitted the model of economic growth promoted by pro-business Liberal Democratic Party state bureaucrats and capital. In particular, the pervasive heteronormative ideology of *ryosai kenbo* promoted the ideal woman as good wife and wise mother: a good wife could work until marriage, should quit wage employment to raise a family, and could re-enter paid work when the children reached adolescence. By implication *ryosai kenbo*, while directed at women, indirectly freed men from domestic responsibilities and caring work so they could spend long hours at their waged jobs. This strong breadwinner model laid the basis for men's advantages and women's disadvantages in the paid labor market in general, and women's predominance in part-time work in particular.

While the ideology of *ryosai kenbo* defined women's work in terms of mandatory motherhood and the heteronormative family for over a century, its meaning has varied over time. The ideological construction of the "professional housewife" accompanied the shift from primary to secondary sector employment in the post-World War II period (Hendry 1993; Carney and O'Kelly 1990). Women, whether professional housewives or not, were expected to manage household affairs (including finances) in the absence of men who worked long hours and commuted long distances. Ironically, men's absence may have "freed" women from direct male control in the household (Hendry 1993). Imamura (1987, 83) argues "freedom of the housewife should be judged less in terms of money... and more in the light of her greater responsibility to manage the household, including finances, by herself and her husband's expectation that she will be able to manage what he can provide." Among wives working part-time, Stockman et al. (1995) found that 73 percent of the female respondents reported exclusively making decisions about family expenditures.

During the pro-growth regime of the 1960s, women's labor force participation dropped, falling to its lowest post-war level of 45.7 percent by 1975. From the mid-1970s, women's wage work took on a distinct shape and type. Women's regular employment declined even as men's regular employment remained constant. The pronounced M-curve pattern of women's employment over their life span reflected the correlation of household responsibilities and paid labor among women (Hunter 1993). These trends suggest that the male-breadwinner reproductive bargain was put in place during the economic expansion.

The Political Basis of the Reproductive Bargain

A strong Japanese state fueled the economic engine of growth during the 1950s and 1960s through industrial planning instruments and minimal direct regulation of industrial relations. State regulation imposed few restrictions on capital and facilitated the success of targeted industries, bolstering large corporate networks, and set the conditions under which labor markets would develop in gender-specific terms. Yet the Japanese state had been an elusive actor, both recognized and underplayed, in the narrative of the economic miracle. Dominant representations of Japan as a "developmental state" explicitly recognized state involvement in picking winners and losers in the economic realm (Johnson 1982). This focus on economic planning agencies diverted attention away from other policy domains affecting women's work.[8]

During the mid-1970s the state turned to women as a flexible solution to rising labor costs. But the major shift came in the 1980s and 1990s when, for the first time, the state coordinated family, employment and welfare policies as an instrument to draw more women into waged work as part-timers and retain them as full-time, unpaid caregivers. The timing of these state initiatives coincided with the rise of nonstandard work among women (evident when comparing Table 2.2, columns 2, 4, 6). A reading of policy debates and subsequent laws suggested that the state formulated part-time employment policy with women in mind. In so doing, it played a leading role both in shaping the terms of employment contracts and the reproductive bargain, and in providing legitimacy to these arrangements.

State bureaucrats promulgated a "new" economic image of women as reflected in a series of policy initiatives. A White Paper issued in 1975 by the Ministry of Labor publicly represented women as both unpaid caregivers in the home and as paid part-timers in the workplace. Further, a repeal of

---

8   Osawa Mari (1994) identified gender-biases in Japanese social policy.

protective principles of regulation served the purpose of removing restrictions on women's labor force participation, including when and where women worked. For example, an amendment to the Labor Standards Law (*Rodo Kijun Ho*) rescinded protection by removing a woman's right to take menstruation leave except in severe cases (Roberts 1994, 173) or nursing leave at the workplace, and by also abolishing limits on overtime, night shifts and hazardous work for women in professional, managerial and technical positions. While removing these restrictions gave women de jure access to a range of jobs once closed to them, they did not remove the de facto barriers to entry into the bastions of male-typed employment.

The 1980s marked the state's effort to facilitate women's labor force participation, but again in a limited capacity as part-time wage workers. Laws enacted neither mandated the hiring of women nor the application of an affirmative action principle to provide a mechanism for promoting women in male-dominated occupations. One central piece of legislation occurred in 1985 with the passage of the Equal Employment Opportunity Law (*Danjo Koyo Kikai Kinto Ho*), which specifically referred to sexual discrimination in recruitment, hiring, promotion, training and retirement (Mackie 1995, 98).[9] The EEOL represented a liberal document more than a radical mandate for change, merely asking firms to "endeavor" to practice equal opportunity and stipulating few sanctions against noncompliance. While some initiatives adopted gender-neutral language, they have had gender-specific effects. In other cases, language, such as "obligation to the family" or "spouse's income" enshrined women as the prototypical part-time worker, and by implication men as full-time wage workers.

By the 1990s the state began to formulate gender-specific policies in an effort to encourage more women to become *paato-taimu* workers. The state faced compelling demographic as well as economic reasons to develop new policy initiatives. A demographic profile had shown that 14.5 percent of the Japanese population was 65 or older in 1995, projected to reach 25.8 percent by 2025.[10] Moreover, the birthrate had continued to decline. These twin demographic trends, along with the rise of medical costs, concerned state bureaucrats who sought political solutions in line with a neo-liberal economic agenda.

---

9   The campaign for the Equal Employment Opportunity Law was organized in the mid-1970s by the International Women's Year Action Group and a coalition of 48 organizations (Mackie 1995, 97).

10   The aging population in Japan contrasts with the rates for other advanced capitalist countries, projected percent increases by 2025 of 18.1 in the US, 19.0 in the UK, 22.9 in Germany and 21.2 in Sweden.

A privatized system of elderly care could minimize costs to both public coffers and private employers. The utilization of women as *paato* workers and as unpaid caregivers threatened less modification of the prevailing gender ideology and the corresponding reproductive bargain.

More directly, the enactment of the Part-Time Labor Law (*Paato Rodo Ho*) was aimed at easing women's entry into and longevity in part-time work. Provision of the Part-Time Labor Law entitled women to childcare and other forms of leave. The law appealed to employers to endeavor to improve work conditions of short-time workers. It encouraged employers to provide *paato* employees with a written contract stipulating conditions of employment (e.g., work hours and wage rates), to utilize social factors, including family obligations, in anticipation of schedule changes, to allocate overtime and holiday work with specific consideration given to family responsibilities, to offer pro-rated paid vacation, to limit contracts to one-year, to provide a minimum of 30 days advance notice of contract non-renewal, to provide opportunities for regular employment, and to "be considerate" in allocation of bonuses, retirement allowances, use of welfare facilities (e.g., recreation, meals, gym, and medical care) and job training. The law also mandated employers with more than 10 workers to formulate regulations and to assign a manager in charge of improvement of working conditions. Despite regulatory rhetoric, enforcement of laws to improve *paato* employment conditions proved difficult, and interviews with national, prefect, and city officials report uneven and limited compliance. Larger companies appeared both better able and more willing than small companies to adopt some of the suggested measures. Kurokawa estimated that only 30 percent of establishments clarified working conditions in writing a few years after the passage of the law (1995, 83). As a result, *paato* employment continued to be largely unregulated and subject to insecure conditions (Chalmers 1989, 245).

Tax law reform acted as a further inducement for women to become *paato* workers. The state raised the upper limits on a spouse's (effectively a wife's) tax-deferred income and exempted the second earner from tax if their income fell below a threshold. Further, the law enabled a household to deduct a portion of income within a specified band at a lower rate and penalized a household for exceeding the thresholds by reducing the amount of benefits received by the full-time wage earner (Hunter et al. 1981). Families thus gained financially from supplying one full-time worker and one part-time worker to the labor force. In this way, the state made it economically rational for households to base their division of labor along traditional gender lines.

A 1994 initiative named the Angel Prelude Plan addressed women's dual roles, both as workers and as mothers. The name "Angel Prelude" reflected the government's cautious approach to influencing "private" affairs through "public" policy. The White Paper of the Ministry of Public Welfare issued in 1995 stated that:

> although the government must refrain from interfering directly in the private matters of marriage and childrearing, diminishing number of children has negative effects on children and society as a whole and thus commands attention. It is possible to remove factors such as difficulties of working, childrearing, physical and psychological burdens accompanying childrearing, burdens of educational costs, housing problems without interfering directly in lives and values individuals' hold.

Women's "private" reproductive choices became the site of urgent public intervention. This policy linked a pro-natalist campaign to the health and wealth of the nation: The health of the nation depended on women increasing their fertility in order to reproduce the future workforce and to care for elderly parents at home, whereas the wealth of the nation depended on women's own labor force participation as part-time workers. The Ministry of Public Welfare put forward the Angel Prelude Plan to promote a set of comprehensive child and family-oriented policies directed at improving the environment "to raise healthy children as well as supporting efforts to make childrearing and employment compatible."

Taken together, the formulation of such a comprehensive policy implicated the state's role in the reproductive bargain. The state skillfully redefined women's dual spheres; women's primary sphere would remain at home but with additional unpaid duties alongside a secondary sphere of gender-specific wage work. Like the ideology of the professional housewife, which emerged during the growth period of the 1960s to keep "middle class" women at home, a new ideological formulation articulated a twofold gender identity for women: as part-time workers and as full-time care-givers. In this way, the state shaped *ryosai-kenbo* ideology to suit the "needs" of capitalist production and to preserve the male-breadwinner reproductive bargain.

Demographic trends and state interests, however, set the state and private enterprise on a possible collision course. The state helped create and maintain women as a pool of cheap, nonstandard labor. However, the state's interest in promoting women's unpaid caring labor as a cost-effective, private solution to rising medical costs and an ageing population potentially conflicts with a firm's desire for women to be on call for "temporary" wage work.

Conclusion

This chapter focused on the period between 1960 and the mid-1990s when Japan's economic model was the envy of countries from the global North to the global South. The analysis uncovered processes gendering work by deconstructing the narrative of the Japanese economic miracle. Conventional accounts, which failed to identify the gendered bodies, spaces and experiences, ignored the subtext of economic development stories. Reading for the gender subtext rendered visible a temporary workforce whose displacement from employing firms relegated women's work to the margins. By virtue of their "temporary" employment status, women had been made invisible in accounts of work flexibility.

Gender has been a salient category used by capital and the state to construct part-time and temporary work as female-typed employment. Both private employers and the state adopted gender-specific policies[11] and practices in response to international economic pressures for restructuring. Nonstandard work condemned many women to what Gonas (1994) called "permanent temporariness."[12] The normalization and feminization of nonstandard employment arrangements and flexibility practices has entrenched gender inequality.

Considering institutional legacies independent of gender contributes to misleading assessments of the Japanese model. Japan's economic miracle and its subsequent decline are not fully explicable without reference to a strong breadwinner reproductive bargain, which provided an institutional foundation and ideological rationale for developing a dual labor market structure; men would devote long hours to wage employment and women would manage family affairs. Japanese employment contracts developed in tandem with the less visible reproductive bargain. Thus, as Glucksman suggests, "women enter the labour market not as 'free agents' like men, but charged with responsibility for childcare (reproduction) and household maintenance (consumption)" (Bradley 2015). More specifically, in Japan's corporate-centered male-breadwinner reproductive bargain, firm-specific skill development and corporate-based benefits rewarded long-term standard employment relationships, under-developing statutory entitlements and the social infrastructure of care services, while training and wage-setting institutions leave nonstandard employment to flourish

---

11   A discursive shift is notable in the use of gender-neutral language in policies formulated during the late-1990s and early decades of the new millennium (JTLP 2014).

12   As evidence, the average length of service of Japanese part-time workers increased from 2.9 years in 1976 to 4.8 years in 1992 (Kurokawa 1995, 81).

unprotected yet not unregulated. Japan's welfare through work narrowed coverage of employment-based benefits to the core male workforce in standard employment and excluded those in nonstandard work from the corporatist bargain.

Both economic and political factors contributed to the rise of nonstandard employment. Economic pressures for restructuring fueled the employers' strategy to shed regular workers and to add short-time workers, a phenomenon which was almost exclusively about the recomposition of women's labor force participation. Restructuring prompted the State to formulate a part-time labor law and family policy whose stated purpose was to ease women's entry into and increase their longevity in part-time work. Nonstandard employment among women was part of an overall strategy to maintain the pro-growth economic regime which, consequently, accentuated gender differentiated labor markets. Politically, a weak labor movement entered into a class and gender bargain that sustained an employment system in which a select core of male workers reaped benefits at the enterprise-level.

This analysis should not leave the false impression that women passively responded to the dictates of state initiatives and ideological injunctions. Women's increased participation in *paato-taimu* work does not simply mean that they slavishly followed state and business dictates. The changing system may have reflected women's active pursuit to create work possibilities without trying to emulate or become men whose intensive work styles may not be desirable.[13] In-depth analysis of micro-level data may provide some insight into how women make decisions concerning *paato-taimu* employment, how they negotiated within and between employment and family spheres, how they resisted narrow gender expectations, and how they construct complex identities.

Whether or not the Japanese bubble economy has burst irreparably, the strategic deployment of women as nonstandard workers and family-based caregivers is no longer functional for the economy. Old institutional arrangements have not been able to forestall and stabilize crises. Women's nonstandard employment central to economic development strategies are no longer sufficient. As the next chapter will show, further analysis of nonstandard employment and economic stasis reveal sources of tension. The following chapter reflects back on the historical construction of the reproductive

---

13   There is evidence to support this interpretation. A campaign to humanize work rejected the male model of long hours and promoted a better balance of wage and non-waged work (see Lenz 1996, 282).

bargain to help explain why a country once celebrated as an economic miracle lost its way. It explores in more depth the logics and trajectories of part-time and agency temporary employment. Trends and tendencies of these two forms are discussed in terms of the reproductive bargain and state-based regulatory reform.

CHAPTER 3

The Logics of Part-Time and Agency Temporary Employment

As indicated in the previous chapter, the concept of reproductive bargain moves understandings of precariousness beyond statistical measurements toward a consideration of the organization of social reproduction. Situating precarious employment and precarity in relationship to the reproductive bargain addresses long-term consequences arising from the institutional logic of this variety of capitalism, including access to training and skill development, and to the systems providing support for the general standard of living and health.

Having established the centrality of gender in Japan's economic trajectory, this chapter highlights the historical terms of the mid-20th century social settlement that supported a standard employment relationship based on a male breadwinner/female care-giver reproductive bargain and company-based citizenship. Identifying the terms of the reproductive bargain illuminates the less visible factors and forces influencing patterns of precarious work and life. Empirical trends are contextualized in the development of Japanese coordinated capitalism from the economic boom during the 1960s through the recession of the 1990s, and ends in the first decade of the 21st century. A case study of Japan, with its high relative and absolute numbers of nonstandard workers, can reveal what happens to economic security when neo-liberalism increasingly encroaches on a highly regulated employment relations system. The age-graded contours and the dramatic increase of nonstandard employment, particularly among women and youth, is rooted in design of the institutional architecture supporting pillars of the Japanese employment system, the reproductive bargain, and its mode of social regulation.

This chapter chronicles regulatory reform aimed at stimulating the growth of nonstandard employment as a cheap source of labor with few benefits and limited employment protections. The precariousness of these employment forms derives in part from a distinct mode of regulation that attenuates the institutional moorings of nonstandard employment. The next section of the chapter reviews the language and logic of regulatory reforms in order to tease out their impact in promoting institutional dualism. This contextualized comparison shows that agency temporary and part-time employment reflects different rationalities yet overlapping precarious conditions. It cautions against assuming that all forms of nonstandard employment become precarious in the same way or even for the same reasons.

The chapter concludes by arguing that precarious work and precarity are driven by more than global competition and deregulatory impulses of neo-liberal policy agendas. While globalization and neo-liberal policy assault traditional forms of employment security, they also combine with pre-existing fault-lines created by the reproductive bargain. Gender, class and other salient social cleavages intersect in ways that are consequential for determining the contours of precarious employment (Vosko et al. 2009).

Trends and Tendencies

The making of precarious employment in Japan is implicated by a corporate-centered male-breadwinner reproductive bargain which has constrained the sites, the subjects and the scale of social protection by emphasizing private solutions to social reproduction (Osawa 2011). Nonstandard employment trends and tendencies in Japan thus need to be examined in light of this male-bread-winner reproductive bargain. During the fast-paced economic transformation the sources of labor from the countryside largely dried up. Then two coincidental "shocks" hit Japan hard in the early 1970s. Internally, the process of state-led industrialization "depleted the resources of cheap labor extracted from rural areas and agricultural sectors" (Yoda 2006, 30; also see Dore 1986), while externally (and globally), oil shocks reverberated throughout this oil-import dependent country. Furthermore, the state could no longer shield Japanese "sunset industries," as global competition intensified particularly from newly industrialized countries (NICs). As a response, from the mid-1970s onward, employers turned to "flexible" nonstandard employment, chiefly among jobs held by women and youth, as a cheap labor buffer to manage high personnel costs associated with the central lifetime employment system.

In the 1970s and 1980s, government officials rhetorically promoted "Japanese-style welfare," framing welfare reform in terms of a supposedly Japanese tradition, simultaneously referencing the past male standard and selectively formulating new regulations, including the passage of the Equal Employment Opportunity Law, and revised tax policies exempting a threshold of income roughly equivalent to most part-time employment. Secondary earners' income below a stipulated threshold qualified families for a tax exemption, which created an economic incentive for some married women to reduce their working hours in order to stay below the legally defined income limit (Gottfried and O'Reilly 2002, 114). Effectively, state reforms encouraged many married women to work part-time.

The economic downturn of the 1990s, due to stagnation and an increase in global competition, further eroded the male standard in favor of other employment statuses. Firms subsidized high wages and security of its aging core workforce by expanding non-regular employment. Even though immigration policies generally foreclosed the possibility of employers filling the large and growing demand for nonstandard employment with low-wage migrant labor, some special work visas for low level jobs in manufacturing were offered to unskilled overseas workers of Japanese descent and a small number of skilled and unskilled workers from other parts of Asia. Though the promise of lifetime employment has not disappeared as either a practice or an expectation, more regular jobs are converted into and new jobs are created in the form of nonstandard employment, most prominently among women, youth and older workers, but also for salarymen who have lost the security once provided by the "three treasures" of lifetime employment, seniority-based promotion and company unions (Roberson and Suzuki 2003, 9). Employment insecurity undermines the ideological and economic basis of the old hegemonic reproductive bargain represented by the salaryman.

Nonstandard employment is <u>not</u> embedded in the corporatist industrial relations system and is not covered by the same contractual rights, social protections and regulations as standard employment. The state codifies the inferior status of nonstandard employment in its official definition of standard employment in reference to those who are employed continuously by the same enterprise immediately following graduation from high school or university (Ministry of Health, Labor and Welfare 2006). Conversely, nonstandard employment includes forms of employment such as part-time, day labor, agency temporary and direct-hire temporary employment, which are not configured around an organizationally based career-track. Neither years of service nor employment experience accumulate to place nonstandard employees in line for in-house promotion, on-the-job training and age-graded wage increases. Standard employment, based on a male-breadwinner norm and its implicit masculine embodiment of non-responsibility for human reproduction, represents one labor market track, but nonstandard employment is constructed in relationship to and belongs on a separate labor market track.

At the turn of the 21st century just over one-third (35.2 percent in 2010) of the total working population occupied jobs in nonstandard employment arrangements (JILPT 2013). An increasing number of new entrants into the labor force begin their working life in nonstandard employment. Though the extent of nonstandard employment predictably declines with the transition to more permanent employment, fewer workers enjoy the expectation of long-term, continuous employment. Between 1985 and 2010, nonstandard employment came to comprise an ever larger share of the overall labor force among workers in all age groups (JILPT 2012, 42). Among men in the labor force the youngest workers experienced the steepest increase of nonstandard employment: a fivefold jump from 4.7 percent to 25.1 for new entrants aged 15–24 and 3.2 to 14.0 for workers aged 25–34; while the rate doubled to 8.1 for older men (ibid.). Women started at much higher levels; like men, the youngest women aged 15–24 saw the greatest percentage increase, quadrupling from 8.3 to 35.4. By 2010, the proportion of women in nonstandard employment had reached 57.7 percent compared to 8.1 percent of men aged 45–54. Substantially, in 2007 around 11–12 percent of individuals in their early 20s to approximately 20 percent of individuals in their late 20s and early 30s entered a legal status of NEET, considered non-employed, neither in employment, in education or in training (Brinton 2011, 28). Taken together, the picture that emerges is of extensive underemployment and precarity.

The dramatic increase of nonstandard employment, particularly among women and youth, is rooted in the design of the institutional architecture supporting pillars of the Japanese employment system, the reproductive bargain, and its mode of social regulation. Still, in 2010, the distribution diverges between men and women across the life-course: men are more likely to experience nonstandard employment as early entrants and as they transition out of the labor force, while over one-third of young women and over half of women at prime ages of 35–54 work in nonstandard employment (JILT 2012).

The gender dimension of this institutional dualism is evident in the growth pattern of nonstandard employment. Female employment and labor force participation lags behind that of men. Young women start out strong with high labor force participation rates, closing the gender gap that existed in 1975. However, the labor force participation of women over thirty falls away, although not as dramatically as in 1975. The M-Curve becomes less pronounced: labor force participation is higher for women of almost all ages in 2010, compared to 1975. Even more striking, the share of part-time employment amongst employed women reached 41.3 percent in 2010. This stands in sharp contrast with men's labor force profile. Employment trends for the aggregate category of temporary employment tell a similar story of gender differences: 21.7 percent of women and 8.3 percent of men worked as temporary employees in 2007.

Already in existence during the 16th century, the origin of day labor predates capitalism while today the day labor force is small and dwindling, it is surprisingly more visible with glimpses of it behind blue tarps in public parks and concentrations near red light districts in cities. Interestingly, the composition of day laborers contrasts with the other nonstandard forms: the majority of day laborers are single men between 45–65 years old, from rural backgrounds, of working class origins and with relatively low educational levels.[1] As day laborers age, they face an even more precarious future. They lack pension rights, typically have no savings, are detached from familial support networks, and unable to easily access social welfare. Despite their legal eligibility, local administrators in welfare offices sometimes refuse to authorize payments unless the applicant can prove incapacitation either due to age (65 years) or physical infirmity (which requires medical documentation) (Gill 1999, 153–154). The dominant image of salarymen as providers contributes to the view of day laborers' unemployment as shameful rather than as a result of unfortunate circumstances beyond the individual's control (ibid.). Interestingly, day laborers are linguistically and geographically (proximate to red light districts) associated with women in the imagery evoked and invoked by day laborers as well as by others. Some day laborers "described themselves using the word *tachinbo*, translated literally as "one who stands" – a similar representation of prostitutes who also stand on street corners in hopes of selling their labor power (Gill 1999, 156).

The analysis that follows disaggregates two prominent employment forms, part-time and agency temporary employment, in terms of gender, age and marital status, in order to provide clues as to how the type of reproductive bargain structure advantages and disadvantages in the labor market. These two forms of employment are legally discrete in that they represent contractually different employment relations covered by specific regulations and that reflect different age-graded patterns by life-cycle stage. Divergent trajectories of part-time employment and agency temporary employment, in both the timing and the reasons propelling adoption, make a compelling case for analyzing each form separately.

Parsing Part-Time Employment

A high proportion of part-time workers punctuate Japan's employment structure. According to OECD figures, part-time employment accounted for 13.9 percent of all employment in 1973, just as the first oil shock reverberated throughout the economy. A consistent rise of part-time employment occurred prior to the start of the recession. In 1990 on the eve of the recession, part-time work inched upward to 15.2 percent for men and women combined, and

---

1 Tom Gill's ethnographic research offers a rich account of the social, cultural and economic conditions of day laborers in Japan.

27.9 percent of women. Thereafter, the economic downturn heightened the pressure on employers to hire more part-time workers. Overall part-time employment reached 26.6 percent by 2010 (JILPT 2013). Throughout the decade of lackluster economic growth, involuntary part-time employment mushroomed from 1.9 percent in 2000 to 6.8 percent in 2009. This reflected a growing share of involuntary part-time employment among part-timers who reported wanting full-time work (8.3 percent in 2000 compared to 23.8 percent in 2009) (OECD extracts 2010).

The large numbers of part-time workers is in part an artifact of the unique definition of the employment form in Japan. A government survey estimates about 30 percent of part-time employees work 35–hours or more. Part-time work is not simply a matter of working fewer hours than a full-time worker, but is clearly linked to an inferior employment status. Japanese women are most likely to come under the employment status of full-time part-timers. We can compare the lower international convention of 30 hours against the higher 35 hours worked threshold in the year 2011: 34.8 percent of women and 10.3 percent of men worked part-time based on the 30 hour per week, increasing to 44.1 percent and 14.7 percent respectively at the upper end.

The widespread use of part-time employees across industrial sectors suggests the ease with which employers choose this form of nonstandard employment, but the uneven pattern concentrated in female-dominated sectors and among married women with children indicates the gendered nature of this employment form. From 1986 to 1996, part-time employment accounted for 93 percent of the growth of women's employment. Women's part-time employment as a percentage of women's total employment increased from 29.1 percent in 2000 to 33.2 percent in 2008, although their share of total part-time work declined slightly from 73.1 percent to 70.4 percent over the same period (JILPT 2010, 117–118). Men's part-time employment grew, but so did their full-time employment, albeit at half the rate over the same time period.[2]

Wage setting structures and institutions tie wages and benefits to employment status. As a result, full-time part-timers earn hourly wages substantially lower than regular employees and nearly the same as "true" part-time workers (Osawa 2001, 185). The low, flat wage scales and the lack of benefits reflects and reinforces the assumption that part-time workers rely on income from other sources, usually a male-breadwinner, to make ends meet. In this way, the

---

2   While 15 percent of male part-time workers worked 5 or more years for the same employer in 1999, the corresponding figure for female part-time workers was as high as 35 percent (Ministry of Health, Labor and Welfare 2000b).

inferior status of part-time employment both assumes and reinforces workers' dependence on a male breadwinner.

The gender composition of an occupation and an industry is correlated to the extent of part-time employment. Those occupations and industries with high concentrations of women have the corresponding higher percentage of part-time employment. Put another way, part-time employment is most prominent in those occupations, firms and industries where workers have low bargaining power. For example, the male-dominated industries of information and computer technologies exhibit lower rates of part-time employment than the more female-dominated information and knowledge-intensive industries (Shire 2007, 73). Women's high rates of part-time employment in sales, retail and restaurants occur in sectors with the lowest wages and most insecure working conditions. Female part-time employment nears parity with female full-time employment in electrical manufacturing and database services/distribution, but exceeds their full-time employment in female-dominated industries, including library, cultural and sports activities, and news agency services (Shire 2007, 73). Likewise, in 2000 part-time employment is concentrated in female-dominated occupations: 24 percent of part-time employees worked as service workers, 23 percent as sales workers, and 20 percent as clerical workers, compared to only 11 percent as managers (Ministry of Health, Labor and Welfare 2000a).

A distinct gendered pattern of part-time employment punctuates the life course. Among male workers, new entrants and those near retirement are most likely to work part-time. Many young men are stuck in nonstandard employment for longer periods of time. Single mothers exhibit a high labor force participation rate of 87.3 percent, marked by high full-time rates of employment, varying with levels of educational attainment (42.8 percent of junior high school graduates as compared to 10.2 percent of university graduates work part-time) (Fujiwara cited in Ezawa 2005, 19). Despite working full-time, single mothers exhibit high poverty rates (Raymo and Shirahase 2014). Contrary to the pattern found in other advanced industrialized nations, higher educational attainment does not translate into significantly higher female labor force participation in Japan. Japanese women with university/tertiary education exhibit similar employment rates compared to women with less than upper secondary education (OECD 2002, 74).[3] A strong breadwinner reproductive bargain poses a particularly stark trade-off for women with family obligations, moderating the returns to education and supporting higher

---

3   Nobuko Nagase (2006, 44) found that 80 percent of mothers with newborn babies living in
    urban areas leave the labor force to become full-time housewives.

rates of non-employment and part-time employment among married women, and affecting poverty levels among single mothers.

The wage gap between full-time and part-time workers was significantly higher in Japan than in other countries: 56.1 of full-time wages in Japan, 71.3 in the UK, 82.1 in Germany, and 83.4 in Sweden, by 2009 (Orcutt and Silver 2014, 209). The gap (as officially classified) has widened in Japan: in 1990, the part-time to full-time wage ratio was 57.8 percent among men and 72.0 percent among women, but it had dropped to 51.2 percent among men and 66.9 percent among women in 2000 (Ministry of Health, Labor and Welfare 2000c). This gap is greater for men than for women because male part-time workers' wage level has not increased as much as that of their full-time counterparts in part due to the increasing shares of young male part-time workers. Still, a higher percentage of female part-time workers reported living mainly on their spouses' income; 66 percent as compared to 20 percent on their own income, while corresponding figures for male part-time workers were 2 percent and 57 percent in 2001 (Ministry of Health, Labor and Welfare 2002). The low, flat wage scales and the lack of benefits reflect and reinforce the assumption that part-time workers rely on income from other sources, usually a male breadwinner, to make ends meet.

Socio-demographics of Agency Temporary Employment

An upward trend of agency temporary employment began in the mid-1980s. Even as the Japanese economy slipped into recession on the eve of the new decade, the temporary help industry grew, dipping slightly at the beginning of pan-Asian financial crisis and then again in the latest global recession. The number of registered general temporary workers steadily increased from 1996 (572,421) to 2000 (1,113,521), dipping slightly in the early 2000s, peaking in 2008 (2,811,987), declining to 1.8 million following the collapse of Lehman Brothers, and picking up again once the world economy began to stabilize in the latter 2010s (JILPT 2013, 37). Of the total workforce, agency temporary employment reached 0.9 percent in 2000, increased to 2.7 percent in 2008 and dropped slightly to 1.9 percent in 2010 (JILPT 2012, 25).[4]

---

4 Notes: Estimates of agency temporary workers vary because of unique contracts in Japan: the LFSS in 2001 defined an agency temporary employee as a person who worked at least one hour during the previous week of the survey, estimating the number at 450,000 or 0.8 percent of total employment, while the *Business Reports from Worker Dispatching Business* (Ministry of Health, Labor and Welfare 2000d) calculated 1.3 million such workers by aggregating all agency temporary employees, including registered workers employed at least once in the previous year.

One of the relatively unique features of dispatched workers in Japan is the two-tiered tracks; Japanese temporary employment firms employ a small but growing number of specialists on regular contracts (*joyo gata*), while the vast majority of workers registered for employment on an as-needed basis (*Toroku Gata*), without explicit or implicit contractual commitments for continuous employment with either the de jure or de facto employer (see Kalleberg 2011). Both direct-hire and agency dispatched temporary employment represented growing segments of the Japanese labor force. Specialists saw a steady increase, starting from 68,941 in 1996 and growing to 293,111 in 2010 (JILPT 2013, 37).

A truncated age profile and highly skewed gender composition characterizes the Japanese temporary agency workforce: initially, women accounted for 95 percent of the total, but declined to 80 percent by the end of the 1990s. Female temporary agency workers are relatively young as compared to their male counterparts: the average age for women is 33, while for men it is 38 (Ministry of Health, Labor and Welfare 2000d). The 1998 White Paper on Working Women (JIL 1999) estimates that women 25 to 35 years old are three times as likely as those less than 25 years old and five times as likely as older women to work for a temporary agency. Given this age profile, it is not surprising that 64 percent of female temporary workers are single and continue to receive support from their families (Weathers 2001). The proportion of agency temporary workers has increased, particularly for women, mainly due to the increase of part-time workers with short, fixed-term contracts. In 2001, 72 percent of women as compared to 52 percent of men worked less than 35 hours a week as an agency temporary employee (Ministry of Health, Labor and Welfare 2001).

More recently, multinational temporary-help firms, such as Manpower Japan, have tailored business practices to local political-economic conditions. The changing reproductive bargain makes available different groups of workers resulting in new socio-demographics of agency temporary work. Older, married women lack career opportunities because an "informal marriage bar" forces many to leave their full-time jobs on the career-track. Recently, agency temporary firms created a new labor market niche by recruiting "housewives" for part-time temporary employment. Packaging two housewives as a full-time equivalent is a tempting option for employers and workers alike in light of legal exemptions built into the tax code. With the growing numbers of out-of-work and underemployed youth, temporary help firms are recruiting young men to fill agency temporary positions, including more secure open-ended contracts for those with recognized skills, known as specialists.

Still, the contours of agency temporary work correspond to larger structures of gender-typed work. A gender division of temporary job assignments concentrates more than 80 percent of female workers in clerical jobs

(Araki 1999, 9), while nearly 70 percent of male workers perform professional or technical work (Sato 2001) in such areas as new media and information technology (Shire and Imai 2000). Although 71 percent of the registered workers had contracts for less than three-month terms in 1999, more than two-thirds of agency temporary employees remained longer than one year with the same client (Kojima and Fujikawa 2000). Likewise, their overall job tenure at the temporary help agency lasts for three-to-five years on average, well below the tenure rate among part-time workers in Japan.

Agency temporary employees receive lower overall compensation than part-time employees, even though they may earn higher hourly wages. Only 66 percent of temporary agency workers enjoy health care coverage (more than the 33 percent of part-time workers in Japan). While two-thirds of temporary agency workers have access to employment insurance and pension insurance, only a small percentage enjoy private enterprise annuities (9.6 percent), bonus payments (28.8 percent), and lump-sum retirement payments (15.4 percent) (Houseman and Osawa 2000), and most forego transportation and vacation allowances (Weathers 2001).

Compared to standard employment, both part-time and agency temporary employment forms are less protected and represent lower cost alternatives. Nonstandard employment is concentrated in occupations and industries with a history of limited institutionalized bargaining power and with a large number of women. Japanese establishments reporting deteriorating performance are especially likely to decrease the number of regular employees and increase most types of nonstandard employees (Morishima 2001). Widespread adoption of both forms is related to their lack of contractual guarantees (both explicit and implicit rights), relieving employers from either the legal or moral responsibility of providing job and income security. Employers use nonstandard employment to gain flexibility over staffing arrangements. Once employed in nonstandard positions, few ports permit entry into full-time, regular jobs. Precarious employment is a product of the sharp institutional dualism between standard and nonstandard employment forms in the Japanese labor market.

Making Precarious Employment: Different Trajectories

The uneven development of part-time and temporary work suggests that different forces and factors might drive how each form becomes precarious. The upward trend of part-time employment began earlier and involved larger numbers than agency temporary employment. Part-time employment emerged as part of the old Fordist production model in a wide-range of older and some new occupations and industries, while temporary employment developed in clerical and newer knowledge-intensive occupations. The nature of the employment relationship and contractual terms make each form precarious in different ways. In Japan, part-time workers on open-ended contracts often have long tenure without contractual guarantees of job security or economic security, since their wages do not significantly increase over time despite many years on the job. Precariousness of agency temporary employment derives from the principle of registration for potential employment and from the use of fixed-term contracts, which make work schedules unpredictable and income streams uncertain.

The type of reproductive bargain illuminates the stark division of labor and the association of employment practices with gender, age and class. Although women predominate in each form, part-time and temporary employment exhibits different age-graded patterns. Part-time employment has been concentrated among married women with children, and increasingly among men at early and later stages of their working lives, whereas temporary employment is found among younger women with no children and a small number of "housewives." Agency temporary firms operating in Japan take advantage of rigid internal labor markets that produce a pool of highly qualified women with limited options for full-time standard employment (Gottfried 2003, 264). Age-graded institutional features, such as rigid internal labor markets, and organizational practices, such as selecting specific gendered bodies, structure patterns of nonstandard employment over the life course. We can only understand part-time and agency temporary employment conditions through a review of regulatory changes and how these legislative initiatives sought to address the rapidly changing labor market.

National Regulatory Reform

The changing mode of regulation crafts a new legal regime, which increases commodification, shifts risks and responsibilities, and formalizes informal conditions of nonstandard employment. Combined with existing policies and legacies of the male-breadwinner reproductive bargain, working-time regulations specifically formulated to address temporary and part-time employment issues have contributed to making nonstandard forms precarious and gendered in Japan.

The passage of the Worker Dispatching Law in 1985 gave the state a tool to regulate temporary agency employment, which was flourishing despite the prior legal ban on the activity. The initial regulation lifted the ban on agency temporary work for 16 sex-typed occupations. By cabinet order of 10 December 1996, this 'positive list' expanded to 26 job categories (Araki 1997), including computer operators, accounting, secretarial work, filing, translation, stenographers, and new media. The focus on sex-typed occupations dictated skill requirements and all but ensured a skewed gender composition of agency temporary employment. Although framed in gender-neutral language, the adoption of a positive list preserved standard employment in core manufacturing associated with men's work and allowed temporary contracts in occupations associated with traditional women's work (Gottfried 2003).

With the ensuing recession in the early 1990s, unions, confined by the corporate-centered male-breadwinner bargain, could only delay neo-liberal reforms. Targeted deregulation protected the largely male union membership in export-oriented production. In the first instance of deregulation, the Older Persons Employment Stabilization Law in 1994 introduced a negative list of jobs for persons older than 60 years. While this amendment only applied to older workers, the regulation anticipated more significant changes and set a precedent for encroachment of neo-liberal reforms. After extensive debate delayed further deregulation for several years, a major revision of the Worker Dispatching Law in 1999 (Araki 1999) switched to a negative list, thereby opening most job areas to temporary agency employment, but conceded to unions a provision that placed one-year time limits on the use of agency temporary contracts in formerly restricted occupations. That same year, an amendment to the Employment Security Law legalized private fee-charging employment services for 29 occupations, allowing them to coexist with public placement services, and fixed a maximum fee for their services. In 2004, incremental reforms permitted temporary staffing in some formerly prohibited sectors, such as manufacturing and medical professions, under the proviso that the temporary position would become permanent (Coe et al. 2006, 3).

The enactment of the Part-time Labor Law in 1993 provided the legal basis for defining part-time employment as a distinct employment status. The provisions of this Act reveal inherent tensions between principles of gender equality and difference; and subsequent changes accepted unequal treatment for all those classified as part-time, regardless of the number of hours worked (Osawa 2001). An advance over previous practice was gained when the amended Labor Standards Act in 1999 codified contractual terms of employment, requiring that employers state in writing the period of the contract, placement of employment, the job to be performed, the scheduled working time, the rest period, the rest days and the annual paid leave in addition to the wage levels.

While in principle all labor laws cover nonstandard employees except in those matters governed by special regulations, including employment, health and pension insurance, and taxes (Araki 2002, 37), in practice many laws do not apply to most workers in nonstandard employment. For example, employees on fixed term contracts and most other nonstandard employees fail to qualify for child and family care leave under the Child and Family Care Leave Act (Nagase 2006, 41), and receive limited coverage from the Employees Pension Plan Act and Employees Medical Insurance Act (Kojima and Fujikawa 2000). Child-care leave is available to employees on request to take care of children who are less than one-year old. While several revisions of the Child Care Leave Act 1992 have enhanced entitlements, including the extension of the provisions to employees in establishments of 30 employees or less in 1995 as well as the introduction of an allowance funded by employment insurance in 1997 (along with an increase to 40 percent of earnings in 2001), only 14 percent of mothers take child-care leave (Nagase 2006, 41). Sick leave and other benefits are not statutory rights, but instead depend on workplace norms. Paid holidays are available after working for an employer a minimum of 6 months and 80 percent of the hours of a full-time equivalent. Such thresholds and exemptions have denied equal access to the same protections for workers in part-time and temporary employment.

Similarly, the failure to explicitly extend principles of equal opportunity and equal pay to nonstandard jobs has subverted the intent and limited the impact of the Equal Employment Opportunities Law (EEOL). For example, the extension of equality regulations aimed at removing barriers to equal opportunities has been undermined by labor and tax policies encouraging married women to work part-time and for lower compensation. Despite attempts to strengthen provisions of the EEOL in 1999, no language explicitly directs employers to apply principles of equal opportunity to those in nonstandard arrangements. Among the OECD countries, Japan stands alone in not explicitly extending equal employment provisions to temporary workers, which has contributed to the skewed female domination of agency temporary work.[5]

Legislative reforms accelerated at the end of the Twentieth Century, due partly to heightened tensions inherent in the male-breadwinner reproductive bargain. The state could no longer rely on the unpaid labor of women in the private sphere for the care of children and elderly parents. Moreover, projected labor shortages due to the declining fertility rate and the ageing population prompted the conservative government to discuss recruitment of workers from abroad. New short-term programs offering industrial training in 1990 and

---

5   While some companies have abolished the dual-track system, women remain underrepresented in management. A survey conducted in 2000–1 found that only 2.2 percent of women found positions on the management fast track (*sogoshoku*) (Orcutt and Silver 2014, 209).

technical internships in 1993 sought to induce the migration of a relatively cheap labor force, especially from other parts of Asia. The temporary status of this labor force avoided provoking too much political opposition from anti-immigration nationalists (Ito 2005, 66). In this way, the state facilitates the growth of low-wage precarious employment among women workers whose legal status prevents them from easily making claims for better working conditions. Still, strict immigration policy limits the number of migrants available to perform reproductive labor in precarious employment relations elsewhere. Policy legacies have restricted the range of policy tools that can adjust the labor supply in the face of a looming care crisis.

In Japan, the mode of regulation supported a reproductive bargain in which nonstandard forms of employment, such as part-time and agency temporary employment, came to be associated with distinct labor force statuses characterized by inferior contractual rights and with increasing risks. On the one hand, the timing, location, and gender composition of agency temporary employment can be traced back to the language and logics of regulatory reform. Agency temporary employment took off after regulation defined the activity as legal for a positive list of female-typed occupations. A shift in the regulatory language permitted agency temporary employment to spread, albeit unevenly, due to the gendered exemptions protecting male preserves. On the other hand, for part-time employment, the passage and framing of regulation came on the heels of an already upward trend. Once in place, regulation legally sanctioned and permitted unequal treatment. A spectrum of regulations along with tax and pension reforms created incentives for married women with children to take up part-time employment without interrupting their fertility decisions and care responsibilities. Political institutions and processes as well as economic exigencies influenced the contractual, temporal and spatial conditions of precariousness.

The coordinated intermediation between labor and capital in large Japanese corporations resulted in the negotiation of a reproductive bargain tying benefits to employment status at the enterprise level and generating strict employment regulations over unfair dismissal that protected core male workers in standard employment. Corporate-centered welfare and industrial regulation left a patchwork of residual policies over work conditions at the national level. What began as strength when the economy was expanding turned into weakness for workers in standard employment, as they (and their unions) were tied to the fate of particular firms. Underrepresented in unions, workers in non-standard employment relied on state-based regulations for protections against risks. Many labor regulations based qualifications for protections, rights and entitlements on time thresholds, which excluded most nonstandard workers from access. Labor regulations centered around the standard employment relationship not only failed to address the existing penalties for dropping out of the labor force or reducing work hours, but also assumed and reinforced the male-breadwinner reproductive bargain, even as the conditions underwriting the bargain were unraveling.

Precarious Employment: Lessons from Japan

In Japan, the origins of precarious employment are rooted in both country spe-cific factors as well as global processes. The rise of precarious employment in this context predates the recession and deregulation during the 1990s, suggest-ing that sources beyond the confines of narrowly defined economic change are responsible. Most accounts of recent labor market changes miss the emer-gence of precarious employment in large part because explanations point to processes of restructuring or the neo-liberal political project as driving the growth of nonstandard employment. In contrast, an analysis invoking the reproductive bargain situates precarious employment within the Fordist accord, and illuminates growing trends and new tendencies within the sys-temic linkages and tensions between production and social reproduction by identifying their structures and agents.

The male-breadwinner reproductive bargain is associated with policies and practices encouraging women to assume responsibilities associated with bio-logical and social reproduction in the absence of adequate social infrastruc-ture of care services, and to derive benefits and rights principally as wives and secondarily as mothers. Precariousness of nonstandard employment is related to the sharp dualism in the Japanese labor market. Firm-specific skill develop-ment and corporate-based benefits reward long-term standard employment relationships, and the underdevelopment of statutory entitlements and the social infrastructure of care services, while training and wage-setting institu-tions leave nonstandard employment to flourish unprotected yet not unregu-lated. The stark trade-off in Japan puts in sharp relief a political process that can also be observed in other countries.

The focus on deregulation has diverted attention away from the regulations that initially shaped the age-graded contours of precarious employment. The precariousness of nonstandard employment is not simply an outcome of less regulation than standard employment, but also a consequence of differential treatment written into the language of regulations and the logic underwriting the mode of regulation. The example of Japan may be somewhat unique with respect to the language adopted in specific regulations. However, the case sug-gests the necessity of inter-referencing regulations and policies governing production and social reproduction by which to examine biases and gaps that affect employment practices and conditions.

Given different historical trajectories of part-time and temporary employment (and day labor), analyses should avoid generalized claims about precarious employment. Part-time employment emerged as Fordism confronted limits of the state-led modernization project. It is significant that the hegemonic framework of the reproductive bargain in Japan kept immigration at a low ebb, despite employers' search for cheap labor. Instead, women in breadwinner households represented an untapped source of cheap labor from which employers could draw for part-time employment further down the production chain. By contrast, agency temporary employment became a viable alternative for women, and increasingly for young men, in administrative and knowledge-intensive work. The demand for agency temporary employees increased as the economy moved from Fordism to neo-Fordism.

In the Japanese variety of capitalism, contractual adjustments and changing regulations are altering the male standard employment relation and employment protections against market risks once at the center of the Fordist manufacturing model and the male-breadwinner reproductive bargain. In general, political neo-liberalism has provided rhetorical justification for dismantling social protections and for deregulation in the name of individual responsibility and austerity, in part, driving the growth of precarious work. Moreover, deregulation has occurred alongside re-regulation with the state more or less facilitating labor flexibility and shifting responsibility for the costs of reproduction onto individuals and families. State-led restructuring of labor and gender regulations and changing contractual arrangements have modified the reproductive bargain, contributing to the skewed gender distribution and the rapid growth and diversification of precarious work.

The demands on and for particular types of bodies are shaped in a gender regime, that is rooted in the larger societal framework of the reproductive bargain and Fordist production. While this chapter focused on the institutional means and mechanisms facilitating the upward trend toward nonstandard employment, the next chapter moves to the organizational level where focus will be more closely on the making of agency temporary work. An in-depth case study of agency temporary employment links organizational embodiment and gendered work to new forms of labor market segmentation and precaritization.

CHAPTER 4

Temp(t)ing Bodies: Shaping Gender at Work in Japan

Japanese enterprises are offsetting high costs of long-term regular employment by expanding "flexible" part-time and temporary employment in a larger effort at work reorganization. Japan, an industrialized country that had led the way in new management styles, can deepen our understanding of organizational gendering of precarity beyond Western experiences. Precarity is not only produced through macro-economic forces, but also through concrete organizational practices in local settings. Temporary-help agencies do more than dispatch workers to client firms. They are global players reshaping career paths and labor markets, both within countries and cross-borders. Even more so, the temporary-help agency performs the alchemist trick of commodifying labor power. These agencies are in the business of creating a mobile workforce for their client firms. What they sell, as both Marx and Polanyi posit in different ways, is a special commodity, a corporeal and a mental capacity to labor.

A case study of temporary employment provided by a multinational temporary-help company situates the global in culturally local contexts of gendered work and employment conditions. The analysis makes visible the situated forms of body management and the production of modes of embodiment in a gender regime as ways of organizing and ordering masculinities and femininities in an asymmetrical valued hierarchy. Organizational embodiment and gendered work are linked to new forms of labor market segmentation and precaritization. The reproductive bargain serves as the framework in which these firms operate and mobilize labor to dispatch to placement companies.

Feminist Theories of Embodiment

The Body at Work and the Work on the Body

Feminists debate the relationship between the "cultural" and the "material" in analyses and explanations of the pattern of gender relations in work and organizations (see Adkins and Lury 1996), and conceptualize embodiment as a new focus on the body at work, in organizations, and as labor (see Acker 1990; Halford et al. 1997; Tyler and Abbott 1998; Witz et al. 1996; Cohen et al. 2013).

A review of feminist scholarship on embodiment highlights the workplace as a site of cultural as well as material (re)production.

The influential literature on the body at work in bureaucratic organizations by Joan Acker (1990), and the more recent study of body work as work on one's own and others' bodies (Cohen et al. 2013), draws attention to the process of gendering and embodiment to explain the fault-lines of labor market segmentation. By using the verb "gendering," Acker emphasizes how gender relations are embedded in the way major institutions are organized. Building on this perspective, Halford et al. (1997) propose a paradigm of "gender and organizations" that sees gender as both embedded and embodied. Embodiment refers to modes of being in bodies (Morgan 1998, 655) and "the ways of inhabiting the world" (Mascia-Lees 2011, 1–2). A mode of embodiment is gendered: "gender rests not only on the surface of the body, in performance and doing, but becomes *embodied* – becomes deeply part of who we are physically and psychologically [and socially]" (Martin 1998, 495, emphasis in the original).

Bureaucratic organizations validate and permit forms of masculine embodiment and invalidate or render impermissible forms of feminine embodiment (Witz 1998, 5). For women, the discursive construction of the reproductive body assumes particular importance in *disqualifying* them from authority positions and is continually evoked as the kernel of embodied difference (Halford et al. 1997, 213; Witz 1998, 6). The sexualized body represents another discursive and material construction of feminine embodiment whereby women have been included, *qualifying* them for certain front-stage and subordinate organizational functions (Witz 1998, 7; also see Adkins and Lury 1996). These dual processes of qualifying and disqualifying particular aspects of feminine embodiment shape the development of sexualized cultures in which organizational gendering takes place.

Feminist organizational analysis links embodiment and gendered work to an analysis of new forms of labor market segmentation around aesthetic labor, particularly but not exclusively in service industries where employees are increasingly being called upon to develop particular forms of embodied skills in the service encounter. According to Witz (1998), "aesthetic labor describes the mobilization of embodied capacities and competencies possessed by organizational participants. This definition foregrounds the sensible components of social interaction." Women must achieve and maintain a particular "state of embodiment" (Tyler and Abbott 1998, 434), expressed through modes of speech, accent and style that conform to a set of gender attributes that embody socially sanctioned but variable characteristics of masculinity and femininity (McDowell 1997, 31). The organization polices and demands "constant vigilance regarding gender self-presentation at work" (Wajcman 1998, 10).

A meso-level analysis complements such micro-level analysis of embodied capacities and modes of embodiment. Witz specifically calls for a shift to the meso-level as a means of "confronting the possibility that modes of embodiment are not only mobilized by individuals but also are produced by organizations" (Witz 1998, 9). Organizations and the workers themselves harness "sexualized bodies" (Cohen et al. 2013, 10–11) to create particular environments. Studies positing that organizations produce modes of embodiment reference some version of Connell's notion of gender regimes to frame analysis in broader structures and processes (Fagan and O'Reilly 1998). I apply the concept of gender regime in a more specific way to describe power relations and identities shaped by social practices at the organizational level (see Acker) informed by the reproductive bargain.

The path-breaking analysis paves the way for thinking about embodied skills and modes of embodiment. Yet many feminist organizational theorists have failed to fully situate the material body in terms of place. An examination of area-studies literature highlights gender and embodiment at work in Japan.

Situated Selves: Gender and Embodiment at Work in Japanese Studies

Anthropologists doing fieldwork in Japan have sought to displace the Western (white male) subject from its privileged position of reason and essentiality, shifting the field of vision to extricate "the East" from the binary valorizing of "the West." This alternative rejects Western dualities premised on the bifurcation of selves, that is, mastery of the mind (rational self) over body (emotional self) with its gender associations and connotations. The perspective of situating selves makes explicit the implicit embodiment of Enlightenment thought, which equates the unmarked West with male reason as dissociated from the female (or emasculated male) embodiment of the unknowable East.

In the introduction to *Japanese Sense of Self*, Rosenberger (1992, 3) summarizes self attainment in the following way: "the self attains meaning in embodied relations to other people, things and ideas." More specifically, Bachnik (1992, 153) points to how the type of interaction affects the organization of self as it moves between discipline/distance and spontaneity/intimacy.[1] Applying the notion of situated selves to gender, Rosenberger (1994) defines fluid gender relations embedded in a field of social relationships with other differences

---

1   These contrasts are commonly expressed as paired sets of terms: *omote* (in front; surface appearance) versus *ura* (in back; that which is kept hidden from others); *soto* (outside) versus *uchi* (inside), *giri* (social obligation) versus *ninjo* (the world of personal feelings); *tatemae* (the surface reality) versus *honne* (the motives or opinions held in the background) (Bachnik and Quinn 1994).

such as age and position. By situating gender in a field of social relationships, Rosenberger rejects prioritizing one set of social differences over another and instead, like Moi (1991, 1035), insists on the "immense variability of gender as a social factor."

Feminist scholars reading the gender subtext of bureaucratic organizational theory find that personalized practices belie the universal ideal of impersonal rules (Pierce 1999, 128–129). In Japanese bureaucracies, affective (emotional) and instrumental rationality do not function necessarily as opposites to construct and manage embodied differences. The construction of women as different is a key mechanism whereby male power is exercised in the workplace (Lenz 1996; Wajcman 1998a, 8). Authority hierarchies are premised on "a type of embodiment privileging the male body" (see Acker 1990), but as Witz et al. (1996, 175) contend, it is a particular version of the male body and expression of hegemonic masculinity.

Japanese employers choreograph bodily and emotional displays directly over both frontline service workers and professionals, including executives (often based on detailed manuals for proper body comportment and style). Donald Richie succinctly captures the distinctive form underlying social conventions in Japan: "Though other countries also have certain rituals that give the disordered flux of life a kind of order, here these become an art of behavior" (cited in French 2001, B6). For example, in the ubiquitous ritualized performance of formal greetings, one slightly bows in the act of presenting one's business card. This small gesture affirms hierarchical status relationships. "By virtue of its gestural, linguistic and normative aspects, it is a total form of social behavior that places the performer in the social order" (McVeigh 1995, 52–53).[2]

Workers learn to fashion bodies in ways that conform to narrow aesthetic codes of femininity and masculinity (Tyler and Abbott 1998, 435). Joy Hendry (1990, 21) gives the example of store clerks' and other service workers' smiling faces as socially sanctioned and instrumentally imposed codes of femininity. Similarly, the requirement for high-pitched female voices calibrates gendered modes of speaking among women in some service jobs. In a jarring juxtaposition throughout the transportation network, male drivers serenely activate recordings of directions from a disembodied female voice. Other types of jobs require specific uniforms as bodily displays: some uniforms camouflage class

---

2   A 'hidden curriculum' in some junior colleges teaches 'an occupation that permits women to remain "dutiful" daughters and suitable wives. … Femininity is donned, draped, hung, and painted on the body. Something spoken, embodied in gestures, expressed in movements and seen in things women carry. It is a way of being, and it involves meticulous attention to the details of self-presentation' (McVeigh 1995, 29–33).

distinctions and gender differences, such as the white lab coats donned by male automobile production line workers (Gottfried 1998), and others accentuate gendered embodiment, such as the kimonos worn by hostesses and the designer accouterments of "office-ladies." By contrast, skilled male workers may forge a sense of self in the process of crafting fine objects through the emphasis of masculine prowess that negates female embodiment (Kondo 1990).

Such body management, both self-imposed and organizationally sanctioned, can generate everyday forms of resistance as well as regulate self-presentation styles. For example, the outer layer of etiquette can provide protection from the possible abuse of or amorous advances toward female lift operators (Hendry 1990, 25). One female part-timer felt compelled by her personal relationship with the employer to maintain a "front" face of friendship. Later, she protested working conditions by turning silent, a communicative practice which derives its force and form from what Hayashi calls "Japanese drama," the tradition of Noh or Kabuki whose masked actors convey a range of emotion through stylized body movement and gestures.[3] Similarly, the refusal to wrap encounters in a *keigo* façade (polite veneer) can be a potent symbol of resistance in Japan. This refusal plays against gender stereotypes of deferential female service. Such betrayals to normative femininity take place through the subjective dis-identification with hegemonic patriarchal relations at work (Lal 2009, 32). Common idiomatic expressions are used in the signification of resistance.

Gendering and aesthetics of the body at work are place-bound organizational processes. The foregoing organizational history shows how global developments of a multinational temporary-help company are negotiated in culturally local contexts of work and labor regulation. More specifically, the organizational gender regime shapes a gender-specific body order in which heterosexual male employees devote themselves to the enterprise-as-family in return for lifelong job security, and female employees are expected to devote themselves to family as an enterprise.

Appropriate Methods

This investigation of agency temporary employment applies multiple methods to collect data for unpacking the global in terms of place-dependent processes. The city is one strategic type of place between the global and the national in that "it allows us to recover the concrete, localized processes through which

---

3   Nagisa Hayashi characterized this form of resistance in a conversation.

globalization exists" (Sassen 2001, 7). In the global city of Tokyo, temporary-help companies have created a niche to satisfy increasing demand for linguistic skills such as interpreting and translation by foreign-owned subsidiaries, and they dispatch employees to perform administrative functions and specialized technical work for large firms spread over decentered business districts that are linked by intersecting private and public rail-lines. This sprawling and densely built environment presents practical problems for the researcher. Growing up and out in bits and pieces, fits and starts, out of the ashes of war destruction, Tokyo defies linearity. The sheer volume of signs, on both horizontal and vertical axes, overloads the visual order of maps and renders the flat surface of a city map less helpful as a navigational guide. Further, the absence of ordinal numbers to locate businesses disorients even Tokyo residents who resort to gestural practices (e.g. the drawing of maps on slips of paper and the giving of impromptu hand directions). The lack of addresses amidst the barrage of signs renders the city unknowable by recourse to "printed culture," such as maps and telephone books. This leads to an emphasis on the visual and the interpretive rather than reliance on the ordinal system of Western maps (Barthes 1982, 33–36).

Such a diffuse field of study eludes easy access for workers and for researchers alike. Using the extended case method enabled me to check my field experiences in the Japanese case against other cases thereby allowing for the possibility of making theoretical and empirical comparisons (Burawoy 2000). Studying a global firm forced me to unbound ethnography from its moorings in a single time and place.

For background information on agency temporary employment, three major sources were used. Statistical data were culled from several official government sources, including the *Japan Labor Bulletin*, the monthly journal published by the Ministry of Labor, January 1988 to May 2012 and Japanese Working Life Profile 2013/14. In addition, using the index for a ten-year period (1988–1998), I scanned articles from two English-language Japanese newspapers, *The Japan Times* and *The Daily Yomiuri*. The review of newspaper articles revealed business practices that became public during the study period. These data were complemented with a three-hour interview with Takashi Araki, Professor of Law at Tokyo University, and a conversation with Keiko Fujikawa, a legal scholar, updating my knowledge of labor regulations (also see Imai 2011).

Entrée into a site often requires personal connections and introductions, which is particularly true in Japan where introductions help to situate the person both personally and socially. A business card imparts one's social status in short order; common in any business or institutional setting. My business card immediately situated me as a sensei, a revered position of professor. I leveraged my position to gain access to upper-level managers and academics.

In Japan snowball sampling is a useful technique, since it relies on personal networks to identify possible respondents. My fieldwork tapped a nested set of relationships, through official and unofficial university hosts, that eased access to sites and opened doors to subjects in strategic positions. An affiliation with a well-known university in Tokyo turned out to be fortuitous; a serendipitous call to make an appointment at Manpower put me in contact with a recent graduate from the same university. She served as a key informant who facilitated interviews with another female manager and several temporary employees.

Overall, the research on temporary agencies occurred over nearly 20 years, from the initial stage of fieldwork in 1995 at the international headquarters of Manpower in Milwaukee, Wisconsin before extending out to the branch office in Tokyo for several months in 1998, followed by shorter visits in 2007 and again in 2014. Interviews covered a range of personnel in the agency temporary business. A two-hour interview with a top executive of Manpower Japan followed up on the same questions posed to his counterpart three years earlier by my graduate assistant, Nagisa Kato Hayashi.[4] Interviews with top executives from Manpower Japan and Manpower headquarters in Milwaukee contained similar questions to address global business trends and practices. Ms. Hayashi interviewed an official from the temporary agency *Rodo-sha Yunion*, a union representing nearly 100 temporary workers in Tokyo. In-depth interviews with two young female permanent managers and two temporary workers lasted one and a half hours each. The female temporary workers were in their mid-20s; one had graduated with a bachelor's degree from a four-year university course and the other was enrolled in a graduate program, and both had prior work experience. Both fit the age and educational profile of agency temporary workers in general: women compose the majority of total agency temporary employment, more than half fall between the ages of 25–39 (Houseman and Osawa 2000), and most have completed junior college education. Interviews with temporary employees consisted of open-ended questions, including motivation for their selection of temporary work, experiences as a temporary worker, their general work history, their relationship to the temporary-help agency, and their supervision on site.

Participant observations occurred at two locations. At one of the branch offices of Manpower Japan in Tokyo, the author observed the intake process for

---

4   Ms. Kato Hayashi not only knew about the topic from her sociological studies, but also had firsthand experience as an agency temporary employee over ten-years earlier. These retrospective data were an invaluable source for understanding the deeply embedded assumptions regarding age- and gender-appropriate work for women.

two hours on one day and four hours another day. During six hours of observations, I shadowed applicants through their intake process.[5] Ms. Kato Hayashi participated in the three-hour intake process at a branch office in Nagoya. A follow-up visit in 2007 took place at the newly relocated headquarters in Yokohama.

Gender, Bodies and Culture in Late 20th-Century Japan

Accounting for Gender Differences: the Rise of Nonstandard Employment

Behind the lifetime employment system are less visible labor market segments of increasing size and importance in the overall Japanese economy. Between 1990 and 2012, the proportion of nonstandard workers (including direct-hired and agency temporary workers) increased from 20 percent to 35 percent (Labor situation 2013/14, 48). Astonishingly, more than half of all women from their mid-30s to retirement age were employed in non-regular jobs (ibid.). Considering agency temporary employment, the disproportionate female composition around 80 percent in Japan contrasts with the pattern in the US and the UK where women account for 60 percent of the total. The temporary-help industry grew even when the Japanese economy slipped into recession in the early 1990s, though agency temporary employment declined on the heels of the financial crisis in 2008. The number of registered "general" workers employed by temporary-help agencies increased from 572,411 in 1996, peaking to over 2.8 million, and settling at 1,055,151 in 2012 (Japanese Working Life Profile 2013/14, 37).[6]

Since the early 1990s, Manpower Inc. surpassed GM as one of the largest employers in the US private sector, employing over a half million workers in the US, operating more than 2700 offices in 48 countries, assigning more than 2 million workers (compared to 600,000 GM employees), and contracting with 250,000 client companies, worldwide. Aggregate sales reached $8.9 billion in 1997, representing a 22 percent increase over the previous year (Manpower brochure). Manpower Japan operates as a wholly owned Japanese subsidiary of Manpower Inc. In 1997, Manpower Japan ranked third among temporary-help companies in the Japanese economy. The company registered 10,000 people in

---

5   The temporary agency designated a young female manager to serve as my translator during the observation phase.

6   The temporary-help industry saw revenues jump 16.3 percent in one-year (1996–7), representing a six-fold increase from a decade earlier (The Daily Yomiuri 1998, 3).

1986, growing fourfold to 41,500 as of 1997, and doubled its active client list from 4456 to 7900 between 1992 and 1997. In 2014, by its own estimates, Manpower Japan employed 439,500 "associates" dispatched from 156 branch offices.[7]

In Japan agency temporary jobs often demand specialized skills, especially in new media and information technology (Shire and Imai 2000). Specialists once numbered around 69,000 in 1996, jumping to 295,983 in 2012, as compared to 1,055,151 general temporary workers (JWLF 2013/15, 37). Clerical workers operating computers account for the largest proportion of agency work for female dispatched employees (Araki 1999, 9). In 2000 more than 80 percent of female dispatched workers were engaged in clerical jobs as compared to nearly 70 percent of male dispatched workers who occupied professional or technical jobs (Sato 2001). During the next decade the gender distribution changed somewhat due to deregulation. A minimum two years of on-the-job experience required by some temporary-help agencies (e.g. Manpower Japan) guarantees a more skilled and somewhat older agency temporary labor force than either their US counterparts or Japanese part-timers, both of whom may have no previous work experience and who often work in low-skilled jobs. These skills boost the pay scales for temporary employees who can earn up to three and a half times more than non-skilled part-timers (Y. Tanaka 1995, 121). Less access to benefits distinguishes all nonstandard employees from regular employees who enjoy corporate-based welfare, such as lump sum bonuses, housing, transportation and family allowances. However, two-thirds of agency temporary employees as compared to one-third of part-timers receive health and pension insurance (Houseman and Osawa 2000).

Most agency temporary workers receive three-month contracts on a repeated basis while overall job tenure lasts from three to five years on average, well below the tenure rate among part-time workers in Japan. These differences stem from the legal distinction between fixed and non-fixed term contracts: The majority (69 percent) receive fixed-term contracts for the period they are assigned to work at a client, whereas the remainder (31 percent) maintain an employment relationship with the agency even when they are not assigned to work at a client (Kojima and Fujikawa 2000). Years of service and employment experience do not place temporary employees in line for promotion or on-the-job training. These disadvantages accumulate faster in the Japanese context where seniority-based systems reward long-term (often lifetime) organizational belonging. Cumulative disadvantages reflect the stark

---

7 Manpower continues to locate offices around the world; nearly 4000 offices operate in 82 countries, serving 400,000 clients, as of 2014.

and rigid employment reality for temporary workers in a seniority system that rewards continuous, full-time employment.

Although the temporary-help industry originated with the establishment of Manpower Japan in 1966, important developments date to the promulgation of the Worker Dispatching Law in 1985 (*Rodosha Haken Jigyo Ho*). Apart from Japan, no other country has regulated temporary employment in terms of occupational distribution. The original law lifted the ban on agency work for 16 allowable occupations. By Cabinet Order of 10 December 1996, this "positive list" expanded to 26 job categories (Araki 1994, 1997), including: computer operators, accounting, secretarial work, filing, translation, stenographers, and new media. The adoption of a positive list preserved jobs in core manufacturing associated with men's work and allowed flexibilization of jobs associated with women's work. Beginning in 1994, however, deregulation introduced a negative list of jobs for persons older than 60 years through amendment of the Older Persons Employment Stabilization Law. Two years later, amendment of Child Care and Family Care Leave Law liberalized agency temporary work for those who take child or family leaves, except for prohibited areas, on the condition that the work period does not exceed more than one-year. In 1999 a revision of the Worker Dispatching Law almost completely deregulated temporary work by switching to a short negative list of prohibited jobs (Araki 1999). A compromise limited the contractual terms of employment to one-year for expanded occupations only. Further deregulation in the 2000s, has opened up new areas formerly restricted, and has encouraged more firms to employ temporary workers in a wider range of occupations already stratified by gender.

In Japan the design of entitlements assumes a masculine embodiment of the prototypical male-breadwinner (Gottfried and O'Reilly 2002). This translates into differential treatment between regular and nonstandard employment contracts with the former enjoying more generous compensation than the latter (Osawa 2001). For example, employees on fixed-term contracts are excluded from the system of child and family care leave under the Child and Family Care Leave Act, and receive limited coverage from the Employees Pension Plan Act and Employees Medical Insurance Act (Kojima and Fujikawa 2000).

Weak labor regulations and selective deregulations motivate clients to deploy agency temporary workers as part of flexible staffing arrangements. Japanese employers not only gain numerical flexibility, but also save on high personnel costs associated with regular employment. In a government survey, employers cited labor costs as the principal reason for increasing nonstandard employment during the worst economic crisis since the end of the Second World War. At the height of the recession, a union official underscored the reason for the client's flexible staffing strategy in the following way: "if they had the same staff for the same jobs for more than two years they may be, in some cases, held liable for the employment of such workers." After the burst of the bubble, "lots of *haken* were laid off as a means of employment adjustment. Some were laid off in the middle of their contracts while others were denied renewal. ... They work to be turned into a safety valve for labor adjustments which are easily lay-off-able." He angrily notes that conditions have worsened citing evidence of increasing contract cancellations from the mid-to-late 1990s. A Tokyo hotline[8] set up for two days in 1991 received 200 calls from agency temporary workers who complained of sudden dismissals and other contract breaches (Y. Tanaka 1995, 121).

But accounting for gender differences requires looking beyond the statistical portrait to the ways gender regimes in organizations produce modes of embodiment. Labor practices and organizational cultures enforce modes of embodiment that make agency temporary employment a tempting option for clients and some female employees.

Temp(t)ing Options: Embodiment and Gender Regimes
The employment contract between the temporary employee and the agency gives the latter control over the employment conditions of the former. As Wacjman (1998a, 8–9) suggests, "the employment contract grants employers command over the bodies of their employees, but these bodies are sexually different." Bodies are sexually differentiated through organizational practices both enacted by the temporary-help service company and the client firms, and enforced by the employment contract. Employment contracts assume the existence of the male-breadwinner reproductive bargain in which women will be available for temporary and part-time work at particular stages in her life course.

Temporary work is one option for Japanese women in their mid-20s who face pressures to drop out of or "retire" from the labor force. Various studies confirmed the practice of "shoulder-tapping" (*katataki*) in which employers pressure workers to retire (around the age of 55 for men and 25 for women) (Y. Tanaka 1995, 203). *Katataki* is a practice that continues despite the enactment of the Equal Employment Opportunity Law (Shire and Ota 1997, 58–59). The flattening of the M-curve employment pattern suggests that more women continue to work during their childbearing years (Y. Tanaka 1995, 100).

---

8 Hotlines are common mechanisms set up for eliciting help regarding perceived injustices experienced on-the-job by a dispersed working population. It is an inexpensive way for advocacy groups (women's organizations, unions) to establish contact with and administer advice to individuals who may suffer discrimination or other violations on-the-job.

Nagase (2000) estimates that 80 percent of mothers with children under three years old drop out of the labor force, and 40 percent take up part-time employment from their mid-30s until they ultimately retire to take care of elderly parents or in-laws. In a more recent demographic trend, women on full-time career tracks either postpone or forego motherhood and marriage and reduce fertility (Ministry of Health and Welfare White Paper 1999).[9]

In a corporate-centered reproductive bargain in which full-time career tracks are configured in terms of masculine embodiment, women may opt for agency temporary employment. This choice allows women to extend their working lives. Temporary staff also may choose this route to gain flexibility in the face of rigid expectations that bind permanent employees to a single employer. Temporary employment frees workers to move from workplace to workplace in search of opportunities. Benefits of such "flexibility" outweigh some costs of opting out of regular employment. Yet the loss of fringe benefits may deter many from seeking temporary employment.

But the choice is constrained by few alternative options available to women in their mid-20s to 30s. Both the union official and a senior Manpower executive at International headquarters acknowledge that Japanese companies' organizational practices and cultural expectations motivate women to seek employment as temporary workers. The executive explains:

> And so there exists in Japan reasonably large groups of women with four years of administrative experience mature in their outlook and in their lifestyle, committed to their profession, because this isn't so important anymore. And their skills are outstanding. They are professional people. And we can just go out and scoop these people up as temporary workers and they're workers. ... A company can't have them on their payroll for social reasons but can bring them in as temporary workers.
>
> GOTTFRIED AND HAYASHI 1998, 29–30

Temporary firms, while preferring a business environment free of regulation, take advantage of rigid internal labor markets that produce a pool of highly qualified women who are available for temporary employment.

Once women reach their mid-to-late 20s they are expected to devote themselves to the family. Women who work full-time contradict the feminized image of the good wife, wise mother on the one hand, and the masculinized embodiment of authority. Japanese women who work full-time may forge

---

9   Ogasawara (1998) observed a small number of office ladies retiring around age 25 only to be rehired for the same job but on a temporary basis.

perverse narratives of self in order to fit into the corporate world. Two young female professionals at Manpower confided to me a "secret" of the older female professional staff, whereby they pretended to have children and families even though they remained single without children. Still, female managers often are given different tasks from their male counterparts. Most of the front-line service representatives at Manpower Japan are women who engage in face-to-face interactions and phone conversations with temporary employees in contrast to male service representatives who are more likely assigned mobile positions involving contact with clients. These women feel out of place in authority positions configured for men.

Employment of women as part-time and temporary workers at a particular stage in the life course contributes to the age-graded gendering of Japanese organizations. Organizations select workers on the basis of an aesthetic code that predisposes the preference for feminine embodiment of temporary work and privilege attributes linked to masculinity and the heterosexual family man in authority positions. The next section elaborates on temporary-help companies' recruitment biases and mobilization of embodied capacities and competencies for placement of employees.

Screening for Temp(t)ing Bodies

Agency temporary-help companies dispatch employees as variable capital to an increasing number of clients who make temporary employees a part of their overall staffing arrangements. As the employing company, the temporary-help company pays wages and benefits to the employee, relieving the client from that variable cost. Yet the temporary-help company must set a price low enough to make temporary employment attractive to clients, but high enough to recruit a prospective pool of employees and to maximize profits. This balancing act requires agency temporary-help companies to continuously re-create a qualified but relatively cheap labor pool.

As a global firm, Manpower Japan adapts labor practices to the local setting. The company cites aesthetic codes of femininity from the cultural milieu. In the case of Japan, the ornamental office lady (OL) serves as the cultural referent for working women. OL is the symbolic abbreviation for a recognized feminine embodiment of office worker in Japan. The ornamental office lady represents a decorative show-piece for both front-stage and backstage jobs. Such ornamental properties have economic as well as aesthetic value in the workplace. Female temp worker's ornamental aesthetic utility joins with her productive capacities to value-added (human capital) features that an employee brings to a firm in the way of increased profits and revenue. By objectifying young talented women, agency temporary companies operating in Japan guarantee a qualified employee who can easily assimilate organizational norms that usually are inculcated through in-house training by client firms. In an interview with a top executive at Manpower UK, she refers to the "personality of organizations" as a factor in matching a temporary worker to a client. Japanese businesses typically transmit their own code of behavior and dress for both wage and salaried employees, both male and female. Thus, temporary companies pay special attention to organizational embodiment in their assignment of workers to a placement site. Agency temporary companies seek to attract and manage qualified female workers who embody certain sexualized body traits and gendered aesthetic features. Through these labor practices Manpower Japan ensures a relatively cheap labor force for their client firms and for increasing their own profit margins.

The agency temporary companies select, produce and manage bodies through an intake process. The intake process at Manpower Japan begins with a pre-screening over the telephone and does not permit walk-in applicants. Applicants who meet the pre-screening criteria (including voice quality and work experience) arrive at an appointed hour either in the morning or in the afternoon. A service representative ushers them into a small, enclosed room in the larger branch office. The intake process follows a scripted procedure that varies in length, ranging from two to five hours, and in content, depending on the applicant's preferences and skill-levels. All applicants watch a 20-minute orientation video on Manpower Japan.

Manpower Japan adapts the screening process from its parent company, Manpower Inc., translating global texts for local contexts. The video represents the global through rational charts that are juxtaposed to the local through bucolic backgrounds. Three young, professionally dressed women walk together in a wooded area, far away from the hustle and bustle of the urban work world, evoking pastoral images of the Japanese countryside. This reference to *furusato* (old village) imagery resonates with ideological constructions of Japanese self and nation (Robertson 1997). Next the women sit around a kitchen table where each in turn recalls her temporary work experiences. A presumed female audience receives the message that the desirable applicant is young, attractive and skilled, while the flashback narration reminds women of their future in the private domestic sphere. Watching the video in a room away from supervisors simulates how temporary workers learn organizational norms and expectations at a placement site.

When the video ends, the supervisor administers a series of exercises and conducts a face-to-face interview. The exercises, in the form of tests, not only measure work abilities, but also monitor and determine the applicant's capacity to self-regulate since many temporary workers have minimal contact with their direct supervisor when on-site (Gottfried 1992). Timed and graded exercises simulate a pressured situation under which the applicant must complete the task quickly and accurately. During these exercises, a service representative notes how composed the applicant stays through the battery of endurance tests. The pressure felt by prospective employees emerges in observations of the intake process. One of the highly skilled applicants shakes perceptibly during her face-to-face interview; she periodically wipes the sweat beading up on her face with a handkerchief discretely folded into a small square (a common prop to cope with the sauna-like humidity of Tokyo summers). In another intake process, Nagisa feels self-conscious about doing well as she compares herself to the younger applicants who complete tasks faster. Applicants are unaware that the company is assessing their conduct under a simulated pressure environment – an aspect of screening disclosed to me at the time of my observations.

The face-to-face interview lasts about 30 minutes, enough time for the service representative to accomplish several objectives simultaneously. She conveys test scores on the assigned tasks/tests, asks the applicant a series of questions about job preferences and work history, and checks on appropriate appearance, demeanor, and behavior. The service representative rates each applicant on a number of embodied skills, including tone of voice (for example rude, polite, high-pitched), posture (for example upright, slouched) and dress (for example professional, clean, neat). Self-presentation (appearance and bearing) and the way she uses her body are central to the selection of applicants, and later to the assignment to particular jobs. Some jobs more than others deploy embodied skills and require aesthetic labor for use on the job. Jobs such as "marketing of products," and "campaign girls" for political campaigns or product campaigns, hire young attractive women whose uniforms may consist of short skirts and high heels, heightening long, thin figures. Women's ornamental appearance becomes an important qualification for attracting the male gaze of the male clients of the temporary agency. The OL's aesthetic labor power is part of the objectified package advertised by the temporary agency and purchased by the client firm. The temporary-help firm and client look for particular aesthetic conventions of femininity to match female employees to placement positions.

A scandal in 1998 made visible an extreme form of heretofore hidden business practice by which temporary-help companies manage and promote sexualized female bodies. As reported in the newspaper and recounted in several interviews, Tempstaff, one of the large Japanese temporary-help companies, engaged in a common, though discriminating practice of grading applicants from "A" to "C" on the basis of physical appearance (*The Japan Times* 1998, 2).[10] The attachment of photographs to resumes, another common business practice, contributes visual data on each applicant. A union official suggests that temporary-help companies deliberately cede to clients the right to reject an agency temporary office worker. According to this same official, male clients often choose young attractive women, irrespective of other qualifications. Aesthetic labor has an economic value. The mobilization of a feminine aesthetic shapes the expression of female embodiment of organizations, qualifying women for temping work.

Age as Embodied Capacities and Competencies

The agency temporary company produces modes of embodiment through its rigorous intake process, especially through selection based on the applicant's age and gender. Preference for young women is not a formal company policy, and in fact is illegal under equal employment law. Whether or not companies deny jobs to women older than 35 or women self-impose the age limit, an informal age ceiling affects who applies and who is deemed qualified for agency temporary employment. My observations of applicants, supported by government statistics, show that women 25 to 35 years old are three times as likely as women less than 25 years old and five times as likely as women older than 35 years old to be agency temporary workers (Ministry of Labour 1998, 47). This truncated age profile tacitly recognizes the potency of the gender regime in which "real" workers are men and "respectable" women are transitory waged workers who drop out for family reasons. Turnover based on age also guarantees a cheaper labor force.

Nagisa fills in details of how age considerations inform the bodily practices of female agency temporary workers. "I put make-up on (you need to look and feel appropriate at formal/official occasions... no woman exposes [her] bare face), got my middle heels on." At the agency for the intake process, "another applicant showed up. Young, just like what/how I was when I was working right after college. I'm beginning to feel the age difference acutely. ... By the end of the video, I started feeling old and inappropriate. After all, I'm 36 and not a new graduate who can market her youth." Her repeated references to her own aging female body as unfit and misfit for agency temporary work articulates the common-sense understanding of appropriate young sexualized

---

10   The revised Worker Dispatching Law introduces provisions regulating personal information and secrets (Araki 1999, 9).

bodies and gender embodiment. By the end of the intake process, Nagisa's anxiety about her age motivates an exchange with the service representative as follows:

Nagisa: As you can see, I'm rather old – 36 years old in fact. Is there a job for a person my age?
Service representative: Yes, there are jobs. Well, jobs such as marketing (*eigyo*) may require youthful looks. Or, jobs at trade shows, such as "campaign girls" should be done by young persons. But, there are jobs for older persons.
Nagisa then comments: I waited for some examples. She didn't elaborate further. The service representative admits that bodies matter. The young age profile ensures desirable, aestheticized female bodies for agency temporary employment.

The desired aestheticized body is reinforced by media images of agency temporary workers. Manpower features a well-known actress in its ads, projecting a youthful image of feminine beauty. A monthly magazine, simply called *Haken*, the Japanese word for temporary workers, can be found among hundreds of similar women's magazines. *Haken* devotes advertising copy from temporary-help companies and employment announcements for agency temporary positions. This commercial publication displays the desired body type, matching other Japanese woman's magazines both in style and in format. It advertises agency temporary jobs and fashion, almost interchangeably, geared to young female "professional" workers. Page after page of fashion, interspersed with job announcements, reinforces a particular feminine embodiment of agency temporary work.

Age-graded organizational embodiment is deeply embedded in Japanese employment practices and labor market structures. Age is the basis for demarcating obligations that frame common-sense understandings and expectations for ordering gender relations and social status. Standard employment wages and promotions advance in regular age-based intervals that assume a male work biography of life-long attachment to the firm. In contrast, agency temporary employees tend to be short-lived within the tight parameters of age in a woman's life-course. The screening process ensures that temporary workers embody the desired look as well as possess the requisite competencies. The life of a temp does not last long. Women's bodies ultimately betray them, unable to resist the aging process. No longer desired by temporary agencies and their clients, middle-aged women enter a different nonstandard labor market segment for part-time work.

Dis-placement in the Organizational Body

The temporary-help company attempts to match temporary employee with clients by assigning women whose competencies and embodied skills fit the organization. Without direct knowledge of day-to-day work life, supervisors from the temporary company rely on cultural citation as the basis of body management by workers. The temporary employee's self-presentation is not a solo act; it is a situated, culturally informed performance. She learns how to wrap herself according to implicit and explicit aesthetic codes of femininity. Temporary employment requires a flexible self, able to respond to both subtle cues and explicit instructions for proper aestheticized styles. Temporary companies prescribe dress codes wrapping female bodies in either official or iconic uniforms. This form of body management facilitates a flexible mode of self-regulation by which temporary employees monitor their own organizational being and look.

The male embodied bureaucracy marginalizes temporary female employees who have no formal place in either the general office or on the career-track. In the Japanese model of bureaucracy, personal favors are part of the work of "doing" authority relationships. Personalized favors become part of elaborate gift-giving rituals that convey, through symbolic means, deference. In her study Ogasawara (1998), who worked as a temporary employee in a large financial institution, reports receiving gifts because of her proximity to the boss, even though she had little personal contact with him. On-site supervisors use their discretion as to whether to include temporary employees in the gift-giving circuit. Exclusion from the formal organizational culture differentiates temporary employees from the permanent staff.

Workers' performance of rituals also reinforces status differences. In one office an invisible hierarchy by employment status became apparent in the allocation of jobs by the full-time clerical staff. Full-time clericals unofficially off-loaded the least desirable jobs to agency temporary workers in defiance of bureaucratic organizational rationality. Ogasawara recalls a scene where an agency temporary worker told her about the full-time clerical staff allocating the detested task of washing teacups and other routinized tasks to older, more experienced agency temporary workers. Another agency temporary with many years of work experience complained to her in private and threatened to quit before the expiration of her contract. The performance of the tea ceremony in the office is a gendered ritual of deference enacted by women regardless of their status. Female temporary workers' lack of organizational belonging puts them in the awkward position vis-à-vis other female employees who may otherwise share common interests.

Temporary employees are expected to blend into the informal organizational culture without belonging to the formal organization. They are called upon to regulate styles of self-presentation and to manage their bodily displays. Displacement from the organizational body order excludes temporary employees from rituals of inclusion, creating new forms of labor market segmentation.

Conclusion

Feminist organizational studies have linked embodiment and gendered work to an analysis of new forms of labor market segmentation around aesthetic labor through which employees are increasingly being called upon to develop particular forms of embodied skills. The treatment of body management in terms of aesthetic labor is particularly resonant in characterizing the Japanese work world where stylized uniforms, along with linguistic and gestural forms, mark workers' places in the social and symbolic order. These practices burdened, excluded and constrained feminine embodiment from the conception of full-time careers in Japan.

A case study of temporary-help in the Japanese context challenges us to think about gender and embodiment as place-bound processes. In determining qualifications, Manpower Japan translates the intake process from the global company for local use. The temporary-help industry provides a good example of aestheticized labor to understand cultural idioms through which bodies are shaped for temp(t)ing work. A desired look, based on a taken-for-granted feminine aesthetic code, qualifies some women for female-typed jobs. Whereas temporary companies worldwide give instructions on proper appearance and enforce aesthetic codes of femininity as a part of body management, Manpower Japan's citations reference the local cultural milieu. Manpower relocated its headquarters from Tokyo to Yokohama where there are lower rents, yet they are still in close geographic proximity via frequent trains leaving the main Tokyo Station to link the agency to old and new clients and workers. The management of bodies, and the body order, occurs at a longer distance as more workers are supervised from afar and through the Internet.

The body order and modes of embodiment also are regulated by employment contracts shaped by the reproductive bargain. Employment contracts assume and reinforce the existence of an organizational gender regime in which women will be available for temporary and part-time work at particular stages in the life course. Age, as a proxy for embodied skills, both qualifies and disqualifies Japanese women to take up agency temporary work. Agency temporary companies operating in other countries exhibit a less sharply delineated age by gender profile in their selection of workers.

An examination of the practical, lived, fleshy body suggests that work re-organization does not constitute an identical process across different contexts. The demands on and for particular types of bodies and embodied capacities are shaped in a gender regime, that is rooted in the larger societal framework of the reproductive bargain. The reproductive bargain remains attached to the iconic salaryman image even though it can no longer accommodate the conditions underwriting middle-class career trajectories for young men starting out in the labor market. Temporary help firms are taking advantage of the availability of these skilled workers by employing specialists alongside female clericals and male laborers. Some firms have introduced a niche market for housewives who represent a "subsidized" and flexible labor force. In creating differentiated tracks and age- and gender-graded tiers, temporary help firms are both responding to and rewriting the terms of the reproductive bargain. Through organizational practices temporary help agencies select, curate, and manage particular modes of embodiment, but also transform labor market institutions.

The in-depth case study of the temporary help industry in this chapter underscores the concrete practices shaping gender at work and the gender distribution of work. Case studies of a single employment form and a single industry need to be situated in the larger context of capitalist development. In this case, global temporary help firms operate both de-territorially in complying with business plans dictated from parent companies and re-territorially in abiding and lobbying for favorable conditions for mobilizing a flexible workforce within the nation-state. By analyzing temporary and part-time work at a macro-level, the next chapter fleshes out the institutional anatomy of the Japanese model of capitalism. A comparison between countries in the next chapter puts in sharp relief the importance of integrating gender into the analysis to explain trajectories of capitalist development.

CHAPTER 5

Compromising Positions: Emergent Neo-Fordisms and Reproductive Bargains

The Japanese model represents the prototypical example of the "Toyota" variant of Fordism. Previous chapters chronicled how and why Japan developed this variety of capitalism. A comparative perspective can show what seems so unique to Japan may in fact represent features of a particular reproductive bargain. By contrasting Japan with Germany and Sweden, this chapter revisits discussions of Fordism, and problematizes the core analytical concepts by making explicit the implicit assumptions about gender relations, that are consequential for explaining complex patterns of inequalities.

In the early 1980s the emergence of new industrial districts in Western Europe and the spread of Japanese "lean" management practices gave rise to theories premised on the "end of Fordism" and the rise of new post-Fordist production paradigms. By the end of the decade, employers and governments more or less embraced neo-liberal conceptions of market imperatives in pursuit of goals unanticipated fully by these post-Fordist models. Employers and social policy-makers sought to achieve major changes in the rules governing social insurance arrangements, and employment relations more generally, including provisions that would relax regulations on the use of part-time and temporary labor. Throughout the 1990s it became increasingly apparent that restructuring cross-nationally followed paths not easily found on any post-Fordist map. Analyses of the major trends reshaping employment relations found advanced capitalist countries facing similar pressures to "innovate" work organization, yet the modalities and tempo of restructuring varied across and within occupations, industrial sectors and by gender.

Theories of restructuring implicitly have been about the end of one production regime and the shift to another. Terms like flexible specialization and post-Fordism evoke a singular meaning. This has blinded observers from seeing tenacious Fordist logic and diverted their attention from seeing how flexible capitalist accumulation strategies and practices are gendered. Any term that abstracts from the most visible forms, particularly as drawn from developments in manufacturing, tends to exaggerate the stability, uniformity, and coherence of each model. Theorists purporting to explain general societal trends end up with a gender-specific narrative that is uncritically rooted in male work biographies, and thus exaggerate a particular set of arrangements in core manufacturing.

Historical narratives trace the roots of emergent neo-Fordisms to negotiation of Fordist reproductive bargains that institutionalized the terms of a political compromise between labor, capital and the state. This chapter argues that Fordism embedded different reproductive bargains compromising women's positions and standardardizing employment contracts around the needs, interests and authority of particular groups of men. Parallel case studies of Sweden, Germany and Japan contrast modalities of institutional change in institutionally "thick" societies among relatively late-industrializers. The comparison highlights the mediating role of social regulation over reproduction as well as over production, which set limits on possibilities for Fordist transformation and the direction of re-regulation. The analysis is based on the comparative case-oriented approach that treats each country as a whole (Ragin 1992, 4–5), and that views the past as neither a unified development story nor a determinant set of standardized sequences. A more contingent theory applying interpretive historical methods recognizes the political agency of organized interest groups that have "chosen" or stumbled into varying paths, and that earlier choices both limit and open up alternative possibilities for social change (Skocpol 1984).

Fordism, Regulation and Reproductive Bargains

Neo-Fordism: What's in a Name

Fordist reproductive bargains were formulated in the post-Second World War period when labor movements throughout the industrialized world entered into class compromises with employers. Organized labor accepted Fordist principles of standardized production forfeiting claims over meaningful and decent work in exchange for relatively good compensation. A system of legally binding agreements, centralized and coordinated bargaining along with a network of laws reinforced what Muckenberger (1989) has called the standard employment relationship (*Normalarbeitsverhaeltnis*). This relationship offered a lifetime of relatively continuous full-time employment in a company structure. Prosperity and rapid economic growth provided the material foundation for sustaining the bargain while political reconstruction efforts to rebuild the war-torn economies through the us Marshall Plan championed the virtues of Fordism worldwide (Jones 1997, 14).

The principles of mass production spread throughout the advanced capitalist world, although the degree of commitment to the mass production paradigm

(Fordism) continued to differ between countries. Increased mechanization enabled manufacture of long runs of standardized products for the expanding mass markets in the industrialized economies. This setup produced a reliance on the narrowly trained, semi-skilled mass worker, a dependence of productive activity on machine rhythms and specialization and fragmentation of tasks in the Taylorist and Fordist image (Rojot and Tergeist 1992, 9–10).

By the late-1960s worker discontent rode a wave of industrial disputes. Patterns of standard employment relations and routine methods for organizing work and adjudicating labor and management disputes began to change around the mid-1970s. As the new international political economy moved towards neo-Fordist and postmodern conditions of greater uncertainty, unpredictability, and decentralization, corporations retooled their production processes, organizational structures, and labor forces to enhance flexibility. Employers' call for flexibility also sounded a note for bargaining decentralization and, to different degrees, for rewriting the reproductive bargain between labor and capital. Bargaining structures came under pressure from capital to devolve from national heights in the most centralized systems to enterprise-levels, and even down to individual worker-levels throughout the advanced capitalist world.

Recontractualization transferred some decision-making prerogatives to individual parties of employment contracts away from collective agents (Muckenberger 1989). Likewise, the welfare state retreated, cutting back on and tailoring benefits, and relaxing regulation on the use of flexible labor forms. This has led to nonstandard working hours, working styles and working arrangements. Yet the instability and uncertainty that characterize the emergence of neo-Fordism in the late-Twentieth century should not exaggerate the passage of former methods of doing work.

Neo-Fordism constitutes a flexible accumulation regime and regulation mode. The regime of accumulation specifies the logic of the production paradigm; that is, the dominant mode of economic growth and distribution, and the corresponding labor process, patterns of consumption, and configuration of inter-firm relationships. A regime of accumulation develops a mode of social regulation as composed of an ensemble of complementary state forms, habits and social norms (Peck 1994, 152). In this way, social regulation delimits spheres of influence "relying primarily on 'positive' measures – the media of money and rights, discipline and classification – rather than merely coercion and repression" (Steinmetz 1993, 68). Table 5.1 presents a comparative template of Fordist and neo-Fordist accumulation regimes and social regulation modes.

84 CHAPTER 5

TABLE 5.1   *Comparative template of Fordism and Neo-Fordism*

	Accumulation regime	
	Fordism	Neo-Fordism
Regime logic	Standardized Production Mass consumption (quantity)	Customized Production Customized consumption (quality)
Labor process	Continuous flow (Taylorism) Assembly line Hierarchical control (proximate)	Discontinuous flow (flexible specialized) Work teams Group/self-control (cyber, distant)
Inter-Firm relations	Vertical Integration	Networks
	Mode of social regulation	
Comparative concept of control	Liberal to social democracy	Neo-liberal
State regulation	Regulatory De-commodification Statutory rule Nationalization Expansion of welfare state Standardized benefits	De-regulatory Re-commodification Re-contractual rule Privatization Retreat of welfare state Non-standardized benefits
Industrial regulation	Standardized settlements Centralized, coordinated bargaining (national, pattern agreements)	Non-standardized settlements Decentralized bargaining (enterprise to individual agreements)
Labor markets	Job title proliferation Defined career paths (long, broad) Standard employment contracts Specialized skilled to unskilled	Job title reduction (functional flexibility) Discontinuous career paths Flexible employment contracts (numerical flexibility) Multi-skilled and deskilled

Compromising Positions: Fordism and Emerging Reproductive Bargains

Regulation theorists have based their investigation on the core male workforce in manufacturing. The embedded nature of this model and the principles of organization in the public and private spheres, however, have been closely coupled to support a strong breadwinner bargain (Pfau-Effinger 1998; Rubery et al. 1997; O'Reilly and Spee 1998). The Fordist compromise assumed and reinforced a less visible gender compromise in which tacit rules governed obligations and rights that "define the relations between women and men, between genders and generations, and finally between the areas of production and reproduction" (Rantalaiho 1993, 2). The resultant reproductive bargain set the terms of gender relations in the family and the integration of men and women into the labor market and other social spheres (Pfau-Effinger 1993).

The male-breadwinner reproductive bargain provided the initial framework for the constitution of major Fordist institutions, including: welfare regimes, the education system, the social security system, and "shaped ideas of masculinity and femininity and of 'proper' kinds of work for men and women" (Crompton and Harris 1998, 132). Men occupied a privileged position to contract their labor power; this gender compromise freed men from domestic responsibility and constructed women's work in relationship to motherhood. Thus, women did not "freely" exchange their labor power in the same way as men because of prior demands made on women's labor by the family (Wacjman 1998b).

Feminist-informed research has related welfare state developments to the unrecognized, unpaid caring work performed by women in the home (Orloff 1999), directing attention to the impact of particular social policies on either modifying or reinforcing the male-breadwinner model (Lewis 1992; Ostner and Lewis 1995). In this classification schema, Germany with its lower labor force participation of women and services provided by unpaid female labor in the family embeds a strong breadwinner reproductive bargain. The high-levels of female labor force participation and extensive social services have modified the reproductive bargain in Scandinavia (O'Reilly and Spee 1998, 262–263; Ellingsaeter 1998; Rantalaiho 1993). However, this research has not systematically explained how and why states and/or regions conform to strong, modified or weak male-breadwinner models (Ellingsaeter 1998, 59), has failed to link the type of reproductive bargain with the type of production regime, and has almost exclusively focused on comparisons between Western European cases.

Charting the Connections

The negotiation of Fordist class compromises arose out of the institutional relationship between labor, capital and the state. Crouch (1993, 61–63) conceptualizes these institutional relationships varying along two axes: the power of organized labor, and the extent and intensity of industrial relations. The power of labor "determines whether employers will be required to come to terms with labor as a bargaining partner" (ranging from high to low). Extent is plotted in terms of levels at which interaction takes place, reflecting the degree of centralization and the locus of bargaining from low (decentralized at the plant or company level), through medium (at the industrial/sectoral level) to high (centralized at the national level). Intensity specifies the particular decision-making fields involved and the form of interaction, tapping institutional density of bargaining relationships ranging from low (pluralist bi-lateralism) to high (neo-corporatism). More intense levels of interaction usually involve political coordination that narrow managerial discretion over both work reorganization and union integration.

All three cases examined are neo-corporatist but to varying degrees. Sweden represents one pole with the strongest and most intense levels of interaction as reflected in highly centralized, tripartite corporatist bargaining. Comparatively weaker, yet still relatively strong, the German labor movement concludes multi-employer agreements at the branch and industry-level without any formal state role. An even weaker Japanese labor movement settles decentralized agreements at the enterprise-level in the context of a "developmentalist" state. Furthermore, the extent to which industrial relations is embedded in law subjects a range of employment conditions and rights to statutory provision (Teague and Grahl 1992, 46). Germany resembles Sweden as countries with high legalistic industrial relations systems providing a wider array of employment protection than Japan where law plays a less interventionist role.

State politics mediate conditions over employment relations and contracts. A hegemonic political party and discourse, either on the right or the left, constructs an easier field for partisan political action aligning policies more closely with the dominant power bloc. The politics of the state determine the sphere of influence of social regulation either expansively through universal distributive principles (social democracy) or selectively through means-tested principles (liberal democracy). Social democracy promotes a public mandate (and discourse) for economic and social interventions improving conditions of employment contracts and modifying reproductive bargains (as in Sweden). The range of caring policies is more constrained when social regulation is framed within conservative social democratic state politics (as in Germany). Enterprise-based welfare limits social benefits even more and circumscribes

TABLE 5.2 *Fordist compromises*

		Corporate Fordism	Company Fordism	Diversified-quality Fordism	Corporatist Fordism
	Case	**US**	**Japan**	**Germany**	**Sweden**
Economic	Intensity of labor and capital relations	Low pattern agreements	Medium	High	High corporatist
	Power of organized labor	Low		Medium	High
	Extent of interactions	Decentralized		Dual	Centralized
Political	Comprehensive concept of control	Liberal Democracy	Developmental	Conservative Social Democracy	Social Democracy
	Distributive principles	Selective	Thresholds	Thresholds	Universal
Social	Male Breadwinner Model	Modified	Strong		Weak
	Gender Contract	Dual Breadwinner Female-care	Male breadwinner Female-care		Dual breadwinner State-care

the social realm (as in Japan). Both conservative social democracy and developmentalist state politics rely more on the family for dependent care. The lack of social support for caring tends to impose a trade-off between family and employment, which in turn reinforces traditional male-breadwinner models (see Table 5.2).

Neo-Fordism and Bargains in Sweden, Germany and Japan

Historical narratives chronicle the bases for class compromises that forged the core institutional characteristics of industrial relations systems, furnished the vocabularies and logics for pursuing goals, and defining what was valued, shaped the norms and rules by which labor and capital were to abide (Hollingsworth and Boyer 1997, 4), and set limits on the terms for subsequent bargaining rounds. An examination of state politics assesses the extent to which organized labor and their political allies expanded social regulation over production and reproduction. Through a review of women's employment status across the life-course, specifically the conditions of part-time employment, the analysis here more explicitly identifies the type of reproductive bargain negotiated as part of Fordism and neo-Fordism.

Social Democratic Corporatist Fordism: Sweden's Third Way
Sweden exemplifies a strong social democratic corporatist regime where the Social Democratic Party enjoyed the longest continuous governance of any capitalist country. A unitary state, as compared to the federal system of Germany, provided an easier field for cohesive political action (Rantalaiho 1997, 23). The resultant strong welfare state generated a set of social policies based on prototypical vocabularies of social democracy (Pempel 1998, 28). In so doing, Sweden forged the Third Way between a liberal market and socialist economies. The social democratic route, emphasizing universal entitlements and social services, and high-level corporatist bargaining, equalized the formal conditions of employment contracts and modified the male-breadwinner model.

The Swedish industrial working class constituted a significant force enhancing the strength of the Social Democratic Party and national-based trade unions (Clement and Myles 1994, 21). The *Saltsjobaden* accord between the *Landsorganisation* (LO), Swedish Confederation of Trade Unions, and *Svenska Arbetsgivareforening* (SAF), the Swedish Employers' Confederation, established an early class compromise that governed industrial relations from 1938 to the mid-1980s (Mahon 1994). Regular wage rounds and parallel talks between the TCO, the Swedish Central Organization of Salaried Employees, and the SAF took place in 1956 (Western 1997, 32). What distinguished Sweden from other countries was the centralized, national character of the Fordist bargain and the intensive interaction between peak-level organizations securing this bargain (Pontusson 1990, 8–9). A high degree of centralization gave trade union confederations, particularly the LO, a strong lever to coordinate collective bargaining and to negotiate a national corporatist framework for improving conditions of employment initially among male industrial workers. At a time of economic expansion during the 1960s trade unions negotiated a solidaristic wage policy that brought low wages in line with industry averages. Nonetheless, "labor contract conditions remained [overtly] patriarchal" up until the late-1960s (Svensson 1995, 31). By the mid-1980s, gender parity in union membership around 84 percent gave women an organized power-base from which to frame gender-specific concerns (Rantalaiho 1997, 29).

The Social Democratic Party's strong commitment to "social" services led to the expansion and integration of the welfare state, satisfying many basic social needs outside of the market economy (Schmid 1994). Extensive, universal entitlements formally equalized employment contracts, realized high social wages, and fostered low-income inequality. As Ellingsaeter (1998, 61) notes, social policies recognized women's individual potential and women's right to paid employment as early as the 1930s but maintained a gender-differentiated identity or, what Rantalaiho (1997, 26) has called, "wage-worker motherhood." By the mid-1970s, a "configuration of integrative social policies" provided an array of entitlements (Gornick and Jacobs 1998, 690) ranging from parental leave, subsidized childcare to tax reform, encouraging and enabling women to enter into the labor force by minimizing the trade-off between employment and family formation. The 1971 tax reform separated taxation for spouses to the benefit of dual earners who spread out income between family members (Clement and Myles 1994, 186). State-provided care supported the development of a dual breadwinner bargain.

The Nordic countries share a history of poor free peasants eking out a living under harsh Arctic climates. Rantalaiho (1997, 21) characterizes this agrarian-based economy as gender-divided but with less full-scale differentiation because demands of survival necessitated a work partnership between men and women. Due to the rapid processes of urbanization and industrialization, Sweden soon became the leading Nordic industrial nation, based on its core metal industry and large firms, and the subsequent development of a large and homogeneous male working class (Ellingsaeter 1998, 61). Swedish women, whose work predominated in the traditional domestic and agricultural sectors, gradually shifted to the commercial and industrial sectors during the interwar period. Their labor force participation, however, reached only 50.1 percent in 1960. This level was surpassed in the 1960s when service expansion catapulted almost two-thirds of Swedish women into public sector employment compared to less than one-third of German women and 6 percent of Japanese women. By contrast, approximately 75 percent of Swedish men worked in the private sector. These public-sector jobs were concentrated in the traditional female occupations of health and education (Melkas and Anker 1998, 354) and many were created as part-time 'for the very purpose of luring women into the labor force' (Nurmi 1998, 135).

Strong corporatist institutions mediated by comprehensive social services supported the most favorable work conditions among female part-timers. A high proportion of Swedish female part-timers worked relatively long hours, enjoyed relative job security and full social benefits. In Sweden part-time work, in principle, was subject to equal treatment with respect to the application of labor and social legislation (Thurman and Trah 1990, 29). Part-time workers were entitled to parental leave, to paid vacations, among other benefits (Sundstrom 1991, 177). Since 1979, mothers had the statutory right to reduced working hours and all employed parents were entitled to reduce their working hours to 75 percent of full-time work until the child turned eight (Ellingsaeter 1998, 63). Yet the Fordist bargain tied access to some benefits (e.g. unemployment benefits) to a minimum number of hours worked (Pettersson 1994, 251). Similarly, the calculation of transfer payments as a proportion of earnings translated into less support for part-time (typically women) workers. Thresholds, however, exerted less negative effect on Swedish part-timers than German and Japanese women because the majority of Swedish part-timers either worked more than the minimum and/or switched back to full-time work. From a comparative perspective, social democratic-informed policies in Sweden positively affected women's labor force longevity as evidenced by less frequent job interruptions. The high labor force participation among Swedish women took the form of additional part-time employment (Clement and Myles 1994, 130); 72 percent of women with children under the age of seven continued participating in the labor force by working part-time (Hong Li and Singelmann 1998).

By the mid-1980s corporatist bargaining shifted from the national-level to the branch-level. The first significant instance of bargaining decentralization occurred in 1983 when the engineering employer's association (VF), led by Volvo, negotiated a separate agreement with *Metall* and its white-collar counterpart (Mahon 1994). At the 1987 SAF Conference employers unveiled a co-worker identity (*metarbetere*), and at the 1990 Conference they hailed the rise of "new flexible companies." Some of the largest companies like Volvo, ABB, and Ericsson endorsed actively the ideas of both co-worker agreements and flexible companies, yet only a few local agreements have been concluded, most notably by ABB (Brulin and Nilsson 1994, 15). In 1995 employers withdrew from most tripartite boards and reorganized at the branch-level. Still, neo-corporatist bargaining remained the dominant form of interest intermediation at decentralized levels and the welfare state maintained a high social wage at slightly reduced levels.

Pressures to adopt neo-liberal market initiatives stalled further expansion of the welfare state and threatened to cut benefits and jobs. These initiatives negatively affected women, both as public sector employees and as clients. Wage drift has occurred, dispersing income, as a result of both unions and employers no longer feeling bound by solidaristic wage principles (Kjellberg 1992). Nonetheless, social democratic state policies contributed to the modification of the male-breadwinner model.

Diversified-Quality Fordism: The German Bargain

The German labor movement and Social Democratic Party (SPD) are comparatively weaker than in Sweden. Political competition between the Social Democratic Party and the Christian Democratic Union (CDU) prevented the former from articulating a coherent political project and from integrating the state into corporatist bargaining. The German state also had less power resources at its disposal given the division of power between central and regional states and between the government and the central Bundesbank. West Germany developed a conservative "social market economy" drawing on a long history of welfare based on the social insurance principle enshrined in the Bismarck model (see Steinmetz 1993). In contrast to Sweden, Germany pursued a high productivity track with few aspirations to full employment, especially with regard to the integration of women. High-level coordination between employers and unions and the relatively strong labor movement produced a unique employment system combining dual training and co-determination. These institutional features supported a standard employment relation among core male workers.

With the guidance of the Occupation forces after the war, reform of industrial relations was oriented toward cooperation. The institution of co-determination was an important symbol of the new cooperative relationship between labor and business (Lembruch 1999, 44). The *Deutscher Gewerkschaftsbund* (DGB), the major West German union federation played no formal role in national bargaining, but the largest affiliate, *IG Metall* among 16 other large industrial unions, engaged in highly centralized bargaining – experiments with tri-partism date back to the Weimar period. Unions faced well-organized employers; the *Bundervereinigung der Deutschen Arbeitgeberverbande* (BDA) consisted of 47 associations covering between 80–90 percent of all private employers (Hollingsworth 1997, 286). Strong peak organizations produced multi-employer industry-wide agreements, a strong vocational training system and co-determination (Streeck 1997). The enactment of the 1972 Works Council Act further strengthened shop-floor organization in large, manufacturing enterprises. By the mid-1980s, union density reached high levels for men but relatively lower levels for women: only 22 percent of women belonged to unions as compared to 47 percent of men.

Germany developed a "social state" whereby generous transfer payments affected extensive redistribution (Schmid 1994, 156), labor laws set high minimum standards, and labor courts monitored the terms of employment contracts. Because many policies tied benefits to long, unbroken employment biographies, unions had a strong incentive to defend the job security of their members over 'outsiders' in order to maintain continuous employment. The adoption of thresholds rather than universal access (as in Sweden) further limited the amount of benefits available to women whose work experience did not fit the standard employment relationship. As a result, male workers more than female workers enjoyed high wages, expensive social rights and strong job security.

The West German class compromise was built on the concept of a family wage that preserved many traditional caring functions in the family. Conservative family policies along with generous social insurance provisions created contradictory experiences for German women (Rubery et al. 1997). Publicly funded child allowances (e.g., *kindergeld* and *erziehungsgeld*) and contract-based family allowances rewarded stay-at-home mothers. The tax system also penalized full-time labor force participation among married women (Gottfried and O'Reilly 1999). On the other hand, women derived generous social security through their status as dependent wives and mothers (Rantalaiho 1997, 27). The non-integration of caring policies, which focused on maternal protection, and strong employment protection, which was based on the standard employment relationship, reinforced the traditional male breadwinner norm.

Part-time employment grew slower than in a number of other industrialized countries, alongside comparatively lower levels of female participation in paid employment. Since the early 1990s the rate of part-time employment became significant, especially marginal part-time employment. In Germany, 74.6 percent of married women worked part-time as compared to 11.8 percent of never married women. The presence of children elevated women's likelihood of working part-time: 56.7 percent for married women with children as compared to 20.1 percent for married women without children. Single female parents exhibited the same low rate of part-time employment at 8 percent as single women without children (O'Reilly and Bothfeld 1998, 23).

A change in the German class compromise took place in the 1984 round of collective bargaining. *IG Metall* conceded flexibility in exchange for reduction in working time (Trinczek 1995, 47) to *Gesamtmetall* (employer's association in the metalworking industry), setting the pattern for successive rounds – Volkswagen, the biggest private employer in Germany, already had settled single-employer agreements (Muckenberger 1997, 9). The breakdown of the old compromise tilted the balance of the dual industrial relations system and delegated new responsibilities to plant-level works councils (Thelen 1992, 225). Still the "rule of pilot contracts" meant that settlement in one district served as a framework for other districts, yielding considerable uniformity of working conditions and wages among union members (Trinczek 1995, 58). Business associations lost capacity to discipline members as more employers either left or insisted on opt-out clauses (Esser 1996, 15). These alterations to industrial relations have destabilized the standard employment relationship. Yet policies and politics continued to assume that standard with its reproductive bargain.

Company Fordism in Japan

The hegemony of the Liberal Democratic Party as a result of more than 38 years of continuous rule fostered a developmental state. Japan's economic bureaucracy supported and "disciplined" big business through monetary instruments and industrial policy in the form of industrial targeting (Johnson 1993). As Pempel and Tsunekawa (1979) have suggested the cooperative relationship between business and the state constituted a form of "corporatism without labor." A combination of weak labor at the national-level, alongside high fusion of labor representation with employers at the enterprise-level, deprived labor of a strong political lever for realizing a broader social bargain.

Japanese industrial relations evolved in the aftermath of the Second World War. Under the command of General Douglas MacArthur, a new constitution was written and labor laws passed, including the Trade Union Law, the Labor Adjustment law, and the Labor Standards Act (Price 1997, 266). Labor historian, Andrew Gordon (1985) chronicles the burst of union organizing and cycles of labor militancy unleashed by these laws. From the end of the war through the early 1960s labor turbulence peaked with union membership reaching its highest level of 45 percent overall (Tsuru 1994, 1) and over 50 percent in the heart of the industrial workforce primarily in steel, automobile and iron (Kosai 1997, 163). The average number of days lost to strike activity exceeded the rate in both West Germany and Sweden (Kume 1998, 8). Women actively participated in these struggles, but unions often segregated them along with young men in separate divisions (Gordon 1998 191). Labor radicalism culminated in workers seizing control over production in several factories. An aborted general strike in February 1947, canceled after the Occupation authorities prohibited the action (Kosai 1997, 163–164), marked a turning point for organized labor (Price 1997, 268). A period of repression against independent labor unions and a concerted campaign by both employers and the state weakened the independent national labor movement. Internal divisions split labor into a more radical group giving primacy to political issues and a more accommodationist group emphasizing economic incorporation (Kosai 1997, 164). Weak at the national level, major trade unions strategically linked their interests with those of their enterprise. Unions were not without horizontal connections; they coordinated negotiations during a Spring Wage Offensive or *Shunto* (Brown et al. 1997) consolidating a trend toward business unionism (Kosai 1997, 164). This "productivity" bargain, however, succeeded in raising wages more broadly and contributed to relatively low-income inequality (Kume 1998 19).

During the decade after the war the majority of women continued to assist in family businesses, on farms or in retail shops. Some middle-aged women worked as day laborers in local food processing plants or in construction. Women employees were concentrated in working-class positions, far outnumbering schoolteachers, secretaries, nurses, doctors, artists and other middle-class jobs (Moloney 1995, 279). Over the next decade family workers rapidly shifted over to wage employment in response to increasing demand for unskilled and semi-skilled workers as factories adopted Fordist production methods (Kumazawa 1996, 165–166).

The Japanese class compromise created strong internal labor markets that ensured job security and an age-graded system of rewards (*nenko*) in large industrial enterprises. Through the *nenko* seniority system, management created a path along which men could rise to supervisory positions. Kumazawa (1996, 167) argues that the removal of women from competitive career-tracks enabled management to open the secure route for male workers. This practice contributed to the fusion of male labor representation with company organization interpolating workers as male "company citizens" (Gordon 1985). The community-type institutions that fostered company citizenship rarely extended beyond the core male work force (Tabata 1998 199). Women, whose jobs were concentrated in small-to-medium sized firms and in nonstandard employment, fell outside union coverage, lowering their access to social wages determined at the enterprise-level. As a result, real wages and social wage disparities between men and women were relatively high in Japan as compared to their European counterparts.

Decentralized trade unions defended the interests of their own firm and the rights of core workers at the enterprise (Suwa 1989, 7), emphasizing enterprise-based over government-sponsored welfare (Goodman and Peng 1997, 208). Unions fought for positive social benefits like childcare leave but for women only. During the mid-1950s unions demanded time-off for women to take care of their babies. It took until the mid-1970s for their efforts to pay off in the form of the first instance of childcare leave in Japan. For the most part, voluntary enterprise welfare supported full-time male workers who occupied positions in large company structures. Further, a piece-meal approach to welfare relied on the family (unpaid labor of mothers and daughters) as the site of welfare service delivery. Family- and enterprise-based welfare relieved the state from a social responsibility for providing a safety net as a collective good. Goodman and Peng write persuasively that the East Asian states consciously re-emphasized the role of the family and invoked gender ideologies in the 1980s, drawing on a Confucian vocabulary to combat demands for a Western-style welfare system.

Employment protection was weak and in regard to women emphasized maternal protection. Moloney (1995, 273) makes a strong case that the Equal Employment Opportunity Law (passed in 1985) while focusing on women's work lives, was framed within the dominant discourse on gender that naturalizes the role of mothers in creating and running a nurturing household. Moreover, tax laws contained financial penalties discouraging full-time, dual-earner families. Families would lose lump sum allowances if a spouse's (wife) income exceeded a threshold of about one million-yen per year, and the second earner received insurance at no additional cost as long as her income fell below the threshold. A study by Abe and Ohtake (1997) confirmed that married women consciously adjusted the number of hours worked to fall below the designated threshold. In this way, the state affected the allocation of labor time that underwrote the tacit male breadwinner bargain.

By the mid-1970s, part-time employment evolved from a mere tool of temporary relief from market fluctuations to a permanent part of a firm's organizational structure and capital accumulation strategy. While part-time employment has increased for both men and women, more than one-third of Japanese women worked part-time as compared to 11.4 percent of men in 1994. Almost 40 percent of Japanese women were part-timers in the prime childrearing years, more than double the level among the younger cohort. Part-time employees received fewer benefits, earned lower compensation (including lower wages and minimal or no lump-sum bonuses), and had access to minimal opportunities for on- the-job training, rotations, and promotions (Osawa and Kingston 1996).

Labor became more politicized in the 1970s led by the leftist public sector union Sohyo (Kume 1998). The moderate unions followed suit after the oil crisis culminating in the formation of the new Japanese Trade Union Confederation (Rengo) in 1989. Unions continued to engage in decentralized bargaining at the enterprise level but became more involved in national-level politics. By 1993 a split in the LDP weakened its hegemony and allowed for a broader base of political contenders to influence policy debates. This political thrust, however, did not dramatically tilt the balance of power between labor and capital. Labor exercised minimal impact on social policy formation, and state politics continued to underwrite the male breadwinner bargain.

Alternative Paths to Emerging Neo-Fordisms: Stability and Change

The legacy of strong labor unions in Sweden and Germany has prevented the breakdown of corporatist industrial relations. Organized labor remains central to negotiation but faces organized employers more willing to challenge accords of the past. The wider scope of collective bargaining and centralized wage setting has compressed the disparity of wages and benefits (Maier 1994, 93). Because democratic-corporatist mechanisms still function for making claims and formally engage participation of organized labor, albeit at more decentralized levels, neo-Fordism in these countries devolves forms of social re-regulation that articulate a modified neo-liberal agenda. Flexibility in this context has not given full reign to market-enhancing initiatives. When returning to office in the early 1990s, the Swedish Social Democrats slowed the pace of neo-liberal change ushered in by the previous conservative government (Ryner 1994). The conservative coalition under Helmut Kohl in Germany met successful resistance from organized labor led by *IG Metall* (e.g. one notable case is the failed attempt by Kohl's Coalition government to drastically reduce sick pay benefits in spring 1997, see Gottfried 1997). In Japan, the Liberal Democratic Party's hegemony and the class compromise intertwined organized labor's fate with the economic fortunes of the enterprise.

Theorists of comparative labor politics have questioned the corollary assumption that the wider scope of corporatist bargaining empowers labor and provides it with more freedom to maneuver in periods of fiscal retrenchment and work restructuring. Thelen (1993) suggests that Swedish social democracy failed to shield labor from the all-out assault by employers whereas the dual system in Germany served as a better safeguard against such attacks since works councils were in a better position to "negotiate decentralization." In a similar argument Kume (1998) claims that institutional-dense networks linking labor and capital at the enterprise level facilitated the recent thrust of unions into national politics in Japan. Neither system, however, has prevented the decline of union density, occurring over a longer period and at a faster pace in Japan (Western 1997, 17). The voluntary, but publicly supported unemployment insurance schemes administered by unions bolstered Swedish trade union power, enabling it to expand at a time when union density declined elsewhere. In Germany and Japan, the emphasis on micro-level bargaining protects a shrinking number of insiders over a larger number of outsiders.

Social democratic corporatism has empowered women as workers. Swedish women have benefited from a class compromise that formulated solidaristic wage settlements and state politics based on the integration of labor market and caring policies (see Table 5.3). A low number of Swedish women work in low paid jobs, and there is a narrow wage differential between men and women. Through their involvement in political parties and trade unions, women workers have widened the scope of thinking on equality beyond the labor market and into the private domain of family-life (Jenson 1991 cited in O'Reilly and Spee 1998, 276). Swedish welfare state policies, supported by social democratic politics, weakened the breadwinner model but did not completely decouple neo-Fordist industrial relations from a male work biography. Nurmi (1998, 135) refers to a "double-bind between women and the welfare state" in which the "state provided both the jobs and the services necessary to enable women to work at those jobs." An interesting argument by Lewis and Astrom (1992 cited in Ellingsaeter 1998, 71) notes two unintended consequences of equality measures. First, the shift in the provision of benefits to Swedish women from entitlements derived on the basis of motherhood to paid workers strengthens policies recognizing women's needs as mothers. Second, the institutionalization of part-time work as an employment right has made this status an acceptable alternative for women. As a result, a conditional equality bargain within the neo-Fordist production framework relegates many working mothers to part-time employment and does not alter significantly the gender division of caring labor. Thus, women's labor force attachment matches men's but the form of integration differ in terms of career paths and placement within the occupational structure.

The strong male-breadwinner in Germany and Japan was sustained despite different Fordist bargains. Germany and Japan exhibit surprisingly similar age-specific labor market profiles; women's labor-force participation rises and falls in a flattened M-curve pattern when graphing female employment by age of worker. The number of women leaving employment during their marriage and childbearing years has declined since 1986 in Japan, making the trough shallower. Born et al. (1996) finds similar results for German women. Japanese women, however, suffer higher penalties for working part-time than either

TABLE 5.3   *Reproductive Bargains: Outcomes of Fordist Compromises*

	Modified dual earner female-care	Modified male-breadwinner Female-care		Weak dual earner state-care
Case	US	Japan	Germany	Sweden
Gender contract				
Trade-off between employment and family	Yes/No	Yes	Yes	No
Female labor force participation	High	Low	Low	High
Family wage	No	Yes	Yes	No
Social rights	Low	Low	Medium	High
Employment contract				
Social wage	Low	Medium	High	High
Industrial rights	Low	Medium	High	High
Part-time work	Marginal	Marginal	Mixed	Secure
Low wage – male	High	Low	Low	Low
Low wage – female	High	High	Medium	Low

Swedish or German women who earn about 90 percent of the full-time wage. It is possible to re-enter full-time employment in Germany as well as in Sweden where women enjoy and have exercised specific rights to return to full-time employment. Institutional rigidities (e.g. a single port of entry into the internal labor market) and the lack of social support diminish Japanese women's likelihood of re-entering as full-time workers. The strong male breadwinner increases the likelihood of women working in a low-paying job. The emphasis on job security at the enterprise-level in Japan and working time in Germany oriented unions toward the defense of lifelong continuous employment among their core male membership. Germany and Japan's employment systems engendered an insider/outsider divide and an enduring, albeit changing, male breadwinner reproductive bargain.

Conservative state politics has been predicated on women's unpaid labor in the family and uneven caring provisions with a different array of advantages and disadvantages for women. In Japan, the 1991 Childcare Law entitled both mothers and fathers to take a year off with the right of return to work. Unlike the German case, there is no compensation after 14 weeks of maternity leave, minimizing this option for working-class women. Japanese enterprise-welfare is a patchwork of derived benefits which amount to modest cash support for mothers. Only women below an income threshold receive a lump-sum payment, and then families can claim a dependent allowance on their tax returns. Japanese employers' wage policies may provide a dependent allowance for kids, but not at the level of German *kindergeld*. The continual rise in men's wages with job tenure (*nenko* system) constitutes the Japanese "family wage" in concrete terms. Childcare leave in Germany holds open the worker's job for three years. The greater availability of day care and after school programs offset some of the negative effects in Japan.

Broader coverage of collective agreements and strong labor laws have reduced flexible labor contracts and brought wages more in line with full-time male workers in Germany (Streeck 1997), whereas lower union coverage and weaker labor regulation in Japan have allowed for a larger percentage of flexible labor contracts. Changes in Japan's Labor Standards Act that removed the remaining protections on night work for non-professionals and the cap on women's overtime hours will likely expand employers' use of women as 'flexible' labor. While the German class compromise had sheltered the workforce from extensive marginal employment, part-time work constitutes a significant and growing share of total employment. Still, women's part-time employment remained high at more than one-third of employment for women in both Germany and Japan. A lower overall share of the population works part-time in Germany, but this employment status work is more feminized.

The Japanese class compromise protected employees in a limited range of enterprises and industrial sectors. Japanese working mothers who switch to part-time work accumulate disadvantages by their limited prospects for movement back to full-time jobs and by the low wages typical of marginal part-time work (Gottfried and Hayashi 1998). Even among Swedish women who enjoy more advantageous employment conditions, part-time work can block career advancement. While fewer Swedish women work part-time than in the past, a comparative study by Clement and Myles (1994) finds part-time work functions as the single most important factor confining Swedish women to the working class.

Mapping Neo-Fordisms and Reproductive Bargains

A map of neo-Fordisms cannot be drawn without uncovering the institutional roots in Fordist class and gender compromises. Sole reference to a class compromise would not have solved the puzzle why relatively similar Fordist bargains in Sweden and Germany are consistent with different reproductive bargains and why relatively similar reproductive bargains appear in Germany and Japan when their Fordist bargains have been relatively different. Reproductive bargains indicate the type of compromise made about the gender division of labor, at work, and by implication, at home. Making explicit the type of reproductive bargain reveals hidden dependencies and helps to account for women's relative position in paid employment and unpaid caring work. The three countries investigated here exhibit different reproductive bargains: Sweden is the furthest along the continuum towards a public gender regime with a dual-earner bargain; Germany and Japan have a semi-public gender regime with a male-breadwinner bargain. These reproductive bargains are articulated with different production regimes and employment relations systems, ranging from the coordinated centralized system in Sweden, industry-coordinated in Germany, to a group-coordinated system in Japan. Institutionalized employment relations systems produce and are built on different bargains over the distribution and the responsibility for the costs of reproduction. Identifying the terms of the reproductive bargain illuminates the less visible factors and forces influencing patterns of precarious work and life.

Historical narratives highlighted the importance of political factors in shaping types of reproductive bargains in varieties of capitalism. Social democratic state politics broadened the realm of social rights and caring services for the organization of everyday life. This weakened the male-breadwinner model toward a conditional equality contract supporting the development of a dual breadwinner and state-provided care in Sweden. In both Germany and Japan the employment system embedded a traditional male breadwinner model in which women depended on income transfers from an individual full-time male worker. As Esping-Andersen (1997, 83) suggests, "[t]he family's virtual dependence on the male earner's income and entitlements meant that unions came to battle for job security (for example, seniority principles, the regulation of hiring and firing practices) and the 'family wage'." Conservative social policies thus "nurtured the emergence of rigid "insider/outsider" labor markets with consequent marginalization and peripheralization, particularly among women workers" (Esping-Andersen 1997, 75), and reinforced a traditional female-provided care model (Pfau-Effinger 1998, 153). Germany and Japan must be differentiated with respect to employment protection. The German social market economy enshrined legal norms for employment protection with the effect of compressing wage differences whereas the Japanese developmental state was not compelled to regulate the terms of employment contracts to the same extent as northern European states.

As Fordism unravels it does so in the context of different bargains. The social regulation of gender relations and reproduction has influenced the kind of Fordist accords that have been bargained, and the reproductive bargains shape the form and terrain of dismantling of those accords. Although women's waged work follows a more continuous pattern through their life span, many women alternate between full and part-time work. As more firms adopt flexible employment strategies, part-time employment status increasingly defines women's work at their prime working ages. The extent of the accumulated disadvantages depends on employment protection and caring support that developed as part of the Fordist bargain in each country.

Neo-Fordism signals the ascendance and proliferation of flexible accumulation strategies and neo-liberal rhetoric combining in different proportions, spreading unevenly within and across industries, unleashing new social forces, and constituting novel sites and subjects of struggle. Changing accumulation regimes and social regulation modes do not constitute a revolutionary leap forward but remain rooted in Fordism even as work processes and organizations deviate from old production concepts. Future trajectories are, more or less, path-dependent, shaped by the strategic actions and by the legacy of Fordist compromises and their reproductive bargains. Neo-liberal globalization and the inability of this employment model to provide a livelihood for an increasing numbers of workers has precipitated a range of responses from below.

With the rise of neo-Fordism the institutions for skill development acquired on-the-job through the training system over one's working life no longer are available to a growing number of people. Brinton (2011) chronicles the fate of the current generation of young non-elite men "Lost in Transition." Like her earlier pioneering research, Brinton focuses on the school to workforce transition, but brings to light how these same institutions now create instability for youth in post-industrial Japan. Young men face more than an unstable labor market and insecure jobs; their prospects are shaped by their inability to secure their own livelihood and identity in the long-run. Brinton is right to focus on young men adrift in an uncertain labor market. This chapter emphasized renegotiation of the reproductive bargain undermining the conditions of existence for these men. Unmoored from the corporate-centered salaryman promise of stable employment, precarious work and unemployment deprives some young men of the social foundations on which male middle-class respectability had been based. Standard employment had provided the material basis of and cultural conditions for hegemonic masculinity of the corporate-centered male-breadwinner system. As the next chapter shows, the growing numbers of men, particularly young men, in nonstandard employment and unemployment compel an examination of the changing norm of the male standard work biography that until recently had been so strong in Japan. The reproductive bargain remains attached to the iconic salaryman image even though it can no longer accommodate the conditions underwriting middle-class career trajectories for young men starting out in the labor market.

CHAPTER 6

Precarity among Youth: Current Challenges, Future Prospects

Introduction

There is a palpable malaise, both embodied and structural, due to the lingering and intractable economic crisis in Japan. This sensory experience of precarity is deeply felt in everyday life as more and more people face economic hardship and an uncertain future. Poverty and inequality are unavoidable social issues confronted by the press, even if their analyses may not recognize the depth and root causes of the problem. Concern about precarious employment has become more pronounced in public discourse now that men increasingly experience unemployment and insecure work, and for longer periods of time.

This chapter scrutinizes trends and tendencies toward widespread youth unemployment and nonstandard employment in the context of an increasingly precarious Japan. Often cited for its low unemployment rate, both absolutely and relative to other countries, the stylized model of Japanese capitalism masked the extent of precarious nonstandard work (temporary, part-time, casual work) in the labor market. For this reason, extant models have failed to recognize growing precarity in society as a whole, the extent of precarious work among women (especially mothers), and increasingly among the young and the elderly (both male and female). By identifying the institutional logic of the corporate-centered male-breadwinner reproductive bargain, we can better understand escalating precariousness and its impact on the "lost generation" of young men entering a transformed labor market. Japan's lost generation faces different constraints and opportunities than those of their parents (Brinton 2011, 13). Standard employment had provided the material basis of and cultural conditions sustaining hegemonic masculinity of the corporate-centered male-breadwinner system. Japan's model of capitalism became unsustainable for larger numbers of workers once the economy slowed down in the early 1990s. The recent growth of unemployment and nonstandard employment compels an examination of the changing norm of the male standard work biography that, until recently, had been so prevalent in Japan.

To fully understand precarity after the initial Lost Decade, the chapter unfolds in three main sections. The first section presents empirical data on employment trends and interprets precarity in light of changing labor market conditions and the unraveling of the reproductive bargain. The emergence and growth of new forms of precarious work and precarity, however, is not simply an outcome of economic forces and factors. Section two shows how the state uses legal and discursive means to shape the conditions of precarious work and precarity. The state coins keywords and reframes employment categories that chastise youth, as a lost generation, for shirking their work responsibility.[1] These keywords emphasize an individual, moral/psychological register rather than structural factors giving rise to youth adrift in the postindustrial labor market. The final section considers the consequences of and response to precarity for jobless and unemployed youth. It reveals the emergence of new labor associations organizing the unemployed and precarious workers in a changing landscape of work and politics.

Interpreting Youth Unemployment and Precarity

Prior to the bursting of the economic bubble, younger workers aged 15–24 exhibited low unemployment rates, only 4.5 percent of men and 4.1 percent of women (See Table 6.1). Since the Lost Decade the rate doubled for both male and female younger workers, reaching 9.4 percent for 15–19 year olds, 9.1 percent for 20–24 year olds, and 7.1 percent for 25–29 year olds, as compared to 5.1 percent overall in 2010 (Labor situation in Japan and its analysis: 2012, 24). From a cross-national comparative perspective, Japanese youth seem to fare better in the labor market. Japanese unemployment statistics, however, misrepresent the extent of "real" unemployment, only counting as unemployed those individuals aged 15 and over, out of work, "capable of immediately accepting work," and seeking work during the survey period (JILPT 2013, 44). Like in the US, omitted from this definition of unemployment are the non-employed, including discouraged job seekers opting out of the labor market, whether by choice or by circumstance. Further, the dichotomous framing of employment and unemployment in conventional statistical language does not accurately take into account employment statuses in between these categories, and therefore underestimates the true levels of less than full employment and the extent of nonstandard precarious employment.

---

1   Like Williams' *"vocabulary of meanings"* in *Keywords*, the emphasis of my own analyses is "deliberately social and historical. In the matters of reference [I] insist that the most active problems of meaning are always primarily embedded in actual relationships, and that both the meanings and the relationships are typically diverse and variable, within the structures of particular social orders and the processes of social and historical change" (1983, 21–22).

TABLE 6.1   *Unemployment by age, gender (1990–2010)*

	1990	2000	2010
Total Overall	2.1	4.7	5.1
Male total	2.0	4.9	5.4
Male 15–24	4.5	10.2	10.4
Male 25–34	1.8	5.0	6.6
Female Total	2.2	4.5	4.6
Female 15–24	4.1	7.9	8.0
Female 25–34	3.4	6.4	5.7

SOURCE: JILPT; JAPANESE WORKING LIFE PROFILE 2012/2013, 42.

The main forms of nonstandard employment include part-time, temporary (agency and direct-hire), casual day labor, and independent contractors. Overall, the proportion of 15–19 year olds working in nonstandard employment jumped from 20 percent in 1982 to 75 percent in 2007. During that same time span, nonstandard employment among 20–24 year olds nearly quadrupled from 10 percent to 40 percent (Brinton 2011, 28). For male workers in the 15 to 24 year old range, nonstandard employment grew from 8 percent in 1991 to just below 30 percent by 2013. Interestingly, young women's nonstandard employment at 10 percent registered a few percentage points more than men in 1991, but then their rates of nonstandard employment mushroomed to 40 percent, twenty-two years later (Labor Situation in Japan 2014, 53). A special category *"fureta,"* signifying young free lancers, totaled 490,000 men and just over one million women in 1997. The number of male *furetas* doubled to 980,000, while the number of female *furetas* increased to 1.9 million in 2003; these numbers slightly declined for men to 920,000 and a major reduction for women to 950,000 in 2007 (Cook 2013, 30). Further, 2013 data tabulated from the Ministry of Internal Affairs and Communications' special Employment Status Survey found, perhaps unsurprisingly, that educational attainment predicted employment status for 25–29 year old men. Male high school graduates were less likely to secure permanent employment (not changing jobs after leaving school) than university graduates: 39.4 percent compared to 57.0 percent, respectively. Correspondingly, men with only a high school degree exhibited higher continuous nonstandard employment at 12.0 percent and more than double the chance of moving from regular to nonstandard employment (5.2) than male college graduates (Labor Situation in Japan 2014, 54). Taken together, the picture that emerges is one of extensive underemployment and precarity.

The growing number of young men in precarious work challenges the dominant image of Japan represented symbolically by the heteronormative, middle-class, citizen worker in Japanese culture and politics (Dasgupta 2003, 2012). New entrants and workers re-entering the labor market often end up in nonstandard employment, further destabilizing career paths over the life-course. The institutions for skill development acquired on-the-job through the training system over one's working life now create instability for youth in post-industrial Japan. Faced with instability, many are postponing family formation and fertility decisions. The dramatic increase of nonstandard employment is rooted in the design of the institutional architecture supporting pillars of the Japanese employment system, the reproductive bargain, and its mode of state regulation.

New Forms of Precarious Work and Precarity: Creating the Lost Generation?

The state is implicated in the definition, size, composition, and conditions of precarious work and employment through extending protections for some categories of work and not to others, through immigration laws, through strict or lax enforcement of labor laws and ordinances, through the formulation of gender and labor regulations,[2] and through the nature of welfare support for different groups in society (Gottfried and O'Reilly 2002). Precariousness is not simply an outcome of less regulation of nonstandard employment, but also a consequence of differential treatment written into (and out of) the language of Japanese state regulations. By using a specialized vocabulary, key words shaped the gendered and age-graded profiles of precarious work and workers. Somewhat uniquely, the Japanese import loan words to indicate that the concept is of "foreign," usually Western, origin (Hirakawa 1995, 94). A kind of "inverse Orientalism" (ibid.) differentiates these employment forms from the standard equated with Japan and sets them apart from Japan, "distancing itself from the Other that is the West" (Endo 2006, 1). Deploying loan words rhetorically detaches the employment form from the exploitative structures of capitalism in Japan. A review of linguistic shifts in national classification of employment statuses can be read as expressions of "instrumental practices in regimes of power" (Krishnan 2014) through which "a state produces segmentation of the citizen body" (Fourcade 2010, 572).

---

2   See Jun Imai (2010) and Gottfried (2009) for a comprehensive review of relevant labor and gender regulations.

Conceived in the cradle of Fordist production, labor regulations standardize benefits around an implicit, heteronormative male-breadwinner whose work biography of continuous stable employment over the life-course is the basis of apportioned rights and responsibilities. Standard employment is the dominant frame of reference determining the subjects worthy of social protection and legal recognition of citizenship rights and entitlements. In Japan, the specific definition of standard employment refers to "those employed immediately after graduating school or university and have been working for the same enterprise" (Ministry of Health, Labor and Welfare Basic Survey on Wage Structure 2006). This official government definition assumes the institutional mooring of standard employment in the tightly coordinated relationship between education and employment, facilitating the transition from school to a port of entry into a firm-specific internal labor market with the expectation of long-term continuous employment as part of the lifetime employment system, a practice rather than a principle written into contracts. Generous benefits associated with standard employment are rooted in company citizenship. By contrast, the state provides minimal statutory social protections and entitlements, and indexes benefits to the standard employment relationship.

Conventional labor statistics and labor regulations use this historical standard as the master category for framing a hierarchy of employment statuses. Typically, unemployment is defined in relationship to standard employment. Japanese labor statistics count as unemployed those individuals age 15 and over and out of work, "capable of immediately accepting work" and seeking work during the survey period (JILPT 2013, 44). This dichotomy leaves out non-waged work and employment statuses in between these categories. Omitted from this definition of unemployment are the non-employed.[3] Non-employment does not simply demarcate non-work or the absence of employment, but also glosses over non-market exchanges, ranging from unpaid reproductive labor to cooperative exchanges outside the orbit of traditional employment relations. In conventional formulations, only wage labor deserves full recognition of rights, rewards and social protection. Labor statistics, conventions and regulations privilege and naturalize wage labor as the primary means of gaining political recognition and economic security.

The frame of reference for determining part-time employment would seem rather straightforward based on an agreed upon conventional threshold of hours worked below a full-time standard. In the early 1990s, Japanese labor law

---

3   For example, only citizens are counted in official unemployment statistics in Singapore and Dubai. Out of work "foreign" workers are not considered unemployed due to their citizenship status, and thus have little legal recourse in claiming their rights and redress for abuse.

enshrined a legally permissible distinction defining part-time employment relative to full-time hours at an enterprise rather than the usual economy-wide standard number of hours worked. The Part-Time Workers' Law of 1993 defined short-time workers as those working shorter hours than regular workers employed in the same undertaking (Kurokawa 1995, 57). In some statistical series, short-time referred to those who worked less than 35 hours in the week the survey was conducted, including seasonal workers and irregular workers. Part-time (*paato-taimu*) was most commonly defined in negative terms: any position that was not a regular position (*sei-shain*), a position, which involved shorter hours than sei-shain, and one that employers merely designated as such. *Sei-shain*, in turn, referred to an employment relationship of an unspecified duration. But like *paato-taimu*, *sei-shain* was a category left largely to the discretion of a firm's human resource office. As a result, some workers classified as part-time actually work 40-hours per week. The inferior employment status is a function of legal classification rather than a threshold of hours worked.

The state also coined key words for the purpose of establishing differential legal statuses. To avoid the historical reference, temporary-help firms and legislators minted the Japanese word *haken*, translated as dispatch, as a more neutral label to disassociate agency temporary employment from the negative connotations of temporary employment in Japan and to overcome the stigma of unskilled labor associated with agency temporary employment in the US. The memory of exploitation of temporary workers during the 1950s informed the framing of labor regulation on the use of agency temporary workers.[4] This history was a well-known chapter recalled by framers of the Dispatching Law that explicitly prohibited the use of temporary employment in some traditional manufacturing jobs.[5]

The terminology of *haken* represents the specific triangular employment relationship between a labor market intermediary, a client firm and an

---

4 Legal frames circulate through various mechanisms. In some respects China has emulated Japan in their enactment of weak labor regulations, including the use of specialized language of "dispatching" instead of the more common nomenclature of "temporary" to identify the agency temporary employee (Shire 2012).

5 Before the Dispatching Law passed in 1985, temporary employment, particularly agency temporary work, flourished largely unregulated except for a law prohibiting the operation of private placement firms. Employing temporary workers to gain flexibility was widespread throughout the 1930s and 1950s, decades before the economic miracle took off. At the Hiroshima Factory of Nihon Steel Works, three-quarters of the labor force held temporary positions in the 1930s (Hazama 1997, 170). These workers suffered deprivations and coercive treatment on the job. Abuse of temporary workers' rights in the manufacturing sector also was rampant during the 1950s.

employee. As elsewhere, this triangular relationship complicates who the employer is and for whom the work is being performed. Though labor law holds the temporary-help firm responsible for supervising and establishing work conditions of the temporary employee, the reality of the triangular relationship creates legal ambiguity for temporary employees seeking to exercise their rights both at the client companies where they work and vis-à-vis the temporary-help firms that employ them. More specifically in Japan, legal ambiguity is in part the result of labor laws and legal norms based on a standard masculine work biography rooted in the corporate-centered male breadwinner model. The exclusion from a firm's internal labor market deprives *haken* of job security and those benefits conferred by the company bargain.

By coining a wholly new term, *haken* conjures up an image of neutral dispatcher acting as a conduit for matching workers to client firms. The resulting placement seems to flow from an objective process rather than from an inferior contractual relationship. In all, the usage of *haken* suggests a different quality as well as quantity of labor power. Temporary-help firms dispatch *haken* to clients on the basis of embodied capacities and competencies (as discussed in a previous chapter). The legal terminology of *haken* codifies differential rights to and at work, which makes this employment form precarious.

Nonstandard employment, such as *paato* for part-time and *arubaito* for a young part-time worker borrow terms from English and Germany respectively. Both *paato* and *arubaito* index the life course in both popular usage and in labor law. In popular usage, *paato* sometimes combines with *obasan* (middle-aged women), or simply with *san*, an honorific ending that can indicate Mr./Mrs. This rhetorical linkage of *paato* to *no obasan* has come to imply a married, middle-aged woman who makes up the vast majority of part-time workers. In this sense, *paato no obasan* suggests that the worker occupies only a part of the status of a full-time employee but never a substantial part. Implicitly, the middle-aged woman is seen as a secondary earner who relies on a male-breadwinner for income security. On the other side of the age spectrum *arubaito* designates a youth's entrance into the labor market, referring to a transitional phase for young workers who might take up temporary part-time employment during their course of studies. When initially introduced, *arubaito* denoted a transitional phase in a typical male work biography before the student entered the "lifetime" employment system. An *arubaito* status was not expected to last more than a short time and was not supposed to negatively impact long-term employment.

As the economic malaise of the Lost Decade lingered into the 21st century, and as more men as well as women remained unemployed or in nonstandard employment long after their student hiatus, the state promulgated new key words shifting the registers for the interpretation of a range of employment relationships. A proliferation of popular and legal terms chastised youth, as a lost generation, for shirking their work responsibility, and thereby strengthening pejorative connotations associated with nonstandard employment, such as: *fureta*, for young people, age 15–34, who are neither students nor housewives and who job hop (Cook 2013, 29); non-employment, including NEET referring to young people not in education, employment or training; *parasaito shinguru*, for young adults who are likened to parasites living off the financial largess of their parents; and net-café refugees, for the homeless, primarily youth, whose main domicile is the Internet café (O'Day 2012). *Arubaito* morphed into the category of *fureta*, combining the English word free with *arubaito*. This hybridized linguistic form implied that *free-arbeiters* or *furetas* willing eschewed conventional employment, and "freely" chose this nonstandard employment form. Initially, *furetas* projected a positive image of a new entrepreneurial, reflexive, self-directed man; a free-lancer who shows initiative in the new economy. Around the same time, the state began using NEET, borrowing from the British expression for youth not in education, employment or training. The Japanese Ministry of Health, Labour and Welfare, however expanded on that definition to cover all individuals from the ages of 15–34 who were not enrolled in school, not in the labor force (thus, not counted as unemployed since they were not currently looking for work), and not married (Labor Situation in Japan 2014, 54).

Into the new millennium, those in nonstandard employment took on the negative mantle of a lost generation or "lost in transition" (Brinton 2011). Young men were represented as slackers, refusing to become adults and forsaking the career-paths of their fathers, and altogether opting out of the old bargain symbolized by the salaryman. Keywords projected an image of young men socially adrift, unproductive members of society, failing to fulfill their masculine citizenship duty as "rights-earning individuals not as needy family members" (Haney and March 2003, 464). Young women in the same employment categories were portrayed as frivolous girls. These categories used an individual moral/psychological register equating nonstandard employment with selfishness and immaturity.

Negative connotations also were reflected in policies critical of *furetas* portrayed as part-time job-hoppers forestalling marriage and childbirth (JILPT 2013, 36). The Work-Life Charter (2007) was one of many legislative attempts to shore up the declining fertility rate (1.25 at the time) by targeting the reduction in the number of *furetas*. Missing from the representation was the structural circumstances leading to the growth of this labor market segment. *Furetas* who do not or cannot pursue a regular career are at a strong disadvantage in the Japanese labor market where length of service is a proxy for nontransferable skills built while working for the same firm (Boyer 1998, 158).

These keywords classify a variety of labor relations and nonstandard employment arrangements. It is important to analyze national classification schemes because words/discourses do not merely reflect power relations, but are "active forces shaping" material lives (Fraser and Gordon 1994, 310). Keywords gain their currency in reference to institutional norms, rules and regulations. In Japan, labor law and employment regulation still bases labor standards on heteronormativity inscribing the male work biography without interruptions for care responsibility. As a result, workers, both male and female, who deviate from this male-breadwinner standard, suffer penalties in terms of foregone promotions and training, lost earnings, limited pensions, and risk social exclusion and experience dislocation. Through the creation of new employment statuses with inferior work conditions, the state actively produces precarious work and precarity. Such statuses are contested and challenged from below.

Organizing Unemployed Youth

Changing employment conditions and precarity are spurring innovative organizational responses among workers in precarious employment and among the unemployed. Consider the example of the Tokyo Youth Union of Contingent Workers (Tokyo Youth Union).[6] It is the oldest and largest union mobilizing young workers in unstable jobs and the unemployed. Smaller youth unions populate other areas surrounding Tokyo (Chiba, Kanagawa, Saitima) as well as in Sendai, Nigata, Nagoya, Okayama, and Okinawa. Common to these youth unions is that they are loosely and informally affiliated; some are dormant and inactive while others maintain strong ties with the Tokyo Youth Union. Following the example of community unions sprouting up during the Lost Decade, the Tokyo Youth Union formed in 2000. It started with a membership of only 30 individuals, growing to around 350 over the next 10years, fluctuating slightly from year-to-year. Members range in age from their early 20's to their early 30's. Many of the original members remain precariously employed, experiencing a difficult time finding secure employment, and their long-term experience of serial insecure jobs leads them to seek redress (voice) rather than through exit. The majority of its members are single men, living on the

---

6 Conversations with leaders of the Youth Union inform my understanding of organizing among young people in Japan.

outskirts of Tokyo or in older apartment buildings. Increasingly, members share a small apartment; fewer live with their parents (which reflect the older age profile of their youth membership).

Tokyo Youth Union organizes around economic issues and legal violations experienced by young workers. Individual workers contact the union for consultation around labor violations.[7] The union initiates collective bargaining for the individual employee when notified about a violation of the Labor Standards Act (LSA).[8] According to the union the company usually recognizes the standing of the union to negotiate. In those cases when the company denies the claim and refuses to recognize the union as a bargaining partner, the union adopts a range of strategies to bring the company to the bargaining table. For example, they may lodge the complaint at the local labor standard's office (organizationally under the Ministry of Health, Labor and Welfare). Other cases result in lawsuits. For example, a court case brought against a ramen noodle company resulted in a victory. The court ruled that the company had violated labor law and directed the company to make restitution. Finally, symbolic protests raise the issue in the public eye. Most spectacularly, 500 temp workers erected a tent village in Tokyo's Hibiya Park to protest their precarious existence made worse after the collapse of Lehman Brothers in 2008. Tokyo Youth Union mobilized temp workers for this spectacle. In so doing, they drew on local idioms of day laborer's makeshift domiciles glimpsed in other city parks for their symbolic protest. The protest raised public awareness of precarious work and the living conditions among a growing segment of the labor force. Mostly, companies recognize the union and agree to participate in collective bargaining, in part because of their previous successes and visibility. Collective bargaining of this type involves only narrow legal issues, since the union only "represents" a single or a few members – though settlements apply to all affected workers.

The union operates both in civil society and in work spaces. Tokyo Youth Union reaches out around specific campaigns, such as lobbying against deregulation of the dispatch law and working with NGOs in their anti-poverty campaign. As a community-based union, their mission and targets extend beyond workplace-based issues to broader social welfare considerations and the state. The precarious existence of this labor force led the union to form an anti-poverty network.

---

7 A common activity of hotlines set up by activist organizations enable individuals to report on rights violations.

8 Japan's Trade Union Law compels employers to bargain with a union even if the union only represents a single worker in an enterprise; that is, the law recognizes a union's right to organize an individual worker and to bargain on this members' behalf (Takasu 2012, 1).

Despite successes at the bargaining table, they have not been able to convert their successes into new membership. While the organization is "socially recognized," organizing remains difficult among this population. Younger workers don't know their rights, don't know about unions, and don't know that their situation may not be temporary. Generationally, youth only have an experience of economic dislocation and union decline and quiescence – the early 1970s marked the last major strike wave in Japan. Smaller activist unions share a common financial challenge; their small and poor membership cannot adequately fund union activities, including hiring of organizers. Unlike the enterprise-based unions, who can rely on dues from a relatively stable membership, these unions actively seek new members across many firms, occupations, and industries to secure resources. Union activists must survive on minimal support from union dues and engage in union activities after work.

The changing nature of work and social precarity may herald the formation of a new precariat class, based both on the loss of long-term employment commitments at the root of organizational career-paths, and on the disconnection from old forms of social protection and sociality (Standing 2011). While many experience precarity in their lives and in their job prospects, a precariat class implies the formation of a structural position shared in common. Precarious work does not in and of itself constitute a new social relation of production. More likely, precarious employment as effect deprives people the ability to establish a long-term career, a vocation, and a livelihood; and precarity as affect is a corrosive condition eroding the foundations for sustaining an identity. As indicated above, precarity has a potentially empowering effect, as nonstandard workers challenge the way we work and live in a capitalist society. New unions populate the political landscape in Japan; these denizens are pursuing a path towards full economic and political citizenship.

Conclusion: Accounting for and Consequences of Precarity among Youth in Japan

The unraveling of former employment guarantees, including lifetime employment and corporate-based welfare, and the role of the state in shaping employment forms create new risks; risks that emerge as more workers are exposed to economic uncertainties and employment insecurities. One of the so-called pillars of the Japanese economic model, the lifetime employment system, was maintained by large-firms that guaranteed job security to core male workers. But lifetime employment has been almost an exclusively male domain supported by the unacknowledged corporate-centered male breadwinner reproductive bargain. In this institutional context, some Japanese men experience unemployment as a social disgrace and consider it shameful to register at public employment agencies. Japanese women may not report unemployment for different social and economic reasons. With few portals into internal labor markets, Japanese women who either lose or cannot find jobs may stop looking for work when confronted by the difficulty of securing re-employment in times of economic crises. These unemployed, discouraged women disappear into the shadow economy of the household as non-employed, no longer counted in unemployment statistics, and expected to derive rights and income security as dependents on a male breadwinner. Thus, the unemployment rate is likely to understate the actual number of men and women out of work.

This chapter excavated the meanings from a cluster of interrelated keywords and frames of references to standard and nonstandard employment. Much of labor law and employment regulation still derives labor standards based on hetero-normative masculine embodiment of work without interruptions for care responsibility. The analysis focused on the consequences of framing benefits, protections and rights around an outmoded male-breadwinner standard. It finds that workers, both male and female, who deviate from this standard, suffer penalties in terms of foregone promotions and training, lost earnings, limited or no coverage of occupational health and safety, pensions and unemployment insurance and are at risk of social exclusion. New subjects in regulation are associated with loosening constraints, not only creating uncertainty as a general condition resulting in new risks and insecurities for individual workers, but also creating new chances for reforming the self and for reconfiguring working time practices.

Guy Standing (2006) offers one of the most far-reaching perspectives on how to think about the implications of casualization. He moves away from simple dichotomies to argue that the freedom to make choices about one's own work biography determines the "double-sided character" of casualization.[9] Nonstandard employment exemplifies the double-sided effects of the change in the mode of regulation. Those with valued skills in the marketplace and without outside work commitments might experience individualization as freedom, while for others it might become a source of insecurity. In the first instance, portfolio and boundary-less careers are meant to capture the flexibility gained by individuals who have more control over how and where they work (Tremblay 2006). As individuals increasingly must negotiate their own

---

9 A political agenda following from Standing's analysis enumerates seven forms of work-related security, including representation security and income security, are fundamental to achieving a new norm of dignified work.

work conditions, the benefits of such individualized arrangements would most likely accrue to single, highly educated women who can best emulate the masculine embodiment of work, in which responsibility for care is a non-issue.

There are possible far-reaching effects of the rise and persistence of unemployment and nonstandard employment on the lives and livelihoods of young men and women. Fewer workers have access to social protections tied to occupational and employment status that was the basis of securing consensus at the center of the old reproductive bargain. Particularly, with the growing numbers of men in nonstandard employment, we need to consider the consequences to hegemonic masculinity. What impact will growing precariousness have on gender identities, relations, power, and on new social imaginaries? What will be the effect on core gender and sexual identities as more men at various stages of their working lives occupy these "feminized" positions? How will masculinity be reconstructed when men no longer can earn a family wage or fulfill the obligations of the breadwinner role? One small qualitative study found that male *furetas* desired to create alternative lifestyles, but their narratives about the future still were framed in terms of normative ideas of the productive male citizen. In this sample, male high school grads whose fathers worked in blue-collar jobs preferred securing stable employment, while university grads favored freedom from white collar work and looked toward carving out their own lifestyle not dictated by the enterprise (Cook 2013, 40). Another study of economic changes and the rise of insecure employment among large swathes of the workforce in former textile towns documents narratives of young working class adults.[10] Gender differences inform the aspirations of these working class youth. On the one hand, young men want to marry eventually but also recognize that the ideal of the male breadwinner, as a potent force in defining masculinity and maturity, is unattainable. On the other hand, young female furetas orient themselves toward securing stable employment rather than marriage.

As we know, the effects of precarity can lead to despair with tragic results, such as the increasing incidence of suicide among young men. Displaced and disconnected from long-term employment prospects, young men are often unable to cope with the accompanying social-psychological trauma. Deconstructing media coverage of a murderous rampage by a young man in Akihabara, the electronics shopping district and home to Japanese gaming culture, Slater and Galbraith (2011) parse out discursive evidence of cultural and social contradictions associated with the loss of stable employment among young men

---

10   This study refers to the research conducted by Professor Kimiko Kimoto of Hitotsubashi University. She summarized her research findings for me when we spoke on July 31, 2014.

in recessionary Japan. In this spectacular case, this male youth's precarious work status is central to the narrative framing the event. What the case demonstrates is the new cultural significance of precarity as embodying loss; loss not only of stable employment, but loss of social moorings. Unmoored from the corporate-centered salaryman promise of stable employment, this precarious status deprives such young men of the social foundations on which male middle-class respectability had once been based. Ironically, national rhetoric now chastises young men for selfishness and not being selfless contributing members of society, blaming them for structural transformations beyond their control. Young men are held accountable for not taking responsibility as productive male citizens; their precarity is attributed to personal failings, not to institutional failings.

Turning inward is a symptom and a response to uncertain times. Hopelessness and despair are not the only responses to precarity: young men and women in nonstandard employment are organizing into new unions. Youth unions are challenging the conditions of precarity for jobless and unemployed youth. The final chapter considers the future of labor in these uncertain times along with an assessment of future trajectories of Japanese capitalism.

CHAPTER 7

Another Lost Decade? The Future of Japanese Capitalism

> Ma Peep: I promise you I'll change everything. And changing everything means changing nothing. You can change the names, but the things remain the same. The old mystifications haven't stood up to psychological and sociological analysis. The new one will be foolproof and cause nothing but misunderstanding. We'll bring the lie to perfection.
>
> IONESCO 1957, 76

In Ionesco's play *The Killer*, Ma Peep's rabble-rousing exhortation captures the emptiness of much political rhetoric; promises to change everything mean changing nothing. Her Orwellian doublespeak portends, ".... We won't exploit men, we'll make them productive. We'll call compulsory work voluntary..." (Ionesco 1957, 77). New "mystifications...cause nothing but misunderstanding" pays homage to the indeterminacy of our times whose meanings often elude sociological scrutiny. Yet political rhetoric is not empty of meaning. Ma Peep's words echoed in my mind, during a few short months over the summer of 2014, when I observed political actors staging political theatre in Japanese institutions. The timing of *The Killer* performance in Brooklyn coincided, not coincidently, with the existential drama unfolding in the twilight of Japan's imperial ruin.

As envisaged amidst the steamy days of late July 2014, residues of empire reside in the "ongoing quality of processes of decimation, displacement, and reclamation" (Stoler 2013, 8). From the judicial branch, the Japanese Supreme Court announced their ruling denying social welfare benefits to all non-citizens regardless of years in residence. In "foreign" relations, the turn toward nationalism and militarism plays out almost daily. Around the same time, the UN Human Rights Committee expressed "concern at the widespread racist discourse" against minority groups including Koreans (The Japan Times July 25, 2014, 1). Not unrelated, the Abe government was rewriting Japanese colonial history, suggesting that "comfort women" were "professional prostitutes" thereby implying a choice among the women who were coerced into sexual slavery (The Japan Times July 2014). On the "domestic" front, the Abe government rhetorically promotes women's employment as an antidote for averting the looming labor shortage. His political rhetoric, under the eponymous agenda, Abe-nomics, encourages women to emulate men's work biography, without proposing corresponding social policies in support of this agenda. In the absence of work restructuring reorganized around responsibility for care, Abe-nomics' proposal asks women to assume a second shift of waged labor in addition to unpaid care work. The proposal does not address or alleviate outsized financial and labor burdens on families, and instead intensifies women's overall labor activities. One government concession contemplates off-loading care work by issuing a limited number of new temporary visas to female migrant workers, but without regard to their labor rights and denying pathways to citizenship and access to welfare benefits. Migrant women hailing from countries across the region complicate gender and class relations, and problematize "foreign" and "domestic" relations reconstituting the political construct of Asia and Asians from the period of empire.

Troubling signs abound in the political field. At this critical conjuncture, rightwing forces are gaining strength both in the government and in the society at large. Abe's aggressive stance has earned him plummeting approval ratings, down to 40 percent from a high of 80 percent at the time he took office. In response, the LDP may split into a "reform" movement even more rightwing than Abe, and a group remaining loyal to the Abe camp. On the other side, the Communist Party of Japan (CPJ) is small while the Democratic Party of Japan (DPJ) has little political currency left after botching the recovery effort in 2011. Growing antagonisms in the region are another source of concern. Abe is embarking on a reinterpretation of Article 9, popularly known as the "peace" clause in the Japanese Constitution. Sounding a lot like Ma Peep, the justification for the reinterpretation spins a ".... logical tautology that Japan can reinterpret the constitution to allow for a broad-scoped exercise of the right to collective self-defense because it falls within the minimum necessary level of self-defense that is already permissible under Article 9" (Drysdale 2014).

Deconstructing the former narrative of the economic miracle in light of the unraveling reproductive bargain makes sense of the current economic outlook. Japan's economy is fundamentally weak due to 15 years of deflationary pressures burbling ever since the major asset bubble burst. In remarks to the Federal Reserve Bank of Kansas City in August 2014, Haruhiko Kuroda, Governor of the Bank of Japan, summarizes the "vicious cycle" brought on by long-term deflation (Janssen 2014). Japanese firms' inability to raise prices because of sagging demand sought to reduce their debt exposure through net savings rather than through new investments, and through their concomitant efforts to contain labor costs by employing a larger share of lower-waged nonstandard workers and by restraining wage increases among both unionized and non-unionized workers. It is notable that the Bank of Japan acknowledges that changes in Japan's wage-setting institutions contribute to shrinking aggregate demand. During this period, firms pulled out of the spring offensive (*Shunto*), which had been a coordinating mechanism for wage negotiations steadily raising pay packages of male-breadwinners. Kuroda's statement hints at the unraveling of the reproductive bargain in his remarks about the abandonment of the *Shunto*, the extensive employment of nonstandard workers, the decline of real wages, and the underutilization of women in the labor force (Kuroda 2014). Japan's difficult recovery must be put in the context of political alliances, both foreign and domestic. Recall the role of US aid giving succor to the fledgling LDP in the 1950s. The initial shock waves continue to reverberate long after the bubble burst, triggering a prolonged recession and a crisis of reproduction. Prior to the onset of deflation, the institutional pillars of Japanese capitalism already stood on shaky ground.

Fukushima further shook up the island nation, revealing the vulnerabilities that lay dormant in society. Japan is entering its third "Lost Decade." These "lost" decades have taken their toll, leaving nothing untouched in their wake. An unusually hot and muggy summer also leaves the indelible impression of widespread precarity. During a few short weeks in July 2014 alone, Tokyo residents woke up to earthquake alerts on their mobile phone devices, and commuters streamed from the Mitaka Train Station in Northern Tokyo, when without warning, the sky darkened and the thunderstorm pelted the rooftops. Just as suddenly, lightning and thunder rumbled, offices went black, and only a glimmer of dusk illuminated interior spaces. A few minutes later, the lights flickered on – a blackout not experienced in Tokyo for 25 years. The extreme weather events are testing grounds for gauging institutional capacities, priorities and political commitments. Abe's government stands at the precipice of restarting two nuclear reactors at the Sendai power plants, despite continuing public distrust expressed in opinion polls and in the 17,800 comments opposing the Nuclear Regulation Authority's recommendation for action (Fackler 2014).[1] The decision to restart the reactors suggests that old political alliances between the nuclear industry and the LDP trump public opinion and perhaps good science, while precarious workers still wade in toxic pools of irradiated water cleaning the area around the nuclear disaster site.

Recent research supports the findings, reported in this book, of changing circumstances toward precarity of work and life. Over the course of many interviews with labor and feminist activists, I sense the depth of this embodied

---

1   "All of Japan's 48 operable commercial nuclear reactors were shut down after the March 2011 triple meltdown at the Fukushima Daiichi Nuclear Power Station created serious public doubts about the safety of atomic power in earthquake-prone Japan" (Fackler 2014).

condition, and the inexorable feeling of loss.[2] These activists embody the unease of a precarious existence. As the previous chapter detailed, young men now experience insecure work for longer periods of time, many into their late 20's and 30's. Some young men, who manage to secure permanent employment associated with what's left of the lifetime employment model, quit after just one year, dissatisfied with a life controlled by the company. Turning inward is a symptom of and a response to uncertain times. Simultaneously, work transformations normalizing precarious work are creating new bases of identity and solidarity, and are prompting and, even necessitating, that workers develop new organizational strategies for representing the interests of a diverse labor force.

On the horizon, like a spectral Hiroshi Sugimoto photograph of the primordial line where sky meets sea in blurred gradations, the future of labor and other social movements is hard to discern. Activists I interviewed look haggard, though undeterred. A number of nongovernmental organizations and worker associations now populate civil society spaces. These emergent organizations represent a variety of identities, desires and orientations. Defying blistering temperatures in July 2014, Pink Dot, donning pink tee-shirts, celebrates the LGBT community in Okinawa; and Anti-Nuke demonstrations occur routinely on city streets around Japan. Rising citizen's movements fight against restarting nuclear power plants and call for a non-nuclear future. One recent anti-nuclear demonstration attracts 100,000 people gathered in front of the Diet, echoing the protests against the US-Japan security alliance in the late 1950s. However, while public opinion polls indicate a majority favors the no nuke's position; senior citizens compose the majority of protestors, among the few groups with discretionary time for protest in the middle of the day. Where is Japan heading?

This book seeks to decipher the enigma that is Japanese capitalism. Preceding chapters evoke a past redolent of success, now overrun by legions unable to stitch together a living, uncertain of their future. This jarring juxtaposition is not easily reconciled if one parses characterizations of the Japanese employment system that once dominated narratives of the economic miracle. The framework outlined throughout reveals the institutional sources of labor

---

2   Data were gleaned from a long conversation with labor activists whose insights and experience enrich my understanding of the past and future of the Japanese labor movement. I want to thank Hirohiko Takasu, Seichii Yamasaki, Jo Nakajima, Matt Noyes and Emiko Aono for taking the time to meet with me in Global Front's air-conditioned office on a stifling hot summer day in July 2014.

insecurities behind this economic juggernaut. Japan's postwar system was composed by a set of institutions, including a developmentalist state implementing a broad industrial policy, trade unions embedded in corporate structures, stakeholder economic governance, and electoral politics dominated by the Liberal Democratic Party. Within any type (variety) of capitalism, crisis and its resolution emerge out of the specific arrangements which distinguish it. Thus, in Japan, the forms taken by the crisis in 1990 and its current efforts at its resolution in 2014 must be understood in terms of the specific features of this version of capitalism and its reproductive bargain. By referencing the reproductive bargain, the analysis not only makes visible how precarity is built into the system of employment relations and eligibility for welfare, but also identifies sources of current demographic tensions seemingly divorced from structures of gender and class relationships.

The historical terms of the reproductive bargain rests on the establishment of company citizenship in support of a standard employment relationship, privileging the male breadwinner in calculations for benefits in exchange for the salarymen working long hours in relatively secure jobs at the enterprise and relying on women's unpaid reproductive labor in the family and increasingly on women's waged work in nonstandard jobs. In what amounted to the male-breadwinner's right to a "family-wage" relieved the state, capital and traditional unions of taking responsibility for supplying socially necessary reproductive labor. Such institutionalized relationships, formerly the engines of growth and stability, drag economic expansion and employment security under new terms of the reproductive bargain. Crucial to labor's future, Japan's reproductive bargain embed union organization in the enterprise. This organizational model benefits company citizenship as long as the companies have "surplus" to distribute, but then becomes a fetter once the fate of their enterprises change. Traditional unions lose members due to downsizing of permanent workers and are robbed of the capacity to organize the increasing number of workers whose livelihoods are not secured by the bargain. In Ma Peep's words, "the old mystifications haven't stood up to psychological and sociological analysis" because former theories that do not integrate gender into their class analytical models underestimate precarity constitutive of the reproductive bargain. Gendering institutional analysis is a key to decoding the enigma of Japanese capitalism.

To make sense of the enduring economic crisis and to reflect on the future of the Japanese model, the remainder of this chapter analyzes institutional and structural factors giving rise to widespread precarity. The chapter assesses the current state of the labor movement and ends on a more speculative note on the future of the Japanese model.

The State of the Labor Movement: From Challenges and Opportunities to Precarity

The Japanese labor movement faces hardship and hard times. Already in Japan, union membership seems to have reached its nadir; overall union density lingers in the low double digits. Membership in traditional unions has declined precipitously; the estimated organization rate[3] peaked around 46.2 percent in 1950, falling to 32.2 percent in 1960, then growing a few percentage points to 35.4 percent during the sixties decade of mass mobilizations by the new left and strike activity by public sector trade unions[4] (Table 7.1). Japanese union membership slid throughout the 1980's and 2000's period of workforce restructuring that included a "hiring freeze, 'voluntary retirement', and replacement of regular workers with non-regular workers" (Suzuki 2004, 10). The union organization rate waned to 17.9 percent overall by 2012, down from 21.5 percent in 2000 (Japanese Working Life Profile 2013/2014, 70). Unionization rates in 1990 correlate with size of company, varying from a high of 61.0 percent for those in firms with 1,000 or more employees to 24.0 percent for 100–999, and a low of 2.0 percent for those in firms with less than 99 employees (Japanese Working Life Profile 2013/2014, 71). By 2012 the corresponding numbers ranged from 45.8 percent of workers in the largest firms to 13.3 percent among workers in middle-sized firms, and 1.0 percent among those in small firms. As the 2012 figures suggest, large enterprises' downsizing had the impact of reducing union density even further. In addition to shedding full-time workers, employers convert jobs and hire more nonstandard workers, which further put a damper on union density rates.

How do we explain trajectories of the Japanese labor movement throughout the course of the mid-20th and 21st centuries? The spatial logics of class formation parallel the development of capitalism in new economic and political

---

3   The organization rate is calculated by dividing the number of union members by the number of employees (Table. 55, Japanese Working Life Profile 2013/14, p.70).

4   "In the late-1940s..., the JCP affiliated 'Sanbetsu Kaigi' (Congress of Industrial Unions of Japan) was the main national confederation but was nearly annihilated by the Red Purge and mass dismissals of 1949 and 1950. Unions critical to the JCP domination formed Sohyo in 1950 with aid from the US occupation. The leadership of Sohyo was in the hands of non-JCP left (the leftwing of the PSJ) and it became the mainstream of the Japanese labour movement. After the 1960s, large enterprise-based unions adopted labour-management cooperative lines and opted to switch their affiliation from Sohyo to the rightwing confederation Domei (Japanese Confederation of Labour). Thereafter, Sohyo remained as a national confederation centred in the public sector. The unification of labour by large enterprise-based unions brought about the dissolution of Sohyo in 1989" (Takasu 2012, 16).

TABLE. 7.1 *Union membership rate, 1950–2012*

Year	1950	1960	1970	1980	1990	2000	2010	2012
Union members (1,000)[5]	5,774	7,662	11,605	12,369	12,265	11,539	10,054	9,892
Estimated Union Organization rate[6]	46.2	32.2	35.4	30.8	25.2	21.5	18.5	17.9
Estimated union organization rate in private industry by size of firm[7]								
1,000 or more					61.0	54.2	46.6	45.8
100–999					24.0	18.8	14.2	13.3
99 or less					2.0	1.4	1.1	1.0
Part-time worker[8] union membership[9]							5.6	6.3
(Percentage of total union membership)							(7.3)	(8.5)

5   Source: Table 55, Trends in Numbers of Unions, Members and Organization Rate (Unit Unions) (Japanese Working Life Profile, 2013/14, p. 70).

6   Rate is calculated by dividing the number of union members by the number of employees (fn. 2, Table 55, Japanese Working Life Profile, 2013/14, p. 70).

7   Source: Table 56, 'Trends in Number of Labor Unions of Private Enterprise by Size of Establishment (Unit Unions) (Japanese Working Life Profile, 2013/14, p. 71).

8   Part-time workers are defined as those workers who work fewer scheduled hours in one-day than general workers at the business establishment, or even if the daily hours worked ar the same, who work fewer scheduled days in a week, and are referred to at the business establishment as part-timers (Japanese Working Life Profile, 2013/14, fn. 1, p.73).

9   The 'estimated organization rate' is based on dividing the number of part-time worker members in labor unions by the number of short-time workers (fn. 2). Source: Table 58, Trends in Part-Time Worker Membership in Labor Unions (Japanese Working Life Profile, 2013/14, p. 73).

geographies. A dialectics of neo-liberal globalization produces new spaces and places for working class formation at different scales. In *Forces of Labor*, Beverly Silver (2003) shows that over the *longue durée*, capital relocates production in search of cheaper and more docile labor (through 'spatial fixes') and transforms organizational and technological processes of production (through 'technological fixes'), both 'making' and emboldening new working classes with "new types of demands, bargaining power and forms of struggle," and at the same time 'unmaking' and weakening the established working classes" (Silver and Zhang 2009, 178). Gender sneaks into the analysis in an ad hoc way, yet her argument about Japan takes into account the ways in which women and part-time work helped to forestall and contain labor unrest apparent in other capitalist countries and among automobile workers in particular. "Cooperative workers" extended to the whole family, as wives and daughters would be held responsible for risking the "lifetime employment security" of the family's (male) breadwinner. When the rural reserves ran out, companies relocated production through subcontracting of the lower tiers to low wage countries in Asia (Silver 2003, 71). To the extent that labor-market dualism has taken on a new spatial form, with the lower and higher rungs of the multi-layered subcontracting system in separate countries, the likelihood that the lower strata will remain quiescent decreases. Under these conditions, the patriarchal family can no longer function as a prop of the system. And once dualism is no longer a "family matter," its other markers – gender, nationality, citizenship, ethnicity – are likely to come to the forefront as mobilizing (rather than demobilizing) facets of labor unrest (Silver 2003, 72). Such global dynamics are only part of the story. Silver's analysis underestimates the national institutional features that contribute to gendering labor market dualism, and that create possible avenues for new labor organizing.

As indicated in the first chapter, the Japanese model of coordinated capitalism developed in the political ferment of the 1950s. Current union organization and class formation reflect these organizational legacies as well as pressures resulting from new structural challenges. By 1960 trade unions had negotiated a reproductive bargain at the enterprise, targeting benefits on the basis of company citizenship for a male-breadwinner, thereby undermining the capacity of labor to mobilize workers across the economy and to protect non-unionized workers. Rooting the reproductive bargain at the enterprise deprived labor of a political lever at the national level from which to advocate for generalized workers' rights and protections. What had been a strength as long as the economy was expanding in the 1960s and 1970s turned into a weakness for workers and their unions whose fate was tied to particular firms, when the Japanese economy entered the lost decade of the 1990s.

Institutional and structural features of Japanese capitalism and the male-breadwinner reproductive bargain help explain the steady decline of union density and the emergence of new union forms. Japanese employers' increasing use of nonstandard workers in all sectors of the economy and in the burgeoning service sector diversifies employment relations and the composition of the labor force. The transformation to a more service-oriented economy, the increasing globalization of labor and capital, the decentralization of work/working, the unraveling of the reproductive bargain, and the casualization of labor, are altering terrains of production/reproduction, restructuring class and gender relations, undermining traditional bases for class formation, and creating the possibility of new bases of identity and solidarity. In the face of these changes, unions no longer can organize around a singular identity, a singular set of conditions, and a singular working class subject derived from a masculine embodiment of the male-breadwinner. New ways of working and new contractual employment relations prompt workers to develop new organizational strategies for representing diverse interests and operate in civil society spaces rather than exclusively or primarily at the worksite. Intersecting fault-lines of gender and citizenship further complicate class formation.

The decrepit state of the labor movement in part is attributed to institutional legacies. The coordinated intermediation between labor and employers in large Japanese corporations resulted in the negotiation of a reproductive bargain tying benefits to employment status at the enterprise level, and generating strict employment regulations over unfair dismissal that protected male workers. Corporate-centered welfare and industrial regulation left a patchwork of residual policies over work conditions at the national level (see Table 7.2). Japanese unions' commitment to protecting the company citizenship of their mostly male membership limited benefits to insiders under the umbrella of collective bargaining at the enterprise. Japan's employment relations system of enterprise-level bargaining with its strong institutional embeddedness "either have weak commitment to organizing activities or prefer organizing strategies based on a partnership model [with management]" (Suzuki 2004, 22). These organizational priorities and practices centering on core male workers undermined the traditional labor movement's capacity to counteract declining union membership when the economy slowed down in the 1980s, and later hit the skids during the recessionary 1990s.

From the 1990s through 2013, much of the growth of employment has been concentrated in part-time and temporary jobs, those areas least touched by enterprise unions (Gottfried 2009a). High levels of part-time employment among women further dampened their overall and relative share of union

TABLE 7.2   *Institutional framework for the study of employment relations*

Production regime	Group-coordinated	
Reproductive Bargain	Family-centric	
	Semi-public	
Male-Breadwinner	Strong	
	Male-breadwinner	
Unfair Dismissal		
Standard	Strong	
Nonstandard	Weak	
Employment Relations		
Extent of Interaction	Decentralized	
Wage setting	Enterprise/Shunto	
Intensity of interaction	Low/Weak	
Institutional embeddedness	Micro-Corporatism/Strong	
Union density	Low	
	2000	2012[10]
Total	20.7	17.9
Male	23.2	
Female	12.4	
Part-time	2.7	6.3
Female % of membership	17.0	

membership in Japan. Yet few traditional unions have successfully extended union membership to part-time and temporary workers – the union membership among part-time workers grew modestly from 2.7 percent in 2001 to 6.3 percent in 2012. Increasing numbers of workers in nonstandard employment depresses union membership. Workers employed in unstable jobs lack the organizational capacity to form unions centered at the workplace. Japanese unions organized at the enterprise are ill-equipped to respond when confronted by a changing political and economic landscape. What lies ahead for labor in Japan? Conversations with labor activists reveal a labor movement at the crossroads.

---

10   Japanese Working Life Profile 2013/14, overall organization rate on page 55 and the organization rate of part-time workers on page 58.

Organizational Transformations and New Forms of Labor Activism

A scan of labor organizing, from the late 1980s to the present, reveals not only new groups being represented, but also indicates the presence of new community unions coalescing in diverse places, spaces, and at different scales, each operating alongside traditional unions.[11] These newer community unions represent workers in smaller enterprises along with unemployed and nonstandard workers, including the Precariat, a community union representing workers in nonstandard employment; the Women's Union Tokyo (WUT), a community union targeting women workers across occupation and industry located in Tokyo; and the Tokyo Youth Union of Contingent Workers (Tokyo Youth Union).

Though relatively new, dating to the 1980s, region-based amalgamated unions already existed in the mid-1950s. Sohyo (General Council of Trade Unions of Japan), a leftist national confederation, founded the first community union, National Union of General Workers (NUGW). Membership in NUGW peaked at more than 130,000 workers in the 1970s, losing ground after the formation of Rengo in 1989 (Takasu 2012).[12] Regional labor councils also nurtured fertile ground for the birth of community unions. One such effort led to community unions joining together to form the Community Union National Network which started with 31 affiliated unions in 1987, added another 33 unions by 1993, and incorporated 72 unions in 30 prefectures, totaling approximately 15,000 members by 2010 (Takasu 2010, 5). Overall, membership in community unions is estimated to account for one percent of the total 10 million union members (Takasu 2010, 13).

Other community unions originate from citizen's and feminist movements (such as the WUT). Many community unions assemble at a city-wide scale, with Tokyo as one main hub of labor organizing activity. Tokyo occupies a privileged place for the growth and cultivation of these unions where it has served as a center of political activism among dense, overlapping networks of activists from social movements in the 1960s-1970s and, more currently, as a nexus of political institutions including the relatively new labor federations.

---

11   My ideas about new unions draw inspiration from interviews conducted over a 14-year time span, including conversations with Tokyo Youth Union representatives on July 12, 2014.

12   For an excellent history of the formation of region-based amalgamated unions, see Takasu (2012), whose analysis is informed by his own personal observations as a labor organizer and as a former general secretary of the National Union of General Workers Tokyo South.

To stem hemorrhaging of union membership, the decade of the 1980s ended with enterprise unions coalescing around three new labor federations, each closely aligned to a political party or political orientation. Most enterprise-based industrial unions unified under the umbrella of the Japanese Trade Union Federation (RENGO). Those trade unions friendly toward the Communist Party of Japan (CPJ) inaugurated a smaller federation, Zenroren, National Confederation of Trade Unions, as a gesture to oppose the dissolution of the more radical Sohyo and the formation of the conservative-leaning Rengo. At the outset, Zenroren counted 1.34 million members (down to 1.2 million in 2009); two-thirds of the affiliated unions had roots in the public sector, and the remainder came out of the industrial sector, primarily representing workers in small-to-medium-sized enterprises (Takasu 2010, 9). Also gestating in 1989, an even smaller labor federation Zenrokyo was established by leftist public sector unions (primarily the National Railway Workers' Union and employees in the Tokyo Metropolitan Government) without ties to CPJ. Even more than the other two federations, Zenrokyo suffered dramatic membership decline, starting with 290,000 before losing more than half its membership (140,000) ten years later (Takasu 2010, 10). Falling membership was a direct result of privatization and resultant downsizing of the workforce.

Japanese union's reform efforts largely have been premised on the idea of creating a new, more democratic structure that serves the needs of marginalized workers. In Japan, dominant unions have generally excluded women, immigrants, and temporary workers from union ranks or have been ineffective in addressing their concerns. A new grassroots reform movement has emerged to overcome these institutional inadequacies and to address longstanding inequities including sexual harassment, pay inequality, and involuntary temporary and part-time employment status as well as new issues that have arisen with Japan's recent economic decline such as layoffs and forced retirement. These new forms of worker organizations include women's unions, community unions, a part-time workers' union, and even a managers' union. These fledgling worker associations have developed outside and against the dominant enterprise union/labor federation model and take as their founding gesture the creation of new democratic structures and egalitarian processes through which marginalized voices can be heard. In response to established labor's perceived inefficacy, worker-based reform movements embraced peer-to-peer networks in building grassroots movements. Peer-to-peer networks are flat (non-hierarchical) and democratic, structured along person-to-person ties across organizations, and based on demographic and geographic rather than enterprise affinity. Such networks have several advantages that facilitate these reform movements' goals. These types of networks aggregate micro-political processes and develop strategies beyond a single organizational logic (in this case, work organizations) relying on and mobilizing information and communication horizontally. Networks tend to support flexibility and efficiency as they make possible the pooling and sharing of resources over time. Basic symbolic and material resources include information, services, time, and money. As an organizational form, a network fosters cooperation for sharing information and for promoting individual and collective interests.

One of the more interesting new organizations is the Women's Union Tokyo (WUT). The WUT plays the dual role of advocating for women's rights as well as for workers' rights. Informed by a democratic impulse, the WUT attempts to maintain an anti-bureaucratic, anti-authoritarian structure; it relies on members' active participation and empowerment. The WUT was founded in 1995 to help women workers otherwise excluded from traditional union membership address issues enterprise unions have typically ignored, such as wage inequality, sexual harassment, gender-based underemployment, and forced retirements. It brings together women from a variety of companies and occupations rather than workers from a single company, industry, or occupation. A census by the union in 2005 counts clerical workers among the largest occupational group (59 percent), but it also includes professionals (22 percent), service workers and store clerks (12 percent) and blue-collar workers (3 percent). Individuals generally approach the WUT for assistance with an on-the-job problem, sometimes gender related, that their company union has not adequately resolved or in cases where union representation is not available. A review of 2,309 grievances handled over a three-year period reveals that the principal issues were layoffs or attempted layoffs (39 percent), sexual harassment (11 percent) and personal disputes (15 percent).[13]

Like the Tokyo Youth Union discussed in Chapter 6, the WUT reached a peak of membership around 250 in 2008, and later waned in the face of internal tensions and insecure work among leaders and members. Many activists worked long hours and suffered from burn-out. A year earlier, WUT leaders used their extensive networks with other similar associations to found Action Center for Working Women (ACW2) in Tokyo, which was launched in a crowded room of 200 women who had arrived via boarded trains from many parts of Japan. ACW2 facilitates networking among small working women's organizations

---

13   Much of this section derives from a project coordinated together with Anne Zacharia-Walsh.

located in other major cities, and looks to Asia for organizing models and strategies. There is an informal transfer of knowledge between groups. Inter-organizational ideas circulate cross borders. ACW2 employs a labor activist in her 40s from Osaka. She brings her local organizing expertise to the ACW2.[14] History suggests, however, that such organizational innovations often become engulfed in the existing institutional framework. To succeed, the WUT and other emerging network organizations will have to overcome resistance from existing institutions and traditions, the inertia of the status quo, and compelling contemporary cries for personal sacrifice for the good of the country.

The current crisis may generate an impulse toward inter-organizational cooperation among community unions. But the future of Japanese labor is in flux. Overlapping networks connect many activists personally and organizationally. The individual nodes of the network are important in maintaining linkages and interconnections. All of these smaller activist unions share a common financial challenge in that their small and poor membership cannot adequately fund union activities, including hiring organizers. In contrast to enterprise-based unions, which can rely on dues from a relatively stable membership, these unions must actively seek new members across many firms, occupations, and industries. Union activists must survive on minimal support from union dues and engage in union activities after work.

Troubling labor is the fragmentation of the movement and the lack of a vision for building a new union movement. Overlapping networks of labor activists ensure communicative exchanges. But strategies and ideological differences divide these small groups. Union activists express ambivalence about their relationship with Rengo, and less so with Zenroren. Like its counterpart in the US, red purges and long simmering political antagonisms drive a wedge between conservative enterprise unions and their leftist-oriented counterparts, but also unions affiliated with the Japan Socialist Party and the Japan Communist Party. Differing visions and structures hamper inter-organizational cooperation that could build social movement unionism.

The left also confronts a generational problem not easily resolved. An older generation of leftwing labor activists is retiring, leaving a leadership vacuum in traditional unions and some of the newer community unions. This is the 1960's generation that came of age during the Vietnam War. Memories of large-scale protests and labor militancy spirited leftwing students to join trade unions and the Communist Party as vehicles for working

14   I am indebted to Midori Ito, Makiko Matsumoto, Kazuko Tanaka, and Naoko Takayama. My analysis of recent events is informed by their recollections and activism.

class struggle. As the 1960s generation of leftists retires, Rengo loses a vocal minority trying to reform the organization from the inside. Outside of Rengo, in the newer unions, the retirement of leftist activists deprives organizations of leadership and social movement experience. In contrast, enterprise unions have a natural succession of leadership based on the union structure. For example, the current president of Rengo comes from the enterprise union at Panasonic. Here again, the history of enterprise unions haunts the possibility for social unionism. Enterprise-based unions need not actively recruit new members who join by virtue of their lifetime job status. Their relatively stable membership ensures a flow of fees and a conduit for new leaders who rise through the ranks. Its organizational form also is a source of weakness. The membership base for the enterprise unions has dwindled as a result of the decline of the manufacturing sector in Japan, partly because of global competition and partly because of Japanese parent firms transplanting factories to low-wage areas elsewhere in Asia. Fewer workers, especially youth unable to secure permanent employment, are in a position to reap benefits from the old reproductive bargain. Attracting new members and transferring leadership to a younger cohort is one of the challenges the progressive labor movement faces today.

The generational argument poses a broader claim about the socio-political milieu informing the political orientations of younger generations of union leaders and potential members (Takasu 2012). Younger leaders neither experience firsthand nor can they tap into the memories of intense working class struggles. Strike activity peaking in the early 1970s, is almost non-existent, along with the disappearance of other demonstrations of labor militancy. Since the mid-1970s labor disputes of all types have declined, and typically take the form of consultation with management away from the public eye. The number of recorded labor disputes more than doubled from 1960 (2,222) to 1970 (4,511), then precipitously declined to 596 by 2012 (Japanese Working Life Profile 2013/14, 75). While disputes over wages saw the sharpest decrease, "objection to discharge or issues of reinstatement" was the only type of dispute steadily on the rise (ibid.), indicative of eroding employment relationships. Narrowing of perspectives also occurs because union members in younger cohorts are often only aware of their own company union. A younger generation of trade unionists is not exposed to alternative points of view because of the waning presence of leftists in their unions. Currently, Zensen the Japanese Federation of Textile, Chemical, Food, Commercial, Service and General Workers' Union, the biggest union, leans toward the right. Even among the more radical unions in the public sector, representing teachers and the Japanese version of AFSCME, a new generation of leaders is too young to know the history of their own unions, particularly strikes in the early 1970s, which produced many of the benefits they currently enjoy.

Progressive labor has not articulated a vision for a "new union" movement in response to changing work relations, the transformation of production, and the unraveling of the reproductive bargain. Left-leaning labor activists are split on the way forward. Some argue for transforming the traditional labor movement. In this scenario, the aim is to restore stable employment and strengthen working conditions for the overall workforce. Others seek a paradigm shift. For them, traditional labor unions are unreliable allies and will not easily reform. More critically, revitalization of the labor movement will require rethinking union organization. In general, labor lacks mechanisms for a comprehensive education of workers and the public on the role of unions in answering big societal issues. "Labor education" is a lost tradition in the labor movement. The informal transmission of labor history is attenuated with the retirement of radicals from union ranks. Formal labor education is not systematically taught within unions. Likewise, university-based labor education is relatively new. One exception is the Hosei Ohara Institute, which has functioned as an archival repository and as a generator of labor history through publications and sponsorship of lectures. The lack of a coherent vision and insufficient mechanisms for the transmission of education to revitalize the labor movement, however, is not simply a matter of arriving at an ideological and political consensus.

The rising numbers of workers in precarious employment both contributes to the decline of the traditional union movement and prompts the building of new labor associations. Those in precarious employment do not necessarily share a coherent interest from which to forge a singular class subject. A so-called precariat does not constitute a class relation in the Marxian sense. For some, precarious work is a transitional position, short-lived and episodic; their possession of symbolic capital (formal qualifications and skills) places them in a contradictory class location. For many in the working class precarity represents an almost inescapable lived reality derived from the restructuring of labor market institutions. Further, the conditions of precarity depend on the nature of the reproductive bargain; that is, the organization of tangible benefits and responsibilities provided by the state for families and for citizens. Thus, precarious employment status is not a sufficient basis for forging a coherent class project. It is also the case that precarious workers' disparate work conditions militate against labor organizing. These workers are spatially disconnected from each other across work sites scattered around the city; their temporally uncertain work schedules – working on-call or as-needed – diminishes reliable channels of communicative action;

and their contractually unpredictable employment prevents them from building up social capital. For this reason, organizing precarious workers cannot follow organizing scripts of the past centered on a stable collectivity at the enterprise. Growth of nonstandard employment undoubtedly has had a negative effect on union membership.

New worker associations, such as networks, organize around multiple, sometimes, conflicting identities and positions. Networks encounter problems related to the very conditions that bring them into existence; they must expend resources toward maintaining and recruiting members who only share an employment status. Further, new borders of class, gender, and nationality are complicating class solidarities and politics. Class politics often remain silent on gender issues. Explicit gender issues regarding responsibility for care and gendered power relations have not been at the center of traditional and many of the new unions. Fragmentation stems from the structures of gender and class relations embedded in the institutions of Japanese capitalism and its reproductive bargain.

Decline of union density in Japan certainly corresponds to conventionally identified causes such as downsizing, deregulations, and privatization. Surely, Silver's (2003) elegant theory correctly documents waves of working class protest ebbing and flowing in accord with the dynamics of global capitalism. However, in mining a new lode of historical data on labor unrest worldwide along with the primary focus on major industries around the world, results in a misreading by Silver as to how gender relates to capitalist dynamics in Japan. It is not so much that dualism is no longer a "family matter," but how family matters. The statement that the patriarchal family no longer forestalls crisis tendencies applies because the reproductive bargain unravels and unsettles certainties. Terms of the reproductive bargain produce specific tensions, which become visible during crisis. Japan's prolonged crisis opens a window for seeing how these tensions unfold, and specifically how unions fare.

From this analysis of the unraveling of the Japanese reproductive bargain, we can observe up close what went wrong along the way. The former reproductive bargain left much of the labor force without social protections, which in turn encouraged firms to renege on the old promise of secure employment. Now enterprises of all sizes and in all industries hire more workers in precarious employment. Before turning to its implications, the next section puts in sharp relief the institutional and legal developments related to the strong male-breadwinner model that contributes to social precarity.

Unraveling of the Reproductive Bargain in Japan

Japan anchors social protection in large corporate structures in support of a strong male breadwinner. In this model, "paid work and family (reproduction/ fertility) are difficult to reconcile given the lack of market-based or publically provided services to replace women's familial care work and the inflexibility of paid work for care givers. The labor market has been focused on "insiders" with little state encouragement to develop services" (Orloff 2008). More specifically, in Japan's corporate-centered male-breadwinner reproductive bargain, firm-specific skill development and corporate-based benefits reward long-term standard employment relationships, under-developing statutory entitlements and the social infrastructure of care services, while training and wage-setting institutions leave nonstandard employment to flourish unprotected yet not unregulated.

A variety of regulations mediate employment relations affecting contractual adjustments; these are implicit and explicit rights and obligations that are both class- and gender-based. In general, labor regulations constrain an unfettered capitalist marketplace by imposing rules on "the exercise of discretion by those with market or institutional power" (Dyson 1992, 1), which can significantly modify both employer and union behavior (Pierson 2001, 5). Yet employers' prerogatives render some subjects out-of-bounds from regulation. Fordist labor regulations standardized benefits around an implicit male work biography of continuous employment over the life-course without regard for care responsibility. Labor regulations fashioned a prototypical male company citizen as the implicit norm for, and the basis of, explicit rights to employment protections and entitlements while at the same time disregarding care responsibility. As such, labor regulations have embodied and reinforced the tacit bargain over the gender division of working time by treating nonstandard employment as an inferior employment status.

Labor regulation designed around the standard employment relationship creates a legal limbo for many nonstandard employees. On the temporal dimension, time thresholds imposed as a basis of qualification for benefits exclude, by definition, nonstandard employment from regulation or subject them to different and often inferior protection. For example, fair labor standards' regulation basing eligibility against a historically negotiated standard work schedule withholds overtime pay from many nonstandard workers when calculating their overall working time. Contractually, new multi-employer arrangements, such as triangular relationship with a labor-market intermediary between an employee and client firm, and 'dependent self-employment' or 'pseudo-self-employment' such as an 'employee-like' worker with 'regular' employment for a single employer, represent new forms of employment relationships that blur the distinction between employee and employer and exceed the standard legal definition of 'who is an "employee" ...and who is the employer' (Dickens 2004, 605). Spatially, company citizenship privileges a small segment of the labor force in standard employment. Labor regulations based on the standard employment relationship thus fail to clearly articulate or parcel out responsibilities for protecting workers in nonstandard employment relationships. Much of labor law and employment regulation still derives labor standards based on a male work biography without interruptions for care responsibility. Those workers, both male and female, who deviate from this standard, suffer penalties in terms of foregone promotions and training, lost earnings, limited pensions, and at risk of social exclusion.

Japan is an example of state-led restructuring of labor and gender regulations that modified the reproductive bargain, contributing to the skewed gender distribution and the rapid growth and diversification of precarious work. The legacy of the large corporate-centered male breadwinner model continues to inform and frame the subjects of regulation, although the state pragmatically re-regulates and selectively deregulates in response to economic, demographic and social pressures. Importantly, many Japanese labor laws fail to extend the principle of equal treatment to nonstandard employees. This failure stems from the assumption that nonstandard employees are marginal workers dependent on a male breadwinner for income security and welfare through work. Japan's *welfare through work* narrows coverage of employment-based benefits to the core male workforce and excludes those in nonstandard work from the corporatist bargain. In the absence of a pool of cheap migrant labor, due to strict immigration laws, Japan has sought to activate maternal employment, especially in nonstandard work, by including a modicum of childcare in its regulatory reforms and through tax policies.

Japan suffers from more than a short-term economic malaise. Precarious work has been, and is becoming a more prominent feature of Japanese capitalism. The degree of adherence to a male-breadwinner principle of household organization in welfare policies, tax policies, equal employment policies (regulation of sexuality and gender relations), and labor regulations has a cumulative impact on the quality and quantity of employment forms/contracts (Osawa 2007), with implications for the extent of precarious work and its gender composition. A strong male-breadwinner employment model treats women principally as mothers and as wives, which privileges the male work biography in standard employment and creates incentives for married women and mothers to work in nonstandard employment or to drop out of the labor force altogether. In this way, the legacy of the strong male-breadwinner reproductive bargain skews insecure nonstandard employment among women, particularly for mothers.

Overall, a rising tide of nonstandard employment spread part-time work to more than one-fifth of the labor market by 2010. However, women's share of part-time employment declined as more young men experience difficulty in acquiring stable employment because the institutions formerly facilitating the transition from education to work have broken down and the internal labor markets have weakened (see Table 7.3). Youth, who the state assumes are dependent on their parents and thus chastised for being parasitic, are over-represented among the precariously employed and unemployed.

Labor market intermediaries take up some of the slack, as discussed in Chapter 4. Though agency temporary employment composes a small share of total nonstandard employment, the intervention of labor market intermediaries contributes to the restructuring of employment relations. In Japan, the temporary help industry developed in concert with the male-breadwinner model. Specific regulations, and later deregulations, facilitated the growth and the occupational, industrial and gender distribution of this employment form. Temporary help firms not only respond to the political-economic context by drawing on a marginal workforce, but also shape temp(t)ing bodies for temp-ing work. As the institutions supporting the male-breadwinner reproductive bargain have eroded, new socio-demographics of agency temporary employment have emerged. Nonetheless, the agency temporary labor force is segregated whereby firms (and their clients) channel men into specialist jobs and women into clerical work.

The boundaries of the old reproductive bargain are shifting. This requires shifting perspectives on how to understand varieties of gender and class relations and their consequences. Shifting boundaries, as discussed in the next section, refer to the renegotiation of the reproductive bargain. Retreat from the former bargain means reorganization not only in production but also in the recalibration of the relationship between production and reproduction.

Shifting Boundaries, Shifting Perspectives

The reproductive bargain that was part of the old postwar social contract developed forms of security and governance "based on hierarchical authority, centralized-bureaucratic administration and formalistic democracy" (Shire 2012, 1). Earlier ways of mitigating risk principally relied on social provisioning by either the state or the family. Both welfare state provision and women's unpaid reproductive labor in the family had buffered old sources of insecurity,

TABLE 7.3   *Employment status by gender, 1995, 2005, 2010*

Gender earnings dispersion	
1995	63
2005	69
2010[15]	63
Part-time total	
1995	16.3
2005	18.3
2010[16]	20.6
Male/female	
1995	7.4/29.1
2005	8.8/31.7
2010	10.3/34.8
Female share of part-time	
1995	73.1
2005	71.8
2010	71.0
Temp total	
1995	12.5
2005	14.0
2010	13.7
(women's share)[17]	(64.0)
Temp agency	
1995	0.8
2005	1.6
% Low wage work overall	
2001	15.7
2005	16.1
2010[18]	14.4
Male	5.9
Female	37.2

15   OECD Employment Outlook 2013, Table O, gender wage gap unadjusted and calculated as dif-
      ference between median earnings of men and women relative to earnings of men. Data for 2011.

16   OECD Employment Outlook, 2003, Table H, part-time defined as less than 30 hours/wk.

17   OECD Employment Outlook, 2013, Table 1. Incidence and composition of temporary
      employment.

18   OECD Employment Outlook, 2013, Table N on low-wage work.

forestalling crisis and stabilizing capitalist social relations. The conditions underwriting the former reproductive bargain are no longer sustainable.

Reproductive bargains are being renegotiated in the face of fiscal crises and the neo-liberal assault on social provisioning with calls for smaller government. Under the banner of neo-liberal rhetoric, debt-strapped national governments justify retreating from the provision of social reproduction. Neo-liberalism pushes states to relinquish responsibility for social reproduction by privatizing risks. Less responsibility for care and social reproduction by the state fuels the growth of more personal services provided either by the market or defaults to the responsibility of family members. On the one hand, the market enlarges vis-à-vis the state, recalibrating the ratio of paid employment and unpaid reproductive labor (Sauer and Woehl 2011, 113–114). On the other, women and households bear "increasing shares of the cost of reproduction of labor" (Pearson 2007). Elson argues that the "reduction of household income and withdrawal or reduction in state-provided services" intensifies the amount of labor women must dedicate to the daily and generational reproduction needs to sustain their households (cited in Pearson 673). As a result, needs are being met by some combination of the market and by paid and unpaid reproductive labor in and for private households.

Through market-based personal services, more paid work takes place in households and extends the working day, both in time and space. The household differs from other workplaces, filtering relationships through the template of the "private" sphere of the family. It is not so much that family life once stood as a bulwark against the heartless world of capitalism, but rather that now most aspects of social life are subject to the logic of profit maximization. The household is both one of the newest and oldest spaces and places for the performance of precarious work. Yet we still know very little about the factors that influence household's decisions either to outsource labor by using low-wage workers (migrants from poorer regions internally or internationally), or to in-source labor by using unpaid reproductive labor. The substitution of paid personal services relieves some women of responsibility from unpaid household tasks by transferring the burden onto other women who perform such feminized (also racialized) labor for low-wages often in insecure employment relationships. With reprivatization of reproductive labor, households with top earners gain a new "employer-function"; integration of women in top positions occur on the basis of broadening of informal feminized working conditions in the home economy (Sauer and Woehl 2011). One of the most dynamic aspects of the new economy in some ways is the least novel. Housework increasingly is privatized and externalized either by locating this waged work outside the household or by bringing other women into the home to perform these tasks usually for low wages.

Even more so today, reproductive labor occurs under different types of employment relations; often exempt from or differentially included in formal employment relations systems and labor regulations. This type of work is place-bound, performed by low-wage and marginalized workers such as women of color and migrants in insecure employment relations, and occurs mostly through face-to-face interaction at the local level. To keep wages low, many women in domestic service occupations are drawn from migrant labor pools. As temporary workers, they do not qualify for a range of benefits. These workers are largely invisible labor confined in the household. Precarious work now inhabits the most intimate relationships around care intra- and inter-households.

The framework outlined in this book genders institutional analysis. It offers a way to theorize varieties of gender relations in terms of the changing relationship between production and reproduction. More specifically, I argue that in the male breadwinner model the division between production and social reproduction relies more heavily on family-centric reproductive labor. "The family was modeled and fed Japan's emerging enterprise-society – work relations that were family-like and allowed men to work long hours" (Allison 2013, 25). Standard employment of the salaryman provided the material basis of and cultural conditions for hegemonic masculinity of the corporate-centered male-breadwinner. A modified reproductive bargain still assumes that women will and can continue to provide informal care in the household while they expand their labor market commitment. However, these two imperatives come into conflict. Women's labor is neither "infinitely flexible" (McDowell et al. 2005, 458) nor is its supply inexhaustible (Elson 2002). An inherent tension exists between the male-breadwinner reproductive bargain and the logic of global capitalism. The capitalist logic of production pushes toward commodification of labor, yet the legacies of the male breadwinner reproductive bargain constrain women's options. Japan faces a deep crisis of reproduction not simply due to fertility decline, the aging population and limited in- and out-migration, but because these demographic trends signal a political economy teetering from dysfunctional institutions.

The unraveling of the reproductive bargain simultaneously stunts union density and creates new conditions for organizing activity. Traditional union's reliance on the largess of the enterprise is not a tenable strategy for the future. Benefits from the former reproductive bargain no longer stretch very far among working class men. New unions and worker associations seek to represent workers left out of and in response to inadequacies of enterprise unions. Precarious work and precarity may supply reasons why workers need protections and give them a collective voice to challenge the conditions of their precarity. Service workers, among the most precarious, are on the threshold of organizing today, empowered by their position at the nexus of work and welfare in the new economy. In this way, reproductive labor that is socially necessary – and not easily off-shored, gives workers in personal service occupations leverage. Still, these fledgling organizations are hampered by structural barriers and institutional legacies. New unions only represent a small percentage of the total eligible workforce. A new political agenda that encompasses a changed labor landscape is necessary if the Japan wants to avoid another lost decade.

Toward a New Political Agenda: Concluding Remarks

The making of a new reproductive bargain between the state, capital and organized labor can destabilize the old gender order. Deciding who will provide care and under what conditions will depend on the outcome of future political negotiations, economic pressures, and possibly the recognition that there are substantive benefits, to both workplace and home, of creating and implementing policies that facilitate caring and working balance. Acker (2004, 36) puts the argument succinctly: "as long as the workplace is organized on the assumption that workers have no other responsibilities, women will carry the responsibility for care." As individuals are "freed" to negotiate their own work conditions, the benefits of such individualized arrangements would most likely accrue to single, highly educated women who can best emulate the masculine embodiment of work, in which responsibility for care is a non-issue.

Labor regulations narrowly frame subjects in the media of rights and money. Rights, which certainly are keys to self-expression, democratic participation and equality of opportunities and outcomes, privilege the individual over the collective. Regulations solely framed in terms of rights run the risk of ignoring communal interests, cooperative arrangements outside the market orbit, and mutual interdependencies. Similarly, regulations framed in the media of money privilege the commodity form of labor over all other forms of non-waged work. This tends to devalue some aspects of workers' lives, especially those related to female-typed work and work biographies, such as unpaid care, intimate practices, and affective labor. Valorization of the wage labor relation and its masculine embodiment in much of labor regulation is premised on the gender "opposition of independence/dependence [which] maps onto other hierarchical oppositions: masculine/feminine, public/ work/care, success/love, individual/community, economy/family, and [rational/emotional]" (Fraser and Gordon 1994, 322). In this sense, the wage labor relation symbolically is connected to meanings of motherhood and fatherhood. More specifically, labor regulations and social policies treat men as independent wage earners not as dependent caretakers; "as rights-earning individuals not as needy family members; and as beneficiaries of cash benefits (unstigmatized) not as recipients of (unearned) services" (Haney and March 2005, 464).[19] A mode of regulation and policy premised on independence over interdependence tends to valorize the masculine worker-citizen whose rights derive from their participation in wage labor and tends to devalue the feminine connected to caring labor. The discourse framed around rights without responsibilities fails to recognize not only the specific needs related to care and caring but also the different prospects and resources that accrue to individuals depend on one's social location.

Deconstructing gender subjects in regulations and key words is a project for orienting political action. By explicating the gender subjects implicit and explicit in grammars of regulation, feminists can critique current work arrangements and denaturalize gendered norms implicit in the language of labor regulation. Moreover, seemingly gender neutral principles when applied to labor regulations and practices may not address fundamental bases of inequality. Extending the principle of equal treatment between standard and nonstandard employment would improve overall employment conditions, but may not significantly alter the gendered character of these employment forms. For example, strengthening equal employment opportunities law will not necessarily bring about the outcome of gender equality. The equal treatment frame aims at "formal equality in the labor market without addressing inequality of circumstances between men and women" (Vosko 2006). Gender inequality will persist as long as the basis for equal treatment refers back to some golden age of industrial or company citizenship based on a standard male work biography of continuous and relatively stable employment. As Vosko (2006) suggests, a broader conception of "labor market membership" must acknowledge that, "workers typically have gaps in employment, fluctuating levels of employment intensity, and jobs of varying duration over the life-course." A life-course perspective is

---

19   The opposition between paired terms, symbolically, discursively, and culturally privilege "masculinity – not necessarily men- [which] is key to naturalizing the (symbolic, discursive, cultural, corporeal, material, economic) power relations that constitute multiple forms of subordination and exploitation...feminist research documents the deeply sedimented normalization of gender as governing code, valorizing that which is characterized as masculine (reason, agency) at the expense of that which is stigmatized as feminine (emotion, dependence)" (V. Spike Peterson 2003, 35).

one way to connect the gender division of labor in households and employment structures into the design of laws aimed at economic security.

Japan's stalled economic growth jars with the celebrated economic success story. Like discovering the ancient burial ground at Pompeii, the excavation of what lays beneath Japan's economic ruins can unearth insights into the inner workings of capitalism. Though Japan's crisis may pale in comparison to Pompeii's cataclysmic end, the tsunami uncovered tensions that laid dormant in society. The disaster allowed for glimpsing the less visible factors and forces influencing patterns of precarious work and life. By deciphering the enigma of Japanese capitalism, we can see the potential obstacles to action directed at growing disparities between good and bad jobs. This in-depth case study also reveals factors and processes that influence the size, composition, and conditions of precarity as effect and as affect and precarious work in its myriad guises. The increasing trend toward nonstandard and precarious employment raises new challenges for labor laws based on a male standard employment relationship and male breadwinner model. Further, the examination of precariousness has implications for the study of the informal economy more generally. Informal and precarious work makes up a substantial part of world economic output. A reflection on Japan's lost decades can contribute to the formulation of a new bargain relevant to changing employment relations, the articulation of a set of policy initiatives for address rising inequalities, the envisioning of a "post-work" politics, liberating life from work that can provoke new political imaginaries beyond work (Weeks 2011), and realize new forms of democratic governance and ways of being.

Bibliography

Abe Says Women are Key to Japan's Future. *Bloomberg Businessweek*. Available (consulted 23 January 2014) at: http://www.businessweek.com/videos/2014-01-22/abe-says-women-are-key-to-japans-future#r=lr-sr.

Abe, Yukiko and Ohtake F (1997) The Effects of Income Tax and Social Security on Part-Time Labor Supply in Japan. *Review of Social Policy* 6: 45–64.

Acker, Joan (1989) *Doing Comparable Worth: Gender, Class and Pay Equity*. Philadelphia, PA: Temple University Press.

Acker, Joan (1990) Hierarchies, Jobs, Bodies: A Theory of Gendered Organizations. *Gender and Society* 2: 139–158.

Acker, Joan (2004) Gender, Capitalism and Globalization. *Critical Sociology* 30(1): 17–42.

Adkins, L. and Lury C. (1996) The Cultural, the Sexual and the Gendering of the Labour Market. In: Adkins L. and Merchant V. (eds) *Sexualizing the Social: Power and the Organization of Sexuality*. London: Macmillan, 204–223.

Adkins, L. and Lury C. (1999) The Labour of Identity: Performing Identities, Performing Economies. *Economy and Society* 28(4): 598–614.

Allison, A. (2013) *Precarious Japan*. Durham: Duke University Press.

Araki, T. (1994) Characteristics of Regulation on Dispatched Work in Japan. *Japan Labor Bulletin* (1 August): 5–8.

Araki, T. (1997) Changing Japanese Labor Law in Light of Deregulation Drives: A Comparative Perspective. *Japan Labor Bulletin* (1 May): 5–10.

Araki, T. (1999) 1999 Revisions of Employment Security Law and Worker Dispatching Law: Drastic Reforms of Japanese Labor Market Regulations. *Japan Labor Bulletin* (1 September): 5–10.

Araki, T. (2002) *Labor and Employment Law in Japan*, Tokyo: The Japan Institute of Labor.

Araki, T. (2013) New Forms of Dispute Resolution: Japan's Labor Tribunal System. In: Stone K. and Arthurs H. (eds) *Rethinking Workplace Regulation: Beyond the Standard Contract of Employment*. New York, NY: Russell Sage Foundation, 174–193.

Arnold, D. and Bongiovi, J. (2013) Precarious, Informalizing, and Flexible Work: Transforming Concepts and Understandings. *American Behavioral Scientist* 57(3): 289–308.

Bachnik, J. (1992) Kejime: Defining a Shifting Self in Multiple Organizational Modes. In: Rosenberger N. (ed.) *Japanese Sense of Self*. Cambridge: Cambridge University Press, 152–72.

Bachnik, J. and Quinn C. (1994) Introduction: Uchi/Soto: Challenging Our Conceptions of Self, Social Order, and Language. In: Bachnik J. and Quinn C. (eds) *Situated*

Meanings: Inside and Outside in Japanese Self, Society and Language. Princeton, NJ: Princeton University Press, 3–37.

Barthes, R. (1982) *Empire of Signs.* Trans. R. Howard. New York, NY: Hill and Wang.

Beck, U. (1999) *World Risk Society.* Cambridge: Polity Press.

Beck, J. and Beck M. (1994) *The Change of a Lifetime: Employment Patterns among Japan's Managerial Elite.* Honolulu, HI: University of Hawaii Press.

Bergeron S. and Puri, J. (2012) Sexuality between State and Class: An Introduction. *Rethinking Marxism* 24(4): 491–498.

Berggren, C. (1995) Japan as Number Two: Competitive Problems and the Future of Alliance Capitalism after the Burst of the Bubble Boom. *Work, Employment and Society* 9(1): 53–95.

Berman, M. (1988) *All That is Solid Melts into Air.* New York, NY: Penguin.

Bernhardt, A. (2014) Labor Standards and the Reorganization of Work: Gaps in Data and Research. University of California, Institute for Research on Labor and Employment, Working Paper #100-14.

Bernstein. (1991) *Recreating Japanese Women.* Berkeley, CA: University of California Press.

Blow, C. (2011) America's Exploding Pipe Dream. *The New York Times*, 28, October. Available (consulted 5 March, 2012) at: http://www.nytimes.com/2011/10/29/opinion/blow-americas-exploding-pipe-dream.html?scp=1&sq=charles%20blow%20bottom%20of%20the%20heap&st=cse.

Born, C., Krueger, H., and Lorenz-Meyer, D. (1996) *Der Unentdeckte Wandel: Annaherung an das Verhaltnis von Strucktur und Norm im Weiblichen Lebenslauf.* Berlin: Sigma.

Boyer, R. (2005) How and Why Capitalisms Differ. Max-Planck Institute for the Study of Societies Discussion Paper 05/4.

Boyer, R. (1998) Wage Determination and Distribution in Japan by Toshiaki Tachibanaki. *Journal of Japanese Studies* 24(1): 155–60.

Bradley, H. (1998) A New Gender(ed) Order? Researching and Rethinking Women's Work. *Sociology* 32(4): 869–873.

Bradley, H. (forthcoming) Gender. In: Edgell, S., Gottfried, H., and Granter, E. (eds) *The Sage Handbook of the Sociology of Work and Employment.* London: Sage.

Brinton, M. (1993) *Women and the Economic Miracle: Gender and Work in Postwar Japan.* Berkeley: University of California Press.

Brinton, M. (2011) *Lost in Transition: Youth, Work, and Instability in Postindustrial Japan.* New York, NY: Cambridge University Press.

Brodsky, M. (1994) Labor Market Flexibility: A Changing International Perspective. *Monthly Labor Review* (November): 53–60.

Bronstein, A.S. (1991) Temporary Work in Western Europe: Threat or Complement to Permanent Employment. *International Labour Review* 130(3): 291–310.

Brown, C., Nakato, Y.F., Reich, M., and Ulman, L. (1997) *Work and Pay in the United States and Japan.* New York, NY: Oxford University Press.

Brulin, G. and Nilsson, T. (1994) New Forms of Work Organization, Trade Unionism and Co-worker Agreements: Sweden, a Case of Union Adaption. Paper presented at the International Symposium.

Burawoy, M. (2000) Introduction: Reaching for the Global. In: Burawoy M., Blum J., George S., et al. (eds) *Global Ethnography: Forces, Connections, and Imaginations in a Postmodern World*. Berkeley, CA: University of California Press, 1–40.

Butler, J. (2004) *Undoing Gender*. New York, NY: Routledge.

Carney, L. and O'Kelly, C. (1990) Women's Work and Women's Place in the Japanese Economic Miracle. In: Ward K. (ed.) *Women Workers and Global Restructuring*. Ithaca, NY: Cornell University Press, 113–145.

Chae, O. (2013) Japanese Colonial Structure in Korea in Comparative Perspective. In: Steinmetz, G. (ed.) *Sociology and Empire: The Imperial Entanglements of a Discipline*. Durham, NC: Duke University Press.

Chalmers, N. (1989) *Industrial Relations in Japan: The Peripheral Workforce*. New York, NY: Routledge.

Chang, D.O. (2011) The rise of East Asia and classes of informal labour. Power-Point Presentation at Sawyer Seminar Colloquium, Chapel Hill, NC. Available at: http://sawyerseminar.web.unc.edu/papers-and-other-readings/.

Chen J., Choi Y.C., Mori K., et al. (2012) Recession, Unemployment, and Suicide in Japan. *Japan Labor Review* 9(2): 75–92.

Chun, J (2014) "The Emotional Politics of Unionism: Organizing Across Gender and Racial Divides" paper presented at the American Sociological Association Annual Meeting, San Francisco, August.

Clement, W. and Myles, J. (1994) *Relations of Ruling: Class and Gender in Postindustrial Societies*. Montreal: McGill Queens University Press.

Cobble, D.S. (2007) *The Sex of Class: Women Transforming American Labor*. Ithaca, NY: ILR Press.

Coe, N., Johns, J. and Ward, K. (2006) The Japanese Staffing Market: Industry Practices and Regulatory Change. Working brief 9, *The Globalization of the Temporary Staffing Industry Research Programme*, Manchester: Manchester University.

Cohen, R.L., Hardy, K., Sanders, T., and Wolkowitz, C. (2013) Introduction: The Body/Sex/Work Nexus. In: Wolkowitz, C., Cohen, R.L, Sanders, T. and Hardy, K. (eds) *Body/Sex/Work: Intimate, Embodies and Sexualized Labor*. Houndsmill: Palgrave-MacMillan.

Cook, E. (2013) Expectations of Failure: Maturity and Masculinity for Freeters in Contemporary Japan. *Social Science Japan Journal* 16(1): 29–43.

Creighton, M. (2009) Japan's Department Stores as a Mirror of 20th Century Japan: Reflecting Societal Shifts, Linking Past and Future Eras. The Department of Anthropology, The Chinese University of Hong. Available (consulted 4 July 2013) at: http://www.cuhk.edu.hk/ant/milliecreighton.pdf.

Crompton, R. and Harris, F. (1998) Explaining Women's Employment Patterns. *The British Journal of Sociology* 49(1): 118–136.

Crouch, C. (1993) *Industrial Relations and European State Traditions*. Oxford: Clarendon Press.

Dasgupta, R. (2003) Creating Corporate Warriors: The 'Salaryman' and Masculinity in Japan. In: Louie, K. and Low, M. (eds) *Asian Masculinities: The Meaning and Practice of Manhood in China and Japan*. London: Curzon Press.

Dasgupta, R. (2013) *Re-reading the Salaryman in Japan: Crafting Masculinities*. London: Routledge.

Dickens, L. (2004) Problems of Fit: Changing Employment and Labour Regulation. *British Journal of Industrial Relations* 42(4): 595–616.

Dore, R. (1986) *Flexible Rigidities: Industrial Policy and Structural Adjustment in the Japanese Economy, 1970–1980*. Stanford, CA: Stanford University Press.

Dower, J. (2000) *Embracing Defeat: Japan in the Wake of World War II*. New York, NY: W.W. Norton and Co.

Drysdale, P. (2014) Re-visiting Japan's Constitution (26 May), *East Asia Forum*. Available (consulted 2 October 2014) at: http://www.eastasiaforum.org/2014/05/26/re-visiting-japans-constitution/.

Dyson, K. (1992) Theories of Regulation and the Case of Germany. A Model of Regulatory Change. In: Dyson K. (ed.) *The Politics of German Regulation*. Aldershot, 1–28.

Eisenstein, Z. (1980) *The Radical Future of Liberal Feminism*. New York: NYLongman.

Ellingsaeter, A.L. (1998) Dual Breadwinner Societies: Provider Models in the Scandinavian Welfare States. *Acta Sociologica* 41 (1): 59–73.

Elson, D. (2002) International Financial Architecture. *Femina Politica* 1:26–37.

Endo, C. (2006) Review of Calichman, Richard F. Contemporary Japanese Thought, H-US-Japan, H-Net Reviews, March 2006. Available (consulted 27 January 2014) at: http://www.h-net.org/reviews/showrev.php?id=11518.

Esping-Andersen, G. (1997) Welfare States without Work: the Impasse of Labor Shedding and Familialism in Continental European Social Policy. In: Esping-Andersen, G. (ed.) *Welfare States in Transition: National Adaptations in Global Economies*. London: Sage.

Esser, J. (1996) The Future of Model Germany: Challenges to the Corporatist System of Business Labor Relations. Programme for the Study of Germany and Europe Working Paper Series #7.4, Harvard University.

Ezawa, A. and Fujiwara, C. (2003) Lone Mothers and Welfare-to-Work Policies in Japan and the United States: Towards an Alternative Perspective. Paper presented at the New Challenges for Welfare State Research, International Sociological Association RC-19 Poverty, Social Welfare and Social Policy, University of Toronto, August 21–24.

Fackler, M. (2014) Three Years After Fukushima, Japan Approves a Nuclear Plant. *The New York Times*. Available (consulted 11 September 2014) at: http://www.nytimes.

com/2014/09/11/world/asia/japanese-nuclear-plant-declared-safe-to-operate-for-first-time-since-fukushima-daiichi-disaster.html?module=Search&mabReward=rel bias%3Aw%2C{%221%22%3A%22RI%3A11%22}&_r=0.

Fagan, C. and O'Reilly, J. (1998) Conceptualising Part-time Work: The value of an Integrated Comparative Perspective. In: O'Reilly J. and Fagan C. (eds) *PartTime Prospect: International Comparisons of Part-Time Work in Europe, North America, and Pacific Rim* . London: Routledge.

Fackler, M. and Sang-Hun, C. (2013) A growing chill between South Korea and Japan Creates Problems for the US. *The New York Times*, 24 November: A6.

Foote, D. (1996) *Judicial Creation of Norms in Japanese Labor Law: Activism in the Service of – Stability?* UCLA Labor Review 43: 635–709.

Foucault, M. (1979) *The History of Sexuality Volume 1: An Introduction.* London: Allen Lane.

Fourcade, M. (2010) The Problem of Embodiment in the Sociology of Knowledge: Afterword to the Special Issue on Knowledge in Practice. *Qualitative Sociology* 33(4): 569–574.

Fraser, N. and Gordon, L. (1994) A Genealogy of Dependency: Tracing a Keyword of the US Welfare State. *Signs* 19(2): 309–336.

French, H. (2001) Can't Resist Telling His Mount Fuji Story Again. *The New York Times* 8 August: B1, 6.

Fujimura-Fanselow, K. and Atsuko, K. (eds) (1995) *Japanese Women.* New York, NY: The Feminist Press.

Galbraith, J.K. (2014) Das Kapital for the Twenty-First Century? A Review of T. Piketty's New Book. *Dissent.* Available (consulted 4 April 2014) at: http://www.dissentmaga-zine.org/article/kapital-for-the-twenty-first-century.

Gill, T. (2003) When Pillars Evaporate: Structuring Masculinity in the Japanese Margins. In: Roberson, J. and Suzuki, N. (eds) *Men and Masculinities in Contemporary Japan: Dislocating the Salaryman Doxa.* London: RoutledgeCurzon.

Geraghty, K. (2008) Taming the Paper Tiger. Cornell *International Law Journal* 41: 503 – 504.

Gonas, L. (1994) *The Transformation of the Welfare State and Its Labour Market.* Swedish Institute for Work Life Research 1.

Goodman, R. and Peng, I. (1997) The East Asian Welfare States: Peripatetic Learning, Adaptive Change, and Nation Building. In: Esping-Andersen, G. (ed.) *Welfare States in Transition: National Adaptations in Global Economies.* London: Sage.

Gordon, A. (1985) *The Evolution of Labor Relations in Japan.* Cambridge, MA: Harvard University Press.

Gordon, A. (1998) *The Wages of Affluence.* Cambridge, MA: Harvard University Press.

Gornick, J. and Jacobs, J. (1998) Gender, the Welfare State and Public Employment. *American Sociological Review* 63(5): 688–710.

Gottfried, H. (1991) Mechanisms of Control in the Temporary Service Industry. *Sociological* Forum 6: 699–713.

Gottfried, H. (1992) In: the Margins: Flexibility as a Mode of Regulation in the Temporary Service Industry. *Work, Employment and Society* 6(3): 443–460.

Gottfried, H. (1997) Duality or Dualism in German Industrial Relations. *Organizations, Occupations and Work Newsletter.* Winter/Spring: 3–4.

Gottfried, H. (1998) Beyond Patriarchy? Theorising Gender and Class. *Sociology* 32(3): 451–68.

Gottfried, H. (2005) Hard Times, New Deals: The Next Upsurge? *Critical Sociology* 31(3): 391–399.

Gottfried, H. (2006) Feminist Thought and the Analysis of Work. In: Korczynski, M., Hodson, R., and Edwards, P.K. (eds) *Social Theory at Work.* New York, NY: Oxford University Press.

Gottfried, H. (2008a) Pathways to Economic Security: Nonstandard Employment and Gender in Contemporary Japan. *Social Indicators Research* 88(1): 179–196.

Gottfried, H, (2008b) Reflections on Intersectionality: Gender, Class, Race and Nation. *Journal of Gender Studies* 11: 23–40.

Gottfried, H. (2009) Japan: The Reproductive Bargain and the Making of Precarious Employment. In: Vosko, L., Campbell, I., and MacDonald, M. (eds) *Gender and the Contours of Precarious Employment.* London: Routledge.

Gottfried, H. (2013) Gender, Work, and Economy: Unpacking the Global Economy. Cambridge: Polity Press.

Gottfried, H. and Graham, L. (1993) Constructing Difference: The Making of Gendered Subcultures in a Japanese Automobile Assembly Plant. *Sociology* 7(4): 611–68.

Gottfried, H. and Hayashi, N.K. (1998) Gendering Work: Deconstructing the Narrative of the Japanese Economic Miracle. *Work, Employment and Society* 12(1): 25–46.

Gottfried, H. and O'Reilly, J. (1999) The Weakness of a Strong Breadwinner Model: Part-Time Work and Female Labor Force Participation in Germany and Japan. Unpublished paper.

Gottfried, H. and O'Reilly, J. (2002) Re-regulating Breadwinner Models in Socially Conservative Welfare Regimes. Comparing Germany and Japan. *Social Politics.* 9(1): 29–59.

Gottfried, H. and Reese, L. (2004) Gendering Comparative Policy Analysis. In: Gottfried, H. and Reese, L. (eds) *Equity in the Workplace: Gendering Workplace Policy Analysis.* Lexington, MA: Lexington Press, 1–28.

Gould W.B., IV (1984) *Japan's Reshaping of American Labor Law.* Cambridge, MA: MIT Press.

Grossberg, L. (2013) Culture. *Rethinking Marxism* 25(4): 456–62.

Haberman, C. (1987) Nobusuke Kishi, Ex-Tokyo Leader. *The New York Times*, 8 August. Available (consulted 22 November 2013) at: http://www.nytimes.com/1987/08/08/obituaries/nobusuke-kishi-ex-tokyo-leader.html.

Halford, S., Savage, M. and Witz, A. (1997) *Gender, Careers and Organisations*. London: Macmillan.

Haney, L. and March, M. (2005) Married Fathers and Chaneyaring Daddies: Welfare Reform and the Discursive Politics of Paternity. *Social Problems* 50(4): 461–481.

Hardt, M. and Negri, A. (2000) *Empire*. Boston, MA: Harvard University Press.

Harootunian, J. and Yoda, T. (2006) Introduction. In: Yoda, T. and Harootunian, H. (eds) *Japan After Japan: Social and Cultural Life from the Recessionary 1990s to the Present*. Durham, NC: Duke University Press.

Harvey, D. (2011) *The Enigma of Capital and the Crises of Capitalism*. Oxford: Oxford University Press.

Hayashi, N.K. (1993) The Japanese State and Female Employment. Unpublished paper.

Hayashi, N .K. (1994) The Role of Paato-Taimu in Recent Restructuring of Japanese Economy. Unpublished paper.

Hazama, H. (1997) *The History of Labour Management in Japan*. London: Macmillan.

Heery, E., Williams, S., and Abbott, B. (2012) Civil Society Organizations and Trade Unions: Cooperation, Conflict, Indifference. *Work, Employment & Society* 26(1): 145–160.

Hendry, J. (1993) The Role of the Professional Housewife. In: Hunter, J. (ed.) *Japanese Women Working*. London: Routledge.

Hendry, J. (1990) Humidity, Hygiene, or Ritual Care: Some Thoughts on Wrapping as a Social Phenomenon. In: Moeran, A.B. and Valentine, J. (eds) *Unwrapping Japan: Society and Culture in Anthropological Perspective*. Manchester: Manchester University Press, 18–35.

Hewison, K. and Kalleberg, A. (2008) Multiple Flexibilities: Nation-States, Global Business and Precarious Labor. Unpublished paper for SSRC, Dubai.

Hirakawa, H. (1995) Inverted Orientalism and the Discursive Construction of Sexual Harassment: A Study of Mass Media and Feminist Representation of Sexual Harassment in Japan. Ph.D. Dissertation, Purdue University.

Hochschild, A. (1983) *The Managed Heart: Commercialization of Human Feeling*. Berkeley, CA: University of California Press.

Hollingsworth, J. Rogers (1997) Continuities and Changes in Social Systems of Production: The Cases of Japan, Germany and the United States. In: Hollingsworth, J.R. and Boyer, R. (eds) *Contemporary Capitalism: The Embeddedness of Institutions*. Cambridge: Cambridge University Press.

Hollingsworth, J. Rogers and Boyer, R. (1997) Coordination of Economic Actors and Social Systems of Production. In: Hollingsworth, J.R. and Boyer, R. (eds) *Contemporary Capitalism: The Embeddedness of Institutions*. Cambridge: Cambridge University Press.

Hong Li, J. and Singelmann, J. (1998) Gender Differences in Class Mobility: A Comparative Study of the United States, Sweden and West Germany. *Acta Sociologica* 41(4): 315–334.

Horiuchi, Y. (2013) America's Role in Making Japan's Economic Miracle: New Evidence for a Landmark Case. Paper presented at the Center for Japanese Studies Noon Lecture, 21 November, University of Michigan.

Houseman, S. and Osawa, M. (2000) The Growth of Non-standard Employment in Japan and the United States: A Comparison of Causes and Consequences. Unpublished paper presented at the Non-standard Work Arrangements in Japan, Europe, and the United States conference, sponsored by WE Upjohn Institute, the Japan Foundation and the Japan Women's University.

Hunter, J. (ed.) (1993) *Introduction. Japanese Women Working*. London: Routledge.

Hunter, J., DeLorme, C., and Charter Hill, R. (1981) Taxation and the Wife's Use of Time. *Industrial and Labor Relations Review* 34(3): 426–432.

Imai, J. (2011) *The Transformation of Japanese Employment Relations: Reform without Labor*. Basingstoke, UK: Palgrave.

Imai, J. (2014) The Link Between Employment and Welfare and the Consequences for Social Inclusion of Non-standard Workers. Paper presented at the XVIII World Congress of Sociology, 13–19 July, Yokohama, Japan.

Imamura, A. (1987) *Urban Japanese Housewives: At Home and in the Community*. Honolulu, HI: University of Hawaii Press.

International Labour Office (1989) *Conditions of Work Digest*. International Labor Conference, 8(1), Geneva: ILO.

Ishida, H. (2006) The Persistence of Social Inequality in Postwar Japan. *Social Science Japan* 35: 7–10.

Ishida, H. and D. Slater (2010) *Social Class in Contemporary Japan*. Oxon: Routledge.

Ito, R. (2005) Crafting Migrant Women's Citizenship in Japan: Taking "Family" as a Vantage Point. *International Journal of Japanese Sociology* 14: 52–69

Jacobowitz, S. (2014) Southward Bound: Voyage Narratives of Japanese Immigration to Brazil. Paper presented at the Center for Japanese Studies Noon Lecture, University of Michigan.

Japan Institute of Labor (1997) *Japanese Working Life Profile, 1996–97*. Tokyo: Japan Institute of Labor.

Japan Institute of Labour Policy and Training (2002) *Japanese Working Life Profile, 2002*. Tokyo: Japan Institute of Labor.

Japan Institute of Labour Policy and Training (2012a) *Labor Situation in Japan and Its Analysis: General Overview 2011/2012*. Tokyo: Japan Institute of Labour Policy and Training.

Japan Institute of Labour Policy and Training (2012b) *Japanese Working Life Profile, 2011/2012*. Tokyo: Japan Institute of Labor.

Japan Institute of Labour Policy and Training (2013) *Labor Situation in Japan and Its Analysis: Detailed Exposition 2012/2013*. Tokyo: Japan Institute of Labour Policy and Training.

Japan Institute of Labour Policy and Training (2014) *Labor Situation in Japan and Its Analysis: General Overview 2013/2014*. Tokyo: Japan Institute of Labour Policy and Training.

Japanese Protest Security Treaty with U.S. and Unseat Prime Minister (2014) *Global Nonviolent Action Database*. Available (consulted 8 April 2014) at: http://nvdatabase .swarthmore.edu/content/japanese-protest-security-treaty-us-and-unseat-prime -minister-1959-1960.

Janssen, R. (2014) Lessons from 15 Years of Japanese Deflation. *Social Europe*. Available (consulted 17 September 2014) at: http://www.social-europe.eu/2014/09/japanese -deflation/.

Jenson, J. (1989) The Talents of Women, the Skills of Men: Flexible Specialization and Women. In: Wood, S. (ed.) *The Transformation of Work? Skill, Flexibility and the Labour Process*. London: Unwin and Hyman.

Johnson, C. (1993) The Institutional Foundations of Japanese Industrial Policy. In: Durlaghji, S. and Marks, N. (eds) *Japanese Business Cultural Perspectives*. Albany, NY: SUNY Press.

Johnson, C. (1982) *M ITI and the Japanese Miracle: The Growth of Industrial Policy, 1925– 1975*. Stanford, CA: Stanford University Press.

Jones, Bryn (1997) *Forcing the Factory of the Future*. Cambridge: Cambridge University Press.

Kandiyoti, D. (1988) *Bargaining with Patriarchy*. Gender & Society 2(3): 274–290.

Kagan, R. (2000) Introduction: Comparing National Styles of Regulation in Japan and the United States. *Berkeley Law Scholarship Repository*, 1 January. Available (consulted 20 November, 2013) at: http://scholarship.law.berkeley.edu/cgi/viewcontent .cgi?article=1494&context=facpubs.

Kalleberg, A. (2011) *Good Jobs, Bad Jobs*. New York, NY: Russell Sage Foundation.

Kalleberg, A., Hudson, K., and Reskin, B. (2000) Bad Jobs in America: Standard and Nonstandard Employment Relations and Job Quality in the United States. *American Sociological Review* 65(2): 256–278.

Kato, T. and Steven, R. (1995) Industrial Relations: Is Japanese Capitalism Post-Fordist? In: Arnason, J. and Sugimoto, Y. (eds) *Japanese Encounters with Postmodernity*. London: Kegan Paul International.

Kawashima, Y. (1987) *The Place and Role of Female Workers in the Japanese Labor Market*. Women's Studies International Forum 10(6): 599–611.

Kingston, J. (2004) *Japan's Quiet Transformation: Social Change and Civil Society in the 21st Century*. London: Routledge.

Kjellberg, A. (1992) Sweden: Can the Model Survive? In: Fermer, A. and Hyman, R. (eds) *Industrial Relations in The New Europe*. Oxford: Basil Blackwell.

Kleeman, F.Y. (2014) *In Transit: The Formation of the Colonial East Asian Cultural Sphere*. Honolulu, HI: University of Hawaii Press.

Kojima, N. and K. Fujikawa (2000) Non-standard Work Arrangements in the U.S. and Japan from a Legal Perspective. Unpublished paper presented at the Non-standard Work Arrangements in Japan, Europe, and the United States conference, sponsored by WE Upjohn Institute, the Japan Foundation and the Japan Women's University.

Kondo, D. (1990) *Crafting Selves: Power, Gender and Discourses of Identity in a Japanese Workplace*. Chicago, IL: University of Chicago Press.

Kosai, Y. (1997) The Postwar Japanese Economy, 1943–73. In: Yamamura, K. (ed.) The *Economic Emergence of Modern Japan*. Cambridge: Cambridge University Press.

Koshiro, K. (2006) Formal and Informal Aspects of Labor Dispute Resolution in Japan. *Law & Policy* 22(3–4): 353–367.

Krippner, G. (2001) The Elusive Market: Embeddedness and the Paradigm of Economic Sociology. *Theory and Society* 30(6): 775–810.

Krishnan, S. (2014) Review of: Allison, A. Precarious Japan. LSE Review of Books. Available (consulted 23 February 2014) http://blogs.lse.ac.uk/lsereviewofbooks/2014/01/29/book-review-precarious-japan-by-anne-allison/.

Kumazawa, M. (1996) *Portraits of the Japanese Workplace: Labor Movements, Workers, and Managers*. Boulder, CO: Westview Press.

Kume, I. (1998) *Disparaged Success: Labor Politics in Postwar Japan*. Ithaca, NY: Cornell University Press.

Kuroda, H. (2014) *Deflation, The Labor Market, and QQE. Remarks in the Economic Policy Symposium*. Federal Reserve Bank of Kansas City. Available (consulted 17 September 2014) at: https://www.boj.or.jp/en/announcements/press/koen_2014/data/ko140824a1.pdf.

Kurokawa, M. (1995) Japan. *Bulletin of Comparative Labour Relations* 30: 45–90.

Lal, J. (2009) Unbecoming Women: Factor Women's Counter Narratives of Domestic Citizenship. Unpublished paper.

Lam, A. (1992) *Women and Japanese Management: Discrimination and Reform*. London: Routledge.

Languillon-Aussel, R. (2014) The Burst Bubble and the Privatization of Planning in Tokyo. *Metropolitiques*. Available (consulted 8 June 2014) at: http://www.metropolitiques.eu/The-burst-bubble-and-the.html.

Lash, S. (1994) Reflexivity and its Doubles. Structure, Aesthetics, Community. In: Beck, U., Giddens, A., and Lash, S. (eds) *Reflexive Modernization. Politics, Tradition and Aesthetics in the Modern Social Order*. Stanford, CA: Stanford University Press, 110–173.

Lembruch, G. (1999) The Rise and Change of Discourses on "Embedded Capitalism" in Germany and Japan and their Institutional Setting. Paper presented at the Japan/Germany Conference, Max-Planck Institute for the Study of Societies, Cologne.

Lenz, I. (1996) On the Potential of Gender Studies for the Understanding of Japanese Society. In: Kreiner and Oelschleger, H.D. (eds) *Japanese Culture and Society*. German Institute for Japanese Studies:12.

Lewis, J. (1992) Gender and the Development of Welfare Regimes. *Journal of European Social Policy* 2: 159–73.

Lie, J. (1996) Sociology of Contemporary Japan. *Current Sociology* 44(1): 1–101.

Literature Science and the Arts (2013) Far Flung Fieldwork. *College of Literature, Science, and the Arts, University of Michigan, Alumni Magazine* Fall 2013: 54–56.

Lo, J. (1990) *Office Ladies, Factory Women: Life and Work at a Japanese Company.* Armonk, New York, NY: M.E. Sharpe.

Locke, R., Kochan, T. and Piore, M. (1995) Reconceptualising Comparative Industrial Relations: Lessons from International Research. *International Labour Review* 134(2): 139–161.

MacArthur Bans General Strike (1947) The Sydney Morning Herald, 1 February. Available (consulted 9 April 2014) at: http://trove.nla.gov.au/ndp/del/article/27906152.

McDowell, L. (1997) *Capital Culture: Gender and Work in the City.* Oxford: Blackwell.

McDowell, L., Perrons, D, Fagan, C., Ray, K. and Ward, K. (2005) The Contradictions and Intersections of Class and Gender in a Global City: Placing Working Women's Lives on the Research Agenda. *Environment and Planning A* 37: 441–461.

Mackie, V. (1995) Equal Opportunity and Gender Identity: Feminist Encounters with Modernity and Postmodernity in Japan. In: Sugimoto, Y. and Arnason, J. (eds) *Japanese Encounters with Postmodernity.* London: Kegan Paul International.

McVeigh, B. (1995) 'The Feminization of Body, Behavior, and Belief: The Cultivation of "Office Flowers" at a Japanese Women's Junior College', *The Asian American Review* 2: 29–67.

Mahon, R. (1994) Wage-Earners and/or Co-Workers? Contested Identities. *Economic and Industrial Democracy* 15 (3):355–83.

Mahler, S. and Pessar, P. (2006) Gender Matters: Ethnographers bring Gender from the Periphery toward the Core of Migration studies. *International Migration Review* 40(1): 27–63.

Maier, F. (1994) Part-Time Employment. In: *Women and Structural Change.* Paris: OECD.

Malinas, D. (2014) Characteristics of the Rebellious Youth in Japan. Paper presented at the Center for Japanese Studies Noon Lecture, 30 October, University of Michigan.

Marquez, G.G. (1970) *One Hundred Years of Solitude.* New York, NY: Harper and Row.

Martin, K. (1998) Becoming a Gendered Body: Practices of Preschools. *American Sociological Review* 63: 494–511.

Marx, K. (1852) *The Eighteenth Brumaire of Louis Bonaparte.* Available (consulted 1 August 2013) at: http://quotes.dictionary.com/history_repeats_itself_first_as_tragedy_second_as#CF5uJvk7vg8DEoZf.99.

Marx, K. and Engels, F. (1848) *Manifesto of the Communist Party.* Available (consulted 3 December 2013) at: http://www.marxists.org/archive/marx/works/1848/communist-manifesto/ch01.htm.

Mascia-Lees, F. (2011) Introduction. In: Mascia-Lees, F. (ed.) *A Companion to the Anthropology of the Body and Embodiment.* Chichester: Wiley-Blackwell.

Mathews, G. (2003) Can 'a Real Man' Live for His Family? Ikigai and Masculinity in Today's Japan. In: Roberson, J. and Suzuki, M. (eds) *Men and Masculinities in Contemporary Japan: Dislocating the Salaryman Doxa.* London: RoutledgeCurzon.

Melkas, H. and Ankar, R. (1998) Occupational Segregation by Sex in Nordic Countries. *International Labor Review* 136(3): 341–364.

Ministry of Health, Labour and Welfare (1995) *Labor Force Survey*, Tokyo: Ministry of Health, Labour and Welfare.

Ministry of Health, Labour and Welfare (1999) *General Survey on Diversified Types of Employment.* Tokyo: Ministry of Health, Labour and Welfare.

Ministry of Health, Labour and Welfare.(2000a) *Labor Force Survey*, Tokyo: Ministry of Health, Labour and Welfare.

Ministry of Health, Labour and Welfare (2000b) *General Survey on Diversified Types of Employment.* Tokyo: Ministry of Health, Labour and Welfare.

Ministry of Health, Labour and Welfare (2000c) *Basic Survey on Wage Structure.* Tokyo: Ministry of Health, Labour and Welfare.

Ministry of Health, Labour and Welfare (2000d) *Business Reports from Worker Dispatching Business.* Tokyo: Ministry of Health, Labour and Welfare.

Ministry of Health, Labour and Welfare (2001) *Labor Force Survey.* Tokyo: Ministry of Health, Labour and Welfare.

Ministry of Health, Labour and Welfare (2002) *General Survey of Part-Time Workers.* Tokyo: Ministry of Health, Labour and Welfare.

Ministry of Health, Labour and Welfare (2006) *Basic Survey on Wage Structure.* Tokyo: Ministry of Health, Labour and Welfare.

Ministry of Labor (1974) *The Status of Women in Japan.* Women and Minor's Bureau, Tokyo, Japan.

Ministry of Labor (1988) *Working Women in Japan.* Women's Bureau, Tokyo, Japan.

Ministry of Labor (1990) *Actual Conditions of Part-Timers.* Policy Research Division, Labour Ministry's Secretariat.

Ministry of Labor (1995) *Labor White Paper: Adjustment to Structural Transformation of Labor Market via Creation of Employment.* Japan Labor Research Organization: Japan.

Ministry of Labor Women's Bureau (1992) (ed.) *Actual Conditions of Working Women.* Finance Ministry. Printing Bureau: Japan.

Ministry of Labor Women's Bureau (1989) (ed.) *Actual Conditions of Working Women.* Finance Ministry. Printing Bureau: Japan.

Ministry of Public Welfare (ed.) (1995) Public Welfare White Paper: Medicine – Quality, Information, Selection and Assent. Public Welfare Issues Study Group Foundation: Japan.

Moi, T. (1991) Appropriating Bourdieu: Feminist Theory and Pierre Bourdieu's Sociology of Culture. *New Literary History* 4: 1017–1049.

Moloney, B. (1995) Japan's 1986 Equal Employment Opportunity Law and the Changing Discourse on Gender. *Signs* 20(2): 268–302.

Morgan, D. (1998) Sociological Imaginings and Imagining Sociology: Bodies, Auto/ Biographies and Other Mysteries. Sociology 4 (November): 647–63.

Morishima, M. (1997) Forward Part II – Japanese Enterprise as Private Sector Bureaucracy. In: Hazama, H. (ed.) *The History of Labor Management in Japan.* London: MacMillan.

Morishima, M. (2001) Contingent Workers in Japan: New Developments and Unexpected Consequences. *Japan Labour Bulletin* 40(3): 5–10.

Muckenberger, U. (1989) Non-standard Forms of Employment in the Federal Republic of Germany: The Role and Effectiveness of the State. In: Rodgers, G. and Rodgers, J. (eds) *Precarious Jobs in Labor Market Regulation: The Growth of A-typical Employment in Western Europe.* Geneva: International Labor Organization.

Muckenberger, U. (1997) German Industrial Relations in a Period of Transition. Unpublished paper.

Nagase, N. (2000) Standard and Non-standard Work Arrangements and Child-Bearing of Japanese Mothers. Unpublished paper presented at the Non-standard Work Arrangements in Japan, Europe, and the United States Conference, sponsored by WE Upjohn Institute, the Japan Foundation and the Japan Women's University.

Nagase, N. (2006) Japanese Youth's Attitudes towards Marriage and Child-Rearing. In: Rebick, M. and Takenaka, A. (eds) *The Changing Japanese Family.* London: Routledge.

Narita International Airport. Available (consulted 7 October 2013) at: http://en .wikipedia.org/wiki/Narita_International_Airport.

National Association of Working Women (1986) *Working at the Margins: Part time and Temporary Workers in the US.* Cleveland, Ohio.

Nurmi, K. (1998) Gender Aspects of Atypical Employment in the Nordic Countries. In: Weiss, D. (ed.) *Flexibles Europa: Die Auswirkungen von Deregulierung und Flexi-bilisierung Europaischer Arbeitsmarkte auf die Arbeits und Lebensbedingungen von Frauen.* Frankfurt: Peter Lang.

O'Day, R. (2012) Review of: M Brinton Lost in Transition: Youth, Work, and Instability in Postindustrial Japan. *Book Reviews* 85(1). Available at: www.pacificaffairs.ubc.ca.

Ogasawara, Y. (1998) *Office Ladies and Salaried Men: Gender, Power and Work in Japanese Companies.* Berkeley, CA: University of California Press.

Onishi, N. (2011) Japan Revives a Sea Barrier That Failed to Hold. The New York Times 2 *November.* Available (consulted on 10 October, 2011) at: http://www.nytimes .com/2011/11/03/world/asia/japan-revives-a-sea-barrier-that-failed-to-hold.html?_r=0.

Orcutt, G. & Silver, N. (2014) The Impact of Foreign Ownership on Gender and Employment Relations in Large Japanese Companies. *Work, Employment & Society* 28(2): 206–204.

Organization for Economic Co-operation and Development (1986) *Flexibility in the Labour Market: The Current Debate*. Paris: OECD.

Organization for Economic Co-operation and Development (1998) *Labor Force Statistics, 1977–97*. Paris: OECD.

Organization for Economic Co-operation and Development (1999) *Employment Outlook*. Paris: OECD.

Organization for Economic Co-operation and Development (2002) *OECD Employment Outlook 2002*. Paris: OECD.

Organization for Economic Co-operation and Development (2007) *OECD Employment Outlook*. Paris: OECD.

Organization for Economic Co-operation and Development (2008) Stats: 'Incidence of Permanent Employment'. Available (consulted on 24 July 2008) at: https://stats .oecd.org/Index.aspx?DataSetCode=TEMP_I.

Orloff, A.S. (1999) Motherhood, Work, and Welfare in the United States, Britain, Canada, and Australia. In: Steinmetz, G. (ed.) *State /Culture: State Formation after the Cultural Turn*. Ithaca, New York, NY: Cornell University Press.

Orloff, A.S. (2002) Gender Equality, Women's Employment. Cross National Patterns of Policy and Politics. Paper prepared for Workshop on Welfare, Work and Family: Southern Europe in *Comparative Perspective*. Florence: European University Institute.

Orloff, A.S. (2009) Gendering the Comparative Analysis of Welfare States: An Unfinished Agenda. *Sociological Theory* 27: 317–343.

O'Reilly, J. and Bothfeld, S. (1998) For Better or Worse? Part-Time Work in Britain and West Germany: A Comparison of the German Socio-economic Panel and the British Household Panel. Unpublished paper.

O'Reilly, J. and C. Fagan (1998) *Part-time Prospects: An International Comparison of Part-Time Work in Europe, North America and the Pacific Rim*. London: Routledge.

O'Reilly, J. and Spee, C. (1998) The Future of Regulation of Work and Welfare: Tie for a Revised Social and Gender Contract? *European Journal of Industrial Relations* 4(3): 259–81.

Osawa, M. (1994) *Bye-Bye Corporate Warriors: The Formation of a Corporate-Centered Society and Gender-Biased Social Policies in Japan*. University of Tokyo Institute of Social Science Occasional Paper, Institute of Social Science, University of Tokyo.

Osawa, M. (2001) People in Irregular Modes of Employment: Are They Really Subject to Discrimination? *Social Science Japan Journal* 4(2): 183–199.

Osawa, M. (2003) Japanese Government Approaches to Gender Equality since the mid-1990s. Wayne State University Occasional Paper Series.

Osawa, M. (2007) Comparative Livelihood Security Systems from a Gender Perspective, with a Focus on Japan. In: Walby, S., Gottfried, H., Gottschall, K. and Osawa, M. (eds) *Gendering the Knowledge Economy: Comparative Perspectives*. Houndsmill: Palgrave.

Osawa, M. and Kingston, J. (1996) Flexibility and Inspiration: Restructuring and the Japanese Labor Market. *Japan Labor Bulletin* 1: 4–8.

Ostner, I. and Lewis, J. (1995) Gender and the Evolution of European Social Policies. In: Leibfried, S. and Pierson, P. (eds) *European Social Policy: Between Fragmentation and Integration*. Washington, D.C.: The Brookings Institution.

Parker, R. (1993) The Labor Force in Transition: The Growth of the Contingent Work Force in the United States. In: Berberoglu, B. (ed.) *The Labor Process and Control of Labor*. Westport, CT: Praeger.

Pearson, R. (1997) Renegotiating the Reproductive Bargain: Gender Analysis of Economic Transition in Cuba in the 1990s. *Development and Change* 28(5): 671–705.

Pearson, R. (2007) Gender, Globalisation and Development: Key Issues for the Asian Region in the 21st Century. Keynote Address, Beyond the Difference. Ochanomizu University 13–14 January.

Peck, J. (1994) Regulating Labor: The Social Regulation and Reproduction of Local Labor Markets. In: Amin, A. and Thrift, N. (eds) *Globalization, Institutions and Regional Development in Europe*. London: Oxford University Press.

Pempel, T.J. (1998) *Regime Shift: Comparative Dynamics of the Japanese Political Economy*. Ithaca, NY: Cornell University Press.

Pempel, T.J. and Tsunekawa, K. (1979) Corporatism without Labor? The Japanese Anomaly. In: Schmitter, P. and Lehmbruch, G. (eds) *Trends Toward Corporatist Intermediation*. London: Sage.

Peterson, S. (2008) Intersectional Analytics in Global Political Economy. In: Klinger, C. and Knapp, G.A. (eds) *UberKreuzungen: Fremdheit, Ungleichheit, Differenz*. Muster: Westfaelisches Dampfboot.

Pettersson, L.O. (1994) Sweden. In: Bosch, G., Dawkins, P., and Michon, F. (eds) *Times are Changing: Working Time in 14 Industrialized Countries*. Geneva: ILO.

Pierson, P. (2001) Investigating the Welfare State at Century's End. In: Person, P. (ed.) *The New Politics of the Welfare State*. Oxford: Oxford University Press.

Pfau-Effinger, B. (1993) Modernisation, Culture and Part-Time Employment: The Example of Finland and West Germany. *Work Employment and Society* 7(3): 383–410.

Pfau-Effinger, B. (1998) Gender Cultures and the Gender Arrangement: A Theoretical Framework for Cross-National Gender Research. *Innovation* 11(2): 147–166.

Pierce, J. (1999) Emotional Labor among Paralegals. *The Annals of the American Academy of Political and Social Science* 561: 127–142.

Polanyi, K. (2001 [1944]) *The Great Transformation*. Boston: Beacon Press.

Pontusson, J. (1990) The Political Economy of Class Compromise: Labor and Capital in Sweden. Paper presented at the Seventh International Conference of Europeanists. Washington D.C.

Post-Kobayashi, B. (1992) Part-Time Work in Japan. In: Ebbing, U. (ed.) *Arbeitspapier 7*, Arbeitkreis Sozialwissenschaftliche Arbeitsmarketforschung.

Price, J. (1997) *Japan Works: Power and Paradox in Postwar Industrial Relations*. Ithaca, NY: Cornell University Press.

Prime Minister's Office (ed.) (1994) *Present Conditions of Women and Policies*. Finance Ministry, Printing Bureau: Japan.

Ragin, C. (1992) Introduction: Cases of 'What is a case?'. In: Ragin, C. and Becker, H. (eds) *What is a Case? Exploring the Foundations of Social Inquiry*. Cambridge: Cambridge University Press.

Rantalaiho, L. (1993) The Gender Contract. In: Vasa, H. (ed.) *Shaping Structural Change in Finland: the Role of Women*. Helsinki: Ministry of Social Affairs and Health.

Rantalaiho, L. (1997) Contextualizing Gender. In: Rantalaiho, L. and Heiskanen, T. (eds) *Gendered Practices in Working Life*. London: MacMillan Press.

Raymo, J. and Shirahasa, S. (2014) Single Mothers and Poverty in Japan: The Role of Living Arrangments. Paper presented at the Center for Japanese Studies Noon Lecture, University of Michigan.

Roberson, J. (1997) Empire of Nostalgia: Rethinking "Internationalization" in Japan Today. *Theory, Culture and Society* 14(4): 97–122.

Roberson, J. and Suzuki, N. (2003) Introduction. In: Roberson, J. and Suzuki, N. (eds) *Men and Masculinities in Contemporary Japan: Dislocating the Salaryman Doxa*. London: Routledge Curzon.

Roberts, G. (1994) *Staying on the Line: Blue-Collar Women in Contemporary Japan*. Honolulu, HI: University of Hawaii Press.

Roberts, G. (1999) Review of *Japan's Minorities: The Illusion of Homogeneity*, edited by Michael Weiner. *The Journal of Japanese Studies* 25(2): 399–403.

Robertson, J. (1997) Empire of Nostalgia: Rethinking 'Internationalization' in Japan Today. *Theory, Culture and Society* 14(4): 97–122.

Robertson, J. (2012) From Uniqlo to NGOs: The Problematic 'Culture of Giving' in Inter-disaster Japan. *The Asia-Pacific Journal* 10(18): 2. Available (consulted 3 January 2013) at: http://www.japanfocus.org/-Jennifer-Robertson/3747.

Rojot, J. and Tergeist, P. (1992) Overview: Industrial Relations Trends, Internal Labor Market Flexibility and Work Organization. *New Directions in Work Organization: The Industrial Relations Response*. Paris: OECD.

Rosenberger, N. (1992) Introduction. In: Rosenberger, N. (ed.) *Japanese Sense of Self*. Cambridge: Cambridge University Press, 1–20.

Rosenberger, N. (1994) Indexing Hierarchy through Japanese Gender Relations. In: Bachnik, J. and Quinn, C. (eds) *Situated Meanings: Inside and Outside in Japanese Self, Society and Language*. Princeton, NY: Princeton University Press, 88–112.

Rosenfeld, R. and Birkelund, G. (1995) Women's Part-Time Work: A Cross National Sample. *European Sociological Review* 11(2): 111–134.

Rowe, P. (2011) *Emergent Architectural Territories in East Asian Cities*. Basel: Birkhauser.

Rubery, J., Smith, M., Fagan, C., and Grimshaw, D. (1997) *Women and European Employment*. London: Routledge.

Ruigrok, W. and Van Tulder, R. (1995) *The Logic of International Restructuring*. London: Routledge.

Ryner, M. (1994) Assessing SAP's Economic Policy in the 1980s: The "Third Way," the Swedish Model and the Transition from Fordism to Post-Fordism. *Economic and Industrial Democracy* 15(3): 385–428.

Sainsbury, D. (1999) *Gender Regimes and Welfare States*. Oxford: Oxford University Press.

Samuels, R. (1981) Kishi and Corruption: An Anatomy of the 1955 System. Working Paper No. 83, Japan Policy Research Institute. Available (consulted 29 May 2014) at: http://www.jpri.org/publications/workingpapers/wp83.html.

Saso, M. (1990) *Women in the Japanese Workplace*. London: H. Shipman.

Sassen, S. (2001) The Locational and Institutional Embeddedness of Globalization. *Political Sociology: States, Power and Society Newsletter* 8(1): 6–10.

Sato, H. (2001) Is "Atypical Employment" a Flexible Form of Working Life? *Japan Labour Bulletin* 40(4): 6–10.

Sauer, B. and Woehl, S. (2011) Feminist Perspectives on the Internationalization of The State. *Antipode* 43(1): 108–128.

Schmid, G. (1994) Women in the Public Sector. *Women and Structural Change*. Paris: OECD.

Shirahase, S. (2009) Delay in Marriage and Income Inequality in Japan: The Impact of the Increased Number of Unmarried Adults Living with Their Partner on the Household Economy. *Deutsches Institut fuer Wirtschaftsforschung SOE Paper 190*.

Shire, K. (2007) Gender and the Conceptualization of the Knowledge Economy in Comparison. In: Walby, S., Gottfried, H., Gottschall, K. and Osawa, M. (eds) *Gendering the Knowledge Economy: Comparative Perspectives*. Houndsmill: Palgrave.

Shire, K. (2012) The Work-Welfare Nexus in Post-Disaster Japan: Deepening Social Risks or New Opportunities for a Better Work-Life Balance? Paper presented at the DFG Research Training Group 1613.

Shire, K. and Ota, M. (1997) The First Decade of Equal Employment Opportunities in Japan: A Review of Research. *The Journal of Social Science* 36: 51–63.

Shire, K. and Imai, J. (2000) Gender and Diversification of Employment in Japan. In: Brose, H.G. (ed.) *Die Reorganisation der Arbeitsgesellschaft*. Frankfurt/Main: Campus Verlag, 117–136.

Silver, B. (2003) *Forces of Labor: Workers' Movements and Globalization Since 1870*. Cambridge: Cambridge University Press.

Silver, B. and Zhang, L. (2009) China: Emerging Epicenter of World Labor Unrest. In: Hung, H. (ed.) *China and Global Capitalism*. Baltimore, MD: The Johns Hopkins University Press.

Skocpol, T. (1984) Emerging Agendas and Recurrent Strategies. In: Skocpol, T. (ed.) *Historical Sociology: Vision and Method in Historical Sociology*. Cambridge: Cambridge University Press.

Slater, D. (2009) The Making of Japan's New Working Class: "Freeters" and the Progression From Middle School to the Labor Market. Available (consulted 2 February 2013) at: http://www.japanfocus.org/-david_h_-slater/3279.

Slater, D. and Galbraith, P. (2011) Re-Narrating Social Class and Masculinity in Neoliberal Japan: An Examination of the Media Coverage of the 'Akihabara Incident' of 2008. *Journal of Contemporary Japanese Studies* 7. Available (consulted 12 August, 2012) at: http://www.japanesestudies.org.uk/articles/2011/SlaterGalbraith.html.

Smith, V. and Gottfried, H. (1998) Flexibility in Work and Employment: The Impact on Women. In: Geissler, B., Maier, F., and Pfau-Effinger, B. (eds) *FrauenArbeitsMarkt: Der Beitrag der Frauenforshung zur sozio-okonomischen Theorieentwicklung*. Berlin: Sigma, 95–126.

Standing, G. (2006) Economic Insecurity and Labour Casualisation – Threat or Promise? Unpublished paper presented at Pathways from Casual Work for Economic Security: Canadian and International Perspectives, 15 September, University of Northern British Columbia.

Standing, G. (2011) *The Precariat: The New Dangerous Class*. London: Bloomsbury Academic.

Steinmetz, G. (1993) *Regulating the Social: the Welfare State and Local Politics in Imperial Germany*. Princeton, NJ: Princeton University Press.

Steinmetz, G. (ed.) (2013) *Sociology and Empire: The Imperial Entanglements of a Discipline*. Durham, NC: Duke University Press.

Stetson, Dorothy McBride/Mazur, Amy, 1995: Introduction. In: Dorothy McBride, Stetson/Amy, and Mazur (eds) *Comparative State Feminism*. London: Sage, 1–21.

Stockman, N., Bonney, N., and Xuewen, S. (1995) *Women's Work in East Asia*. London: University College London Press Limited.

Stoler, A. (2013) *Imperial Debris: On Ruins and Ruination*. Durham, NC: Duke University Press.

Streeck, W. (1992) *Social Institutions and Economic Performance: Studies of Industrial Relations in Advanced Capitalist Economies*. London: Sage.

Streeck, W. (1996) Neo-Voluntarism: A New European Policy Regime. In: Marks, G., Scharpf, F., Schmitter, P., and Streeck, W. (eds) *Governance in the European Union*. London: Sage, 64–94.

Streeck, W. (1997) German Capitalism: Does it Exist and Can it Survive? In: Crouch, C. and Streeck, W. (eds) *Political Economy of Modern Capitalism: Mapping Convergence and Diversity*. London: Sage.

Stucky, N.K. (2013) The Phantoms of Narita Airport: The Forgotten Warriors in Fading Green Fields. *Japan Subculture Research Center*, 23 April. Available at: http://www

.japansubculture.com/the-phantoms-of-narita-airport-the-forgotten-warriors
-in-fading-green-fields/.

Sugimoto, Y. (1997) *An Introduction to Japanese Society.* Cambridge: Cambridge University Press.

Sundstrom, M. (1991) Part-time Work in Sweden: Trends and Equality Effects. *Journal of Economic Issues* 25(1): 167–78.

Suwa, Y. (1989) Why are Part-Time Workers Not Well Unionized? *Japan Labor Bulletin* 1: 5–8.

Suzuki, A. (2010) The Possibilities and the Limits of Social Movement Unionism in Japan. Paper presented at the Conference on Cross-National Comparison of Labor Movement Revitalization. December.

Svensson, L. (1995) Closing the Gender Gap: Determinants of Change in the Female-to-Male Blue Collar Wage Ratio in Swedish Manufacturing 1913–1990. Doctoral Dissertation, Lund University.

Swenson, Peter (1989) *Fair Shares.* Ithaca, NY: Cornell University Press.

Tabata, H. (1998) Community and Efficiency in the Japanese Firm. *Social Science Japan Journal* 1 (2): 199–215.

Tabb, W. (1995) *The Postwar Japanese System: Cultural Economy and Economic Transformation.* New York, NY: Oxford University Press.

Tabuchi, H. (2011) Braving Heat and Radiation for Temp Job. *The New York Times,* 9, April. Available at: http://www.nytimes.com/2011/04/10/world/asia/10workers.html?pagewanted=all&_r=o#.

Tabuchi, H. (2014) Fukushima Cleaned Up by Poor and Unskilled. *The New York Times,* 17 March, A1, A10.

Taira, K. (1997) Factory Labor and the Industrial Revolution in Japan. In: Yamamura, K. (ed.) *The Economic Emergence of Modern Japan.* Cambridge: Cambridge University Press.

Takasu, H. (2012) The Formation of a Region-Based Amalgamated Union Movement and Its Future Possibilities. In: Akira Suzuki (ed.) *Cross-National Comparisons of Social Movement Unionism: Diversities of Labour Movement Revitalization in Japan, Korea and the United States.* Berlin: Peter Lang.

Tanaka, Y. (1995) *Contemporary Portraits of Japanese Women.* Westport, CT: Praeger.

Taylor, M. (2004) What Derrida Really Meant. *The New York Times,* 14 October, A29.

Teague, P. and Grahl, J. (1992) *Industrial Relations and European Integration.* London: Lawrence and Wishart.

The Daily Yomiuri (1998) New Temp Agencies are Uniquely Japanese. 10 June, 3.

Thelen, K. (1992) The Politics of Flexibility in the German Metalworking Industries. In: Golden, M. and Pontusson, J. (eds) *Bargaining for Change: Union Politics in North America and Europe.* Ithaca, NY: Cornell University Press.

Thelen, K. (1993) West European Labor in Transition: Sweden and Germany Compared. *World Politics* 46: 23–49.

Thurman, J. and Trah, G. (1990) Part-Time Work in International Perspective. *International Labor Review* 129(1): 23–40.

Tremblay, D.G. (2006) From Causal Work to Economic Security: The Paradoxical Case of Self-Employment. Unpublished paper presented at Pathways from Casual Work for Economic Security: Canadian and International Perspectives, September 15, University of Northern British Columbia.

Trinczek, R. (1995) Germany: The Case of the Metal Manufacturing Industry. *Flexible Working Time: Collective Bargaining and Government Intervention.* Paris: OECD.

Tsukamoto, T. (2012) Why is Japan Neo-liberalizing? Rescaling of the Japanese Developmental State and Ideology of State-Capital Fixing. *Journal of Urban Affairs* 34(4): 395–418.

Tsuru, T. (1994) Why Has Union Density Declined in Japan? *Japan Labor Bulletin* 1: 4–8.

Tyler, M. and Abbott, P. (1998) Chocs Away: Weight Watching in the Contemporary Airline Industry. *Sociology* 3: 433–50.

Uno, K. (1993) The Death of 'Good Wife, Wise Mother'? In: Gordon, A. (ed.) *Postwar Japan as History.* Berkeley, CA: University of California Press.

Vidal, M. (forthcoming) Fordism and the Golden Age of Capitalism. In: Edgell, S., Gottfried, H., and Granter, E. (eds) *The Sage Handbook of Sociology of Work and Employment.* London: Sage.

Visser, J. (2000) From Keynesianism to the Third Way: Labour Relations and Social Policy in Postwar Western Europe. *Economic and Industrial Democracy* 21: 421–456.

Visser, J. and van Ruysseveldt, J. (eds) (1996) *Industrial Relations in Europe: Traditions and Transitions.* London: Sage.

Vosko, L. (2006) Temporary Work in Transnational Labour Regulation: The Limits of a SER-Centric Model in Forging Pathways from Gendered Precariousness. Unpublished paper presented Pathways from Casual Work for Economic Security: Canadian and International Perspectives, September 15, University of Northern British Columbia.

Vosko, L. (2010) *Managing the Margins: Gender, Citizenship, and the International Regulation of Precarious Employment.* Oxford, Oxford University Press.

Vosko, L., MacDonald, M., and Campbell, I. (eds) (2009) *Gender and the Contours of Precarious Employment.* London: Routledge.

Wajcman, J. (1998a) *Managing Like a Man: Women and Men in Corporate Management.* University Park, PA: Pennsylvania State University Press.

Wajcman, J. (1998b) Personal Management: Sexualized Cultures at Work. Paper presented at Work, Employment and Society Conference, Warwick, UK.

Walby, S. (1999) The New Regulatory State: The Social Powers of the European Union. *British Journal of Sociology* 50(1): 118–140.

Walby, S. (2004) The European Union and Gender Equality: Emergent Varieties of Gender Regime. *Social Politics* 11(1): 4–29.

Walby, S. (2006) Theorizing the Gendering of the Knowledge Economy: Comparative Approaches. In: Walby, S., Gottfried, H., Gottschall, K., and Osawa, M. (eds) *Gendering the Knowledge Economy: Comparative Perspectives*. Basingstoke, UK: Palgrave.

Walby, S. (2009) *Globalization and Inequalities: Complexity and Contested Modernities*. London: Sage.

Walby, S., Gottfried, H., Gottschall, K., and Osawa, M. (2007) *Gendering the Knowledge Economy: Comparative Perspectives*. Basingstoke, UK: Palgrave.

Weathers, C. (2001) Changing White-Collar Workplaces and Female Temporary Workers in Japan. *Social Science Japan Journal* 4: 201–218.

Weeks, J. (1989) *Sex, Politics & Society. The Regulation of Sexuality since 1800*. 2nd Edition. London: Trans-Atlantic Publications.

Week, K. (2007) Life within and against Work: Affective Labor, Feminist Labor, Feminist Critique, and Post-Fordist Politics. *Ephemera* 7(1): 233–249.

Weeks, K. (2011) *The Problem with Work*. Durham, NC: Duke University Press.

West, M. (2003) Employment Market Institutions and Japanese Working Hours. University of Michigan Law School, Paper #03-016. Available (consulted 1 November 2013) at: http://law.bepress.com/umichlwps/olin/art22/.

Western, B. (1997) *Between Class and Market: Postwar Unionization in the Capitalist Democracies*. Princeton, NJ: Princeton University Press.

White Paper on Working Women (1997) General Survey: Widening Working Conditions between Part-time and Regular Female Workers – 1996. *Japan Labor Bulletin* 3(March): 1.

White Paper on Working Women (1998) *Japan Labor Bulletin* 4(April): 2.

Williams, R. (1983) *Keywords: A Vocabulary of Culture and Society*. Revised Edition. New York, NY: Oxford University Press.

Wissen and Brand (2011) Approaching the Internationalization of the State: An Introduction. *Antipode* 43(1): 1–11.

Witz, A. (1998) Embodiment, Organization, and Gender. Paper presented at the International Conference on Rationalization, Organization and Gender, Sozialforschungsstelle Dortmund.

Witz, A., Halford, S. and Savage, M. (1996) Organized Bodies: Gender, Sexuality and Embodiment in Contemporary Organizations. In: Adkins, L. and Merchant, V. (eds) *Sexualizing the Social*. London: Macmillan, 173–190.

Wood, S. (1989) The Transformation of Work? In: Wood, S. (ed.) *The Transformation of Work? Skill, Flexibility and the Labour Process*. London: Unwin and Hyman.

Yoda, T. (2006) The Rise and Fall of Maternal Society: Gender, Labor, and Capital in Contemporary Japan. In: Yoda, T. and Harootunian, H. (eds) *Japan After Japan: Social and Cultural Life from the Recessionary 1990s to the Present*. Durham, NC: Duke University Press.

Subject Index

Names Index